The Post-Resurrection
Words of Jesus

The Post-Resurrection
Words of Jesus

Vinu V Das

Tabor Press

© 2025 Tabor Press. All rights reserved. No part of this publication may be reproduced, distributed, or transmitted in any form or by any means without the prior written permission of the publisher, except in the case of brief quotations embodied in critical reviews and certain other noncommercial uses permitted by copyright law.

ISBN 978-1-997541-22-6

Table of Contents

Chapter 1. Outside the Garden Tomb – Mary Magdalene 11

1.1. The Setting of the Garden Tomb 12

1.2. Profile of Mary Magdalene 14

1.3. The Encounter with the Risen Jesus 16

1.4. The Commission to Go and Tell 19

1.5. Interpretive and Theological Themes 21

1.6. Implications for Contemporary Discipleship 23

Chapter 2. On the Path from the Tomb – "The Other Women 26

2.2. The Early Morning Journey 31

2.3. Angelic Encounter and Instruction 35

2.4. The Path from Tomb to City 39

2.5. The Sudden Encounter with the Risen Christ 43

2.6. Theological Significance of the Women's Witness 46

2.7. Harmonizing Gospel Accounts 48

2.8. Implications for Contemporary Discipleship and Mission 50

Chapter 3. Road to Emmaus – Two Disciples 54

3.1. Historical and Geographical Setting of the Emmaus Road 55

3.2. Profiles of the Two Disciples 58

3.3. Walking in Despair: The Psychological Landscape 62

3.4. The Stranger's Exposition of Scripture 65

3.5. Hospitality at Emmaus: Breaking Bread and Recognition 68

3.6. The Burning Hearts Phenomenon 71

3.7. Return to Jerusalem: From Private Epiphany to Communal Witness 74

3.8. Theological and Missional Implications 76

Chapter 4. Private Appearance to Simon Peter 80

4.1. Biblical Record and Witnesses of the Private Appearance 81

4.2. Psychological and Spiritual Landscape of Peter 83

4.3. Theological Significance of Jesus Appearing to Peter First Among the Twelve 86

4.4. Possible Locale and Timing of the Appearance 88

4.5. Dynamics of Forgiveness and Reconciliation 90

4.6. Implications for Ecclesial Authority and Shepherd Imagery 92

4.7. Lessons for Contemporary Discipleship 93

Chapter 5. First Evening in the Locked Room – Ten Disciples 97

5.1. The Atmosphere Behind Shut Doors 98

5.2. The Appearance of the Risen Christ 100

5.3. Gifts of Peace and Joy 101

5.4. The Scars That Speak 103

5.5. Breath of the Spirit and Apostolic Commission 104

5.6. Transformation and Future Trajectory 105

Chapter 6. One Week Later – Thomas Included 108

6.1. The Setting Eight Days Later 109

6.2. The Character of Thomas 111

6.3. The Second Appearance of Jesus....................................113

6.4. The Confession of Thomas...115

6.5. Theological and Pastoral Implications 117

Chapter 7. Dawn on the Shores of Galilee – Seven Disciples and the Miraculous Catch 121

7.1. Galilee's Quiet Liminal Space..122

7.2. A Night of Futile Labor..124

7.3. The Stranger's Dawn Directive 126

7.4. Full Nets and Thundering Hearts 127

7.5. Breakfast by Charcoal Fire 129

7.6. Re-Commissioning on the Shore 130

7.7. Contours for Contemporary Discipleship 131

Chapter 8. Mountain in Galilee – The Great Commission 134

8.1. Setting the Scene on the Mountain in Galilee.............135

8.2. The Declaration of Cosmic Authority..........................137

8.3. The Mandate to Make Disciples of All Nations...........139

8.4. The Promise of Perpetual Presence..............................141

8.5. The Great Commission in Canonical and Covenantal Context 143

8.6. Contemporary Implications: Theology, Mission, and Ethics 144

Chapter 9. Appearance to "More Than Five Hundred" Believers at Once 147

9.1. Historical and Cultural Coordinates of the Locked-Room Gathering..148

9.2. Interior States: Fearful Hearts and Flickering Faith 151

9.3. Actions and Words of the Risen Christ 153

9.4. Doctrinal and Practical Reverberations 156

Chapter 10. Appearance to James (the Lord's Brother) 159

10.1. Scriptural Attestation and Early Witness Tradition 160

10.2. Historical Context and Sociological Dynamics 162

10.3. Psychological Phenomena in Group Revelation 164

10.4. Theological Significance of Large-Scale Manifestation 166

10.5. Pastoral and Ecclesial Applications............................167

Chapter 11. Final Instructions on the Mount of Olives – Immediately before the Ascension 171

11.1. Historical Profile of James Prior to the Resurrection..172

11.2. Scriptural Witness to the Appearance and Intertextual Echoes 175

11.3. Chronology, Locale, and Context of the Appearance .177

11.4. Psychological and Spiritual Transformation of James 179

11.5. Theological Ramifications of the James Appearance .181

11.6. James's Post-Appearance Leadership and Martyrdom 183

11.7. Pastoral and Missional Lessons for Contemporary Faith Communities 184

Chapter 12. Post-Ascension Conversations - To Saul of Tarsus..187

12.1. Historico-Cultural Profile of Saul of Tarsus Before the Encounter 188

12.2. The Damascus-Road Encounter: Narrative Anatomy and

Theological Symbolism 190

12.3. Mediation Through Ananias and Early Community Reception 193

12.4. Early Formation, Desert Solitude, and Apostolic Confirmation 194

12.5. Doctrinal Contributions Rooted in the Damascus Revelation 196

12.6. Missional Legacy and Contemporary Resonances 197

Chapter 13. Post-Ascension Conversations - To John on Patmos 200

13.1. Political Exile and Prophetic Readiness 201

13.2. The First Christophany: Voice, Vision, and Commission 204

13.3. Seven Letters: Diagnostic Conversations with the Churches 206

13.4. Invitation to the Throne Room: Heavenly Dialogue and Covenant Scroll 208

13.5. Prophetic Re-Commission: Eating the Scroll and Measuring the Temple 210

13.6. Final Dialogues: "Behold, I Am Coming Soon" and Eschatological Consolation 211

13.7. Theological, Pastoral, and Missional Implications 213

Chapter 14. Why These Jesus' post-resurrection Words Matter 216

14.1. Historical Reliability and Canonical Memory 217

14.2. Theological Architecture of the Risen Christ's Speech 219

14.3. Ecclesial Formation and Missional Identity 221

14.4. Pastoral Consolation and Transformative Discipleship 222

14.5. Apologetic Coherence and Cultural Engagement 224

14.6. Missional Imagination and Global Horizons 225

14.7. Spiritual Formation and Contemplative Encounter 226

Chapter 1. Outside the Garden Tomb – Mary Magdalene

The story of Mary Magdalene outside the garden tomb unfolds in the predawn stillness of Jerusalem, yet its resonance stretches far beyond that hushed moment in the first century. This encounter not only inaugurates Jesus' resurrection appearances but also reshapes the grammar of Christian witness, turning grief into proclamation and bewilderment into commissioned purpose. Rather than focusing solely on the emotional pivot of recognition, this chapter probes the layered historical, cultural, and theological dynamics that converge when the risen Christ speaks Mary's name. Appreciating the full weight of the scene requires entering the material realities of Second-Temple burial customs, the social location of Galilean women, the narrative artistry of John's Gospel, and the eschatological horizon that frames resurrection as the dawn of a new creation.

1.1. The Setting of the Garden Tomb

The garden locale described in John 20 evokes deliberate echoes of Eden, signaling that a work of re-creation has begun in the very sphere where death once reigned (John 19:41; cf. Genesis 2-3). Tombs hewn in limestone caves around Jerusalem often belonged to wealthier families, suggesting that Joseph of Arimathea's resources provided the physical stage for this redemptive drama. The placement of the tomb "near" the crucifixion site allows continuity between cross and resurrection, underlining Johannine motifs of glory revealed in both suffering and victory. Early morning darkness mirrors the disciples' cognitive and spiritual obscurity, a darkness that is soon to be dispelled by the Light of the world (John 1:4-5; 8:12). The narrative's emphasis on physical details—stone, linen cloths, spices—grounds the resurrection claim in concrete history rather than mythic abstraction, inviting readers to consider empirical evidence.

1.1.1 Second-Temple Burial Practices and Tomb Architecture

Rock-cut tombs commonly featured an antechamber leading to burial niches (kokhim) where bodies rested until skeletal remains were later collected into ossuaries, a practice evidenced by archeological finds in the Kidron and Hinnom valleys. The use of linen wrappings and aromatic spices such as myrrh and aloes, mentioned earlier in John 19:39-40, conformed to Jewish purity regulations that sought to mitigate corpse defilement. Rolling stones (golal) could be disk-shaped or square blocks depending on the wealth of the patron, and their sheer weight—often exceeding one ton—renders the later displacement of the stone a striking sign within the narrative. Tombs situated in gardens provided a measure of both honor and seclusion, distancing burial activity from the crowded residential quarters of the city while simultaneously evoking prophetic imagery of fruitful renewal (Isaiah 65:17-25). Inscriptions recovered from that era attest to the family status of tomb owners, reinforcing the social capital Joseph of Arimathea risked by publicly aligning with Jesus. Purity laws required that bodies be entombed before sundown, compressing Mary's Friday observation of burial into a brief, emotionally charged window preceding Sabbath rest (Luke 23:55-56). The presence of a "new" tomb where no one had yet been laid (John 19:41) neutralizes any confusion about identity, for only one corpse would be associated with that location. Limestone chambers also moderated temperature and slowed decomposition, enabling attentive disciples to verify the absence of Jesus' body with minimal olfactory distraction. Archaeological reconstructions of similar garden tombs in the vicinity of first-century Jerusalem corroborate the plausibility of the evangelist's spatial description, lending historical texture to theological proclamation. Gentile skepticism that burial narratives arose from later legend falters in the face of such concrete particularities. Placing the event in a real tomb also signals God's transformative intent to sanctify the very spaces most tainted by death. Finally, the garden setting anticipates the eschatological promise of renewed creation where burial grounds give way to resurrection life.

1.1.2 Chronology of Resurrection Morning

The Gospels converge on the first day of the week, yet each provides complementary time markers that enrich the reconstruction of events. John notes the still-dark pre-dawn hour (John 20:1), Luke describes early dawn (Luke 24:1), and Mark specifies "very early" with the sun having just risen (Mark 16:2), indicating a window between approximately 4:30 a.m. and 6:00 a.m. in early April. Jewish reckoning regarded days from sundown to sundown, so Sunday began on what modern readers would consider Saturday evening, but the narrative interest lies in the symbolic correlation of first-day light with new creation. Mary arrives apparently before the other women cited in the Synoptics, perhaps motivated by restless grief or deeper relational devotion, showing how multiple visits to the tomb can harmonize the accounts. After finding the stone removed, she runs to alert Peter and the unnamed disciple whom Jesus loved (John 20:2), generating the well-known footrace that verifies the vacant chamber. Those men depart, leaving Mary alone again in the garden, thereby setting the stage for her unique encounter (John 20:10-11). The confluence of angelic announcements recorded in Matthew 28 and Mark 16 with Mary's personal dialogue in John 20 likely occurred in overlapping waves as different witnesses arrived and departed. Jerusalem's pilgrim population, swollen for Passover, had not yet fully stirred, granting relative privacy to these early proceedings. The Roman guard detail implied in Matthew 27:65-66 may have withdrawn in confusion or terror after the angelic descent described by Matthew 28:4, accounting for their absence in John's report. This mosaic of chronological data underscores the historical credibility of the evangelists, who preserve independent memory strands converging on the same transformative morning. Synchronizing the events also illuminates the psychological cadence by which despair yields, not instantly but progressively, to dawning belief. The resurrection timeline thus emerges not as a simplistic sequence but as a tapestry woven from multiple perspectives converging on a single, epoch-making claim.

1.2. Profile of Mary Magdalene

Mary of Magdala enters the Gospel narratives as a woman healed of seven demons (Luke 8:2), yet she emerges as a paradigmatic disciple whose devotion outpaces that of many male counterparts. Magdala, a prosperous fishing town on the western shore of the Sea of Galilee, exposed her to cosmopolitan influences while still anchoring her in Jewish piety. Economic independence is suggested by her capacity to provide material support for Jesus' itinerant ministry alongside other women of means (Luke 8:3). Mary's persistent presence at the crucifixion (John 19:25), burial observation (Matthew 27:61), and resurrection site underscores rhetorical intention to amplify female solidarity when male disciples faltered. Church tradition's later conflation of Mary with the repentant sinner of Luke 7:36-50 or with Mary of Bethany obscures her distinctive witness, but careful exegesis restores her primary identity as healed follower turned first herald of Easter. Modern feminist hermeneutics rightly celebrate her agency while also cautioning against romanticizing her role beyond the text's boundaries.

1.2.1 Magdalene in the Synoptic Tradition

Matthew, Mark, and Luke uniformly identify Mary as a leader among the Galilean women who traveled with Jesus to Jerusalem, emphasizing her steadfast accompaniment at decisive moments (Matthew 27:55-56; Mark 15:40-41; Luke 23:55-24:10). Her earlier healing signifies liberation from spiritual bondage, foreshadowing the deliverance the resurrection will proclaim universally. The Synoptics record her as one of several witnesses rather than the sole discoverer of the empty tomb, highlighting the communal dimension of resurrection testimony. Mark's "young man dressed in white" (Mark 16:5) and Matthew's radiant angel (Matthew 28:5) both entrust Mary and the other women with the directive to inform the disciples, confirming the thematic pattern of divine message coming first through marginalized voices. Luke's note that the apostles initially regard the women's report as "idle talk" (Luke 24:11) reveals entrenched cultural biases that God deliberately overturns. In each Synoptic account Mary is named first, implying leadership within the group and lending historical verisimilitude, for inventing a female primary witness would have weakened apologetic strategy in patriarchal antiquity. Patristic commentary from Tertullian and Augustine affirms Mary's privileged role while also exploring typological resonances between Eve, who heralded death, and Mary, who announces life. The Synoptic presentation thus supplies a complementary frame for John's more intimate portrayal without contradiction, as multiple visits and evolving recognition can explain apparent divergences. Literary analysis observes that the frequency of Mary's name in these resurrection episodes functions as a mnemonic anchor for oral tradition, ensuring fidelity across communal retellings. Synoptic depictions also equip the church to counter later Gnostic speculations that would detach Mary's authority from the canonical narrative.

1.2.2 Discipleship Journey and Transformation

Mary's spiritual journey traces a movement from bondage to belonging, exemplifying the soteriological arc of the Gospel itself. Delivered from demonic oppression, she channels her restored agency into tangible service, financing the mission that will eventually lead to Jerusalem's climactic events. Her willingness to remain near the cross despite Roman intimidation and potential association with a condemned criminal evidences courage grounded in gratitude. Observing Joseph and Nicodemus complete burial rites (Mark 15:47) positions her to serve as a witness both to Jesus' death and to the precise location of His interment, thereby nullifying later theories of misplaced tomb. The inequality of gendered testimony in ancient courts did not deter her resolve, illustrating how the kingdom revalues social constructs by empowering those historically silenced. Mary's tears at the tomb embody raw lament, but they also create space for divine consolation, echoing Psalm 30:5 where weeping may endure for a night but joy comes in the morning. Recognition, when it comes, is catalyzed not by visual perception but by auditory familiarity; hearing her name spoken by the Shepherd recalibrates her identity (John 10:3-4). Transformation reaches its zenith when Mary migrates from personal clinging—"do not hold on to Me" (John 20:17)—to outward mission, demonstrating that authentic encounter propels disciples beyond devotional intimacy toward communal responsibility. Patristic exegesis often highlights this pivot as paradigmatic of Christian maturation: the believer must release possessive religiosity to embrace apostolic calling. Mary's narrative also underscores the eschatological tension between present experiential fellowship with Christ and the promise of a fuller communion mediated by the Spirit. Her trajectory, therefore, offers pastoral reassurance that honest grief is not antithetical to faith but can become the soil in which resurrection hope takes root and bears witness.

1.3. The Encounter with the Risen Jesus

John's narrative artistry slows the pace as Mary stoops to peer into the tomb, where two angels occupy the spaces once filled by Jesus' head and feet, subtly invoking the cherubim over the mercy seat in Exodus 25:18-22. The angels' question, "Woman, why are you weeping?" surfaces the affective center of the scene, yet Mary's response focuses on the practical dilemma of a missing body (John 20:13). Turning around, she sees Jesus but mistakes Him for the gardener, an identification that resonates theologically with Adam's vocation to tend Eden (Genesis 2:15), hinting that the Second Adam is inaugurating a restored creation. Misrecognition serves a narrative function by verifying the physical reality of Jesus' resurrected body rather than a mere spiritual apparition, for a hallucination would conform to Mary's expectations. The moment of recognition hinges on the intimate address "Mary," at which point cognitive dissonance resolves into joyous confession "Rabboni" (John 20:16). Jesus' subsequent instruction not to cling physically signals both continuity and transformation: bodily reality persists, yet modes of relating will now be mediated by the impending gift of the Spirit (John 20:17; cf. 14:16-20). The dialogue foregrounds personal relationship, emphasizing that resurrection faith arises not merely from empty artifacts but from encounter with the living Lord who knows His sheep by name. Narrative theologians observe that speech, rather than sight, functions as the decisive hermeneutical key, underscoring the centrality of the Word in Johannine theology. The question posed by many modern believers—"Why does Jesus not appear plainly to all?"—finds partial answer here: revelation remains both gift and summons, inviting recognition shaped by prior discipleship. Mary's movement from despair to proclamation thus mirrors the existential journey many readers undertake as Scripture addresses them personally. The episode also reinforces the continuity between Jesus' earthly ministry, where hearing precipitated faith, and His resurrected ministry, where the Shepherd's voice still calls forth familiarity and obedience.

1.3.1 The Experience of Grief and Misrecognition

Psychologically, grief often dulls perception and constricts interpretive horizons, a phenomenon exemplified in Mary's failure to identify Jesus while He stands directly before her. Cognitive science of religion notes that expectation heavily influences recognition, and Mary anticipates only a corpse, not a living interlocutor. Her misidentification of Jesus as the gardener further demonstrates that resurrection is not simply wish fulfillment, for her desires would have recognized Him immediately were she projecting hope. Theologically, the garden motif recasts Genesis' tragedy: where the first humans hid from God among garden trees, the Second Adam graciously hides His identity long enough to invite authentic question. Angelic presence, though extraordinary, does not resolve her sorrow; only personal encounter with Christ suffices, illustrating that mediating signs point beyond themselves. New Testament scholarship often contrasts this vignette with the Emmaus narrative (Luke 24:13-35), where disciples likewise misrecognize until symbolic action (breaking bread) reveals Jesus, underscoring a pattern of progressive disclosure post-Easter. Mary's weeping thus becomes a catalyst rather than a barrier, for heartfelt lament opens conversational space for divine initiative. Pastoral theology draws from this dynamic to affirm that emotional honesty before God need not delay revelation; rather, it may precipitate it. The scene thereby confronts modern stoicism that suppresses sorrow, reminding believers that resurrection hope integrates, not erases, human affect. Scripturally, her tears echo Lamentations 1:16 and Psalm 56:8, inviting readers to see continuity between Israel's lament tradition and Christian resurrection joy.

1.3.2 Recognition through Name and Voice

When Jesus utters "Mary," the single word accomplishes what angelic explanation and empirical observation could not, revealing the uniquely relational character of Christian revelation. Linguistically, the vocative use of her native Aramaic name underscores intimacy and authenticity, countering any suggestion of late Greek literary invention. Johannine themes concerning the Good Shepherd (John 10) converge here, as sheep recognize the shepherd's voice and follow. Mary's reciprocal address "Rabboni," a form signifying both reverence and affectionate familiarity, consolidates recognition while also anchoring her role as disciple rather than secular acquaintance. Voice recognition, as contemporary neurology affirms, activates limbic system pathways associated with belonging and emotional memory, illustrating the psychosomatic integration of faith experience.

Narrative criticism observes that the direct speech contrasts with the indirect characterization of angels, highlighting Jesus' superiority and the climactic nature of the moment. The naming tradition resonates with Isaiah 43:1, "I have called you by name; you are mine," reinforcing covenant fidelity now confirmed through resurrection. Contemporary spiritual formation literature draws on this exchange to encourage practices of contemplative listening where believers rehearse their identity as personally addressed by God. The episode also anticipates Pentecost, where the Spirit will mediate Christ's voice to the wider community, democratizing the relational dynamic Mary experiences firsthand. Ultimately, recognition through voice underscores that Christian faith is irreducibly personal, rooted in encounter yet oriented toward communal proclamation.

1.4. The Commission to Go and Tell

Immediately after recognition, Jesus redirects Mary from private devotion toward public mission, commanding her to announce His impending ascension to the "Father and your Father, to my God and your God" (John 20:17). This statement not only anticipates the event in Acts 1:9-11 but also articulates the new familial relationship secured through resurrection, aligning believers with Jesus' filial intimacy. The commission overturns cultural expectations by appointing a woman as first messenger, a fact that modern scholars regard as one of the strongest historical criteria for authenticity given the patriarchal context. Mary obeys, reporting to the disciples, "I have seen the Lord," thereby providing the earliest kerygmatic formula encapsulating Christian testimony. Her announcement shifts the narrative locus from tomb to community, signifying that resurrection cannot remain a privatized mystical experience but must be ecclesially shared. The imperative "Go" echoes earlier sending motifs in John 4 and John 17, demonstrating continuity between pre- and post-Easter mission. Jesus' reference to ascending underscores that resurrection inaugurates, but does not exhaust, the glorification process, orienting the disciples toward the next redemptive installment: the gift of the Spirit.

Theologically, Mary's role exemplifies "eschatological reversal," where the last become first and marginal voices become primary heralds of salvation history. Pastoral application sees in her example a template for Christian witness grounded in personal encounter yet obedient to divine command rather than subjective preference.

1.4.1 Apostolos Apostolorum – Mary as Sent One

The title "Apostle to the Apostles," later bestowed upon Mary by Augustine, encapsulates her mediating role between Jesus and the Twelve. Canonical usage of apostolos in the New Testament centers on those sent by Christ with authoritative message (Matthew 10:2; Acts 1:2), and although Mary is not numbered among the Twelve, her function momentarily parallels theirs. Ecclesiological implications arise: mission precedes formal office, and the Spirit's gifting determines vocational boundaries more than societal conventions. Medieval spirituality often portrayed Mary as prototype of contemplative-active synthesis, balancing encounter with service, and this duality undergirds numerous monastic charisms. Feminist theologians leverage the apostolic language to advocate greater recognition of women's leadership within church structures, finding precedent in the resurrection narrative. Counterarguments caution against anachronistically imposing later ecclesial categories onto the text, yet even conservative scholarship concedes the narrative's radical inclusion. Comparative studies explore how other Second-Temple Jewish movements occasionally featured prophetic women, but none elevates female testimony to foundational creed as boldly as the Gospels. In homiletics, Mary's proclamation offers a concise Easter sermon model: experiential sight, Christological identification, and communal announcement. As "Apostle to the Apostles," Mary exemplifies how every believer, regardless of social rank, becomes envoy once transformed by the living Christ.

1.4.2 Theological Significance of the Commission

By exhorting Mary not to cling and instead to witness, Jesus delineates post-resurrection spirituality that values presence yet prioritizes mission. The commission reframes eschatology: resurrection life already penetrates history, but consummation awaits ascension and Spirit-outpouring, drawing disciples into participatory delay. Trinitarian patterns emerge as Jesus references His Father and foretells the Spirit's mediation soon to come, positioning Mary's message within divine economy. Soteriologically, the phrase "my God and your God" bridges Christ's unique sonship and believers' adopted status, anchoring Christian identity in relational communion rather than moral performance. Missiologically, the instruction underscores that resurrection news belongs in the public domain, resisting privatized spirituality. Ethical ramifications follow: if death is defeated, then oppressive systems predicated on fear lose leverage, empowering marginalized voices to speak boldly as Mary does. Liturgical traditions integrate this insight through Easter antiphons that proclaim, "Christ is risen," inviting communal response echoing Mary's first acclamation. The commission also models narrative-critical movement from sight to speech, illustrating that revelation seeks expression, not mere experience. Finally, the instruction functions apologetically, for the empty tomb, verified by the disciples post-announcement, corroborates Mary's testimony and dismantles hypotheses of theft or hallucination.

1.5. Interpretive and Theological Themes

The encounter between Mary and Jesus brims with theological freight that continues to inspire scholarly reflection and devotional application. Among these themes are new creation imagery, reversal of gendered expectations, scriptural fulfillment, and the interplay between faith and empirical inquiry. Resurrection morning thus serves as both hermeneutical key for Johannine Christology and generative symbol for Christian spirituality.

1.5.1 Resurrection as Creation's Dawn

John's deliberate alignment of resurrection day with the first day of creation invites readers to perceive the event as cosmic reboot rather than isolated miracle. Garden setting, early light, and gardener misrecognition collectively point to Genesis motifs, suggesting that Easter morning marks day one of a renewed world. Pauline theology corroborates this cosmic reading by describing Christ as firstfruits of those who have fallen asleep (1 Corinthians 15:20-23), implying agrarian new-creation sequence. Patristic writers from Irenaeus to Athanasius connect resurrection with recapitulation, interpreting the Second Adam rectifying the fall begun in Eden. Liturgical calendars reinforce the motif by positioning Sunday worship as weekly commemoration of new creation. Ecological theology draws on this theme to assert that bodily resurrection affirms material creation, resisting gnostic disparagement of the physical realm. Mary, as firsthand witness within a garden, becomes emblematic caretaker of the news that creation's sabbath rest is now suffused with resurrection life. Contemporary preaching leverages new creation imagery to address environmental stewardship, insisting that resurrection mandates hope for the cosmos as well as individual souls. Artistic traditions often paint the scene with verdant backdrops to visualize this eschatological flourishing. The theme thus beckons believers to inhabit creation not as doomed terrain but as arena of promised transformation.

1.5.2 Gender Dynamics and Witness Credibility

The privileging of Mary's testimony undermines patriarchal assumptions entrenched in both ancient culture and, at times, modern ecclesial structures. Historians note that women's court testimony lacked formal standing in first-century Judaism, rendering the choice of Mary as primary herald counterintuitive if the story were fabricated for persuasive effect. Such criterion of embarrassment strengthens historical plausibility of resurrection accounts, as multiple independent traditions maintain female prominence despite apologetic disadvantage. Feminist theologians mobilize the narrative to critique ongoing marginalization of women's voices in church leadership, urging retrieval of Mary's legacy as impetus for reform. Conversely, some traditionalists caution against using narrative precedent to establish doctrinal polity, yet even they acknowledge testimonial centrality of female disciples at Easter. Modern missiology records parallel phenomena where women in cultures with restricted public roles nonetheless become primary evangelists, mirroring Mary's commission. The narrative thus challenges readers to evaluate credibility not by societal rank but by transformed character and divine entrustment. Academic skepticism that dismisses resurrection as patriarchal invention confronts the inconvenient historical reality of its inaugural female testimony. Mary's example hence serves as apologetic fulcrum, hermeneutical corrective, and pastoral encouragement for those whose voices remain undervalued.

1.6. Implications for Contemporary Discipleship

Mary Magdalene's encounter invites believers today into practices that emulate her openness, honesty, and obedience. Beyond historical interest, the narrative poses discipleship questions: How do we process grief without losing hope? How do we recognize Christ's voice amid cultural noise? How do we translate personal encounter into communal witness? Addressing these questions situates resurrection faith within daily praxis.

1.6.1 Spiritual Practices of Encounter

Lectio Divina, contemplative silence, and imaginative prayer emerge as disciplines through which modern disciples can listen for the Shepherd's voice, paralleling Mary's auditory recognition. Honest lament, modeled in the Psalms and in Mary's tears, remains vital for emotional integrity before God, counteracting triumphalist tendencies that bypass suffering. Participating in corporate worship on the first day of the week echoes the narrative rhythm and situates individual experience within the body of Christ. Retreating to natural spaces, gardens included, can create sensory environments that recall resurrection dawn, fostering receptivity to divine initiative. Spiritual direction offers frameworks for discerning when clinging to past modes of relating hinders new movements of grace, an echo of Jesus' injunction not to hold on in restrictive ways. Examination of conscience at day's end may incorporate the question, "Where did I hear my name today?" nurturing attentiveness to God's personal address. These practices collectively shape a lifestyle of expectancy, mirroring Mary's transition from sorrow to proclamation.

1.6.2 Witness in a Skeptical Culture

Post-Christendom societies often dismiss religious claims as subjective preference, making Mary's concise testimony—"I have seen the Lord"—a model of experiential authenticity coupled with communal accountability. Apologetics today benefits from integrating narrative evidence, historical data, and personal transformation, reflecting the multi-layered assertion Mary embodied. Digital platforms provide unprecedented avenues for proclamation, though they risk fostering disembodied interaction, so integrating embodied service—feeding the hungry, comforting the grieving—grounds witness in tangible love. Interfaith dialogue requires respectful articulation of resurrection hope without triumphalist hubris, recognizing that Mary's message, while bold, remained invitational. Addressing gender inequalities within church and society validates the credibility of a Gospel that first empowered female witness. The practice of telling resurrection stories in diverse cultural idioms echoes Mary's transmission of news to disciples who spoke multiple languages, preparing them for global mission. In environments hostile to faith, the resilience displayed by a lone woman in a garden encourages contemporary believers to trust divine calling over social approval.

Conclusion

The predawn meeting between the risen Christ and Mary Magdalene radiates theological, historical, and pastoral significance that continues to shape Christian imagination. From the limestone contours of Joseph's tomb to the intimate cadence of a name spoken in Aramaic, every narrative detail converges to announce that death is decisively conquered and that the first herald of this victory is a once-marginalized woman turned apostle. By situating the episode within

Second-Temple burial customs, Johannine Christology, and contemporary discipleship practice, this chapter has sought to show how ancient testimony pulses with present-tense relevance. The garden tomb no longer stands as a monument to loss but as an open portal through which new creation bursts into history, inviting each reader to recognize the Shepherd's voice and carry resurrection hope into every sphere of life.

Chapter 2. On the Path from the Tomb – "The Other Women

The dawn of resurrection morning is crowded with witnesses, yet the canonical focus rarely lingers on the collective known simply as "the other women." In Matthew's account these nameless disciples—Mary the mother of James, Salome, Joanna, and others—rush from the tomb in a mixture of awe and trembling, only to find their path interrupted by the risen Lord Himself (Matthew 28:8-10; Mark 16:1-8; Luke 24:1-11). While subsequent Christian memory often elevates Mary Magdalene as the first herald of Easter, the testimony of her companions provides indispensable corroboration, theological depth, and pastoral breadth. Their experience is neither peripheral nor redundant; it is the Spirit-curated prism through which the resurrection's seismic reverberations spread from a borrowed tomb to the ends of the earth.

2.1. Historical Context of the Women at the Tomb

The presence of multiple female disciples at Jesus' crucifixion and burial constitutes a striking counter-narrative to first-century expectations, for women's public roles were typically restricted by both Greco-Roman and Judaic conventions. These women had traveled from Galilee to Jerusalem, funding the Galilean mission out of their private means and witnessing the entire Passion sequence (Luke 8:1-3; 23:49, 55). Their inclusion in each Synoptic resurrection account signals authorial intent to preserve an unbroken chain of female testimony despite its apologetic drawback in patriarchal courts where women's words were often deemed inadmissible. Josephus, for instance, discounts female witness as unreliable, yet the Gospel writers insist on its centrality, thereby underscoring divine subversion of cultural norms. The women's capacity to purchase spices for anointing (Mark 16:1) implies financial autonomy unusual for the era, hinting at social standing that allowed them to traverse markets at dawn. Their devotion stands in stark relief against the male disciples' flight, illustrating Luke's thematic emphasis on great reversals wherein the humble are exalted (Luke 1:52). Early church fathers, including Origen and Chrysostom, explicitly defended the historicity of these female witnesses against pagan ridicule, noting that no sane author inventing a hoax would choose women as principal heralds. Furthermore, second-temple literature such as the Mishnah lists burial obligations primarily for men, yet the Gospels record women initiating these rites, thereby portraying them as courageous custodians of covenantal love. Jewish festival pilgrimage records reveal that Galilean families sometimes lodged communally near the Mount of Olives, making the women's sustained presence in Jerusalem logistically feasible. Their determination to honor Jesus with proper burial spices, even after observing Joseph and Nicodemus' hurried preparations before the Sabbath (John 19:38-42), reflects scrupulous adherence to purity laws. Roman governance during festivals intensified military presence, yet the soldiers' withdrawal from the tomb after the angelic event (Matthew 28:2-4) left these women traversing a briefly unguarded zone, accentuating the providential timing of their movements. Sociologically, the collective identity of the women models the early church's inclusive community where gender, economic status, and region converge in egalitarian mission. Taken together, their historical context elevates them from narrative backdrop to pivotal conduits through whom the resurrection burst onto the public stage. Recognizing this framework guards interpreters against dismissing their journey as sentimental folklore and instead appreciates it as divinely orchestrated historiography. Their witness thus stands as both a challenge to cultural prejudice and a testament to the Spirit's preferential empowerment of underestimated voices. Every subsequent mention of Easter discipleship owes an implicit debt to the threshold they first crossed at dawn. In sum, these women embody the paradox of the Kingdom: those considered least qualified become first entrusted. Their context is not an antiquarian footnote but a mirror reflecting God's enduring strategy of strength perfected in apparent weakness.

2.1.1 Profiles of the Women

Mary the mother of James, sometimes identified with Mary of Clopas (John 19:25), emerges as a matriarchal figure who likely experienced socioeconomic hardship after losing her husband, yet her persistence alongside her sons testifies to intergenerational discipleship. Salome, traditionally interpreted as the wife of Zebedee and thus the mother of James and John, bridges familial ties with apostolic leadership, suggesting that her early exposure to Jesus' ministry cultivated a household culture of radical commitment. Joanna, wife of Chuza, Herod Antipas' steward (Luke 8:3), represents an unexpected intersection of royal court access and prophetic proclamation, underscoring the Gospel's reach into political structures. Other unnamed women, referenced collectively by Luke 24:10, symbolize the broader, often invisible network of female disciples who formed the logistical backbone of itinerant ministry—cooking, arranging lodging, and mediating communal disputes. Patristic glosses propose that Susanna, listed earlier among Jesus' supporters, may also have been present, thus expanding the witness circle. Each woman's personal narrative carries unique socioeconomic coordinates, yet all converge in shared devotion, demonstrating how the resurrection weaves disparate stories into cohesive mission. Their multi-regional origins—Magdala, Capernaum, Tiberias—mirror the geographic diversity of first-century Galilee, indicating that

Jesus' message already transcended local tribalism before Pentecost's global outpouring. Feminist theologians emphasize that these women provide a necessary corrective to androcentric readings by illustrating mutuality in Kingdom ministry. Their literate capacity to comprehend angelic messages and articulate them coherently to the apostles suggests greater educational exposure than stereotypes allow, challenging modern assumptions about ancient female illiteracy. Iconography from catacomb frescoes often depicts them bearing torches or alabaster jars, visually situating their profiles as liturgical archetypes for vigilance and sacrificial service. Early Syriac liturgies commemorate them collectively on the second Sunday after Easter, affirming their canonical stature. The profiles collectively reveal that resurrection faith is not monolithic; it thrives in a tapestry of personalities, professions, and pieties. Recognizing each contributor curbs the modern tendency to flatten biblical women into a single homogeneous category and instead honors the Spirit's nuanced artistry. Their memory challenges contemporary communities to cultivate spaces where every demographic finds purpose in God's redemptive story. Without their distinct yet united voices, the church's foundational narrative would stand impoverished, lacking the polyphonic resonance God evidently desired. Therefore, exegetical attention to their profiles is an act of justice, restoring their rightful place in salvation history.

2.1.2 Relationship to Jesus' Ministry

The women's sustained logistical support—financial, relational, and organizational—was indispensable to the Galilean campaign, which spanned numerous villages, incurred travel expenses, and required food distribution networks (Luke 8:1-3). Their presence provided relational continuity; as Jesus' male disciples were occasionally dispatched on trial missions (Luke 9:1-6), these women offered stabilizing hospitality upon return. Studies of patron-client systems in antiquity reveal that benefaction elevated status not only for the donor but also for the recipient community, suggesting that the women's generosity bolstered public perception of Jesus as a legitimate rabbi under reputable female patronage. Their firsthand experience with deliverance—some healed of demonic oppression, others liberated from social marginalization—fostered experiential authority when later proclaiming resurrection. Unlike the Twelve, who sometimes disputed rank and misread messianic expectations (Mark 9:33-34), the women consistently exemplified humble service, foreshadowing the servant leadership model Jesus codified at the Last Supper (John 13:14-15). They navigated cultural boundaries skillfully, accompanying a male rabbi in a manner that avoided scandal by traveling in groups and likely coordinating with familial networks for lodging. Their relational equity with Jesus refuted contemporary mischaracterizations of gendered hierarchies within discipleship, presenting instead a mosaic of mutual honor and respect. Rabbinic literature acknowledges learned women like Beruriah, indicating that female theological engagement was not unheard of, and the Gospel narratives further normalize such engagement through these women's participation in resurrection dialogue. Their relationship with Jesus was pastoral as well as logistical; He ministered to their emotional wounds and affirmed their dignity, thereby equipping them for future leadership. Post-resurrection, Acts 1:14 records women praying with apostles in the upper room, demonstrating continuity of mission forged by years of shared ministry. The women's relational investments cultivated trust, making their resurrection report credible within the disciple community despite initial skepticism. This dynamic underscores a crucial principle: enduring relationships established in pre-crisis ministry become vital channels for post-crisis revelation. Contemporary missional praxis can learn from this pattern, recognizing that sustainable ministry requires diversified relational networks. The women's alliance with Jesus thus models holistic discipleship that integrates economic stewardship, emotional loyalty, and theological receptivity. Their relationship trajectory illuminates how pre-Easter faithfulness prepares disciples for post-Easter commission. Consequently, their involvement was not auxiliary but constitutive of Jesus' earthly mission strategy. Modern readers are invited to reassess ministry paradigms that marginalize certain demographics, recognizing that the Gospel's advance historically relied on such inclusive partnerships. By examining the relational texture of these women's journey with Jesus, the church gains insight into cultivating resilient, collaborative communities today.

2.2. The Early Morning Journey

In the dim hush preceding sunrise, the women embarked on a solemn procession toward Joseph of Arimathea's garden tomb, their footsteps echoing mingled grief and duty (Mark 16:1-2). The trajectory from their likely lodging site near the southern slope of the city to the garden north of Golgotha traversed narrow limestone streets, already fragrant with Passover remnants and cool spring air. Historical climatology suggests that nighttime temperatures in Jerusalem during late March or early April often fell below 15°C, necessitating shawls that doubled as veils for modesty. Although Jewish law prohibited work on the Sabbath, preparing spices beforehand and commencing travel at first light complied with Halakhic boundaries, allowing them to honor both piety and affection. The purchase of myrrh and aloes after sunset Saturday indicates resourcefulness; traders operating near the Fish Gate offered after-hours commerce to festival pilgrims. Their discussion en route—"Who will roll away the stone?"—reflects practical realism rather than naïve optimism, showing that their love did not eclipse logistical awareness (Mark 16:3). Anxiety over Roman guards likely intensified their apprehension, as soldiers tasked with securing political order would not hesitate to detain mourners violating sealed tombs. Nonetheless, the women prioritized covenantal loyalty over personal safety, mirroring Esther's resolve to risk royal displeasure for covenant people (Esther 4:16). Rabbinic commentaries on Sabbath boundaries permitted compassionate acts for the dead, which the women leveraged to justify their mission, exemplifying creative fidelity to Torah. Their early departure ensured minimal male escort, exposing them to potential harassment in pre-dawn alleys, yet their solidarity provided collective protection. Luke's notation that they arrived "very early in the morning" underscores thematic reversal: darkness becomes the womb of new light (Luke 24:1). Spiritual formation literature often amplifies this motif by encouraging predawn prayer as a posture of expectancy. The journey's liminality—poised between night and day, despair and hope—mirrors the theological threshold between death and resurrection. Had the women delayed until full daylight, the tomb event might have become a public spectacle too chaotic for intimate revelation, illustrating Providence's choreography of timing. Archaeological reconstructions of Jerusalem's first-century street network show that the likely route passed by ritual mikva'ot used by pilgrims for purification, infusing their walk with symbolic undercurrents of cleansing anticipation. In sum, the early morning journey weaves together grief-laden obedience, practical foresight, cultural boundaries, and divine timing, demonstrating how the ordinary act of walking becomes sacramental when propelled by covenant love. Their itinerary, though brief in distance, traversed the expansive terrain between desolation and dawning faith, setting the stage for angelic interruption.

2.2.1 Motivations and Emotional State

Grief, duty, and residual hope coalesced to propel the women out of sheltered rooms into the chilled dawn air. Each carried personal sorrow: Salome mourned the dashed messianic dreams she once prompted her sons to chase (Matthew 20:20-23); Joanna lamented the violent miscarriage of justice perpetrated by the ruler she once served through her husband. Their collective motivation was not primarily theological speculation about resurrection—an idea peripheral in mainstream Second-Temple Judaism—but covenant faithfulness manifest in burial honor (cf. Daniel 12:2; Acts 23:8). Psychologically, bereavement studies reveal that performing rituals for the dead offers survivors a sense of agency amidst uncontrollable loss, a dynamic evident in their determination to anoint Jesus properly. Cultural anthropologist Victor Turner's concept of liminality aptly describes their journey: between the statuses of follower and witness, they traversed a threshold of transformation. Despite lingering terror after witnessing crucifixion brutality, they resisted avoidance behaviors typical of trauma response, instead moving toward the source of pain. Their emotional palette included cognitive dissonance, for Jesus had predicted rising on the third day (Mark 8:31; 9:31), yet experiential reality contradicted messianic triumph. This inner conflict heightened their vigilance as they walked, attuning them to any sign that could harmonize prophecy and circumstance. Prayerful lament likely accompanied their steps, echoing the Psalter's pattern of pleading and trust, particularly Psalms 22 and 130. Contemporary bereavement therapy underscores narrative reconstruction as vital for healing; the women's forthcoming encounter would re-author their story entirely. Social neuroscience asserts that group solidarity modulates cortisol levels during stress, suggesting that their shared presence mitigated trauma's physiological impact. Missionally, their motivations aligned with the Kingdom ethic of loving devotion rather than strategic influence, yet God transformed that devotion into cosmic proclamation. Their willingness to confront unresolved questions—guard presence, stone weight, potential hostility—exemplifies faith that acts amidst uncertainty, a virtue extolled in Hebrews 11. Gendered expectations likely amplified anxiety, for public spaces at dawn were male-dominated, and women risked reputational damage. Nevertheless, love proved stronger than social stigma, embodying the Song of Songs' assertion that "love is as strong as death" (Song 8:6). By documenting such emotional nuance, the Gospels validate the complexity of faith experiences that encompass fear, confusion, and courage simultaneously. Their motivational tapestry becomes theological witness: authentic discipleship integrates affective honesty with steadfast obedience. Therefore, their emotional journey invites modern readers to bring full-spectrum feelings into encounters with the risen Christ rather than compartmentalizing spirituality. Their example also challenges communities to honor lament as a legitimate precursor to breakthrough revelation.

2.2.2 The Role of Spices and Burial Customs

Anointing the deceased with aromatic spices served dual functions in Jewish burial custom: mitigating odor during decomposition and symbolically honoring the body as fearfully and wonderfully made (Psalm 139:14). Nicodemus' lavish allotment of myrrh and aloes weighing about seventy-five pounds (John 19:39) signified royal treatment, yet the women's additional spices underline meticulous devotion to completeness, reflecting similar care at Lazarus' tomb (John 11:38-39). Myrrh, harvested from Commiphora resin and costly due to import routes from Arabia, carried connotations of both burial and kingship, as referenced during Jesus' infancy (Matthew 2:11). The use of nard, a Himalayan spikenard referenced in prior anointing episodes (Mark 14:3-9), may also have been intended, signifying prophetic foresight into His burial. Halakhic guidelines in tractate Semahot prescribed washing and anointing within twenty-four hours, but Passover restrictions necessitated the women's return on the third day, raising concerns about early decay in Jerusalem's mild climate. The act of preparing spices required grinding, mixing with oil, and storing in alabaster jars, tasks demanding both time and dexterity, underscoring their premeditated care. Archaeological discovery of first-century spice shops near the Tyropoeon Valley corroborates the availability of such ingredients during festival weeks. The women's intention to enter a tomb rendered them ritually unclean for seven days according to Numbers 19, yet their willingness underscores prioritizing covenant loyalty over personal ceremonial purity. Early Christian writers such as Cyril of Jerusalem spiritualize the spices as virtues—faith, hope, and love—offered to the risen Lord, but the historical act itself remains profoundly tangible. Modern embalming practices differ drastically, making it crucial for contemporary readers to appreciate ancient olfactory realities that motivated prompt burial rituals. The spices also foreshadow baptismal chrism in early church rite, wherein anointing symbolizes participation in Christ's death and resurrection. Economically, the purchase of such spices represented a significant investment, perhaps depleting travel funds reserved for Passover accommodations. The weight of their jars adds practical complexity to their journey, amplifying the miracle that angels rather than women roll away the stone. Liturgically, Eastern Orthodox tradition commemorates these "Myrrh-Bearing Women" on the second Sunday of Pascha, preserving collective memory of their aromatic devotion. Their actions thus bridge tangible care for the deceased with eschatological proclamation, for the spices prepared to honor a corpse instead attend a living Lord, transfiguring funerary ritual into festival. This reversal anticipates eschatological imagery wherein death-soaked cloths become wedding garments (Revelation 19:7-8). Therefore, the women's spice mission is not narrative filler but sacramental pivot where human compassion intersects divine surprise. In practical theology, pastoral care ministries can draw on this paradigm to integrate acts of mercy with expectancy for resurrection renewal.

2.3. Angelic Encounter and Instruction

Arriving at the tomb, the women encountered an angel whose appearance, described as lightning-like with garments white as snow (Matthew 28:2-3), reconfigured their reality from grief to awe. Earthquake imagery accompanying the angel underscores the cosmic upheaval of resurrection, echoing Old Testament theophany patterns at Sinai (Exodus 19:16-19). The angel seated on the displaced stone functions both as herald and interpreter, clarifying that Jesus' absence signifies resurrection, not robbery. Linguistic analysis of the angel's imperative "Do not be afraid" reveals a present middle imperative in Greek, conveying ongoing release from fear rather than a momentary command. The message refutes potential rumors of body theft by affirming divine agency and instructing the women to notify the disciples that Jesus will precede them into Galilee (Matthew 28:7). This Galilean rendezvous prophecy reconnects the post-resurrection community with its ministry roots, reinforcing continuity amid transformation. The angelic instruction includes an evidential invitation: "Come, see the place where He lay," blending empirical verification with theological declaration, thereby endorsing faith that welcomes tangible inquiry (cf. John 20:27). Paralytic guards become as dead men (Matthew 28:4), ironically dramatizing the power reversal in which living soldiers mirror corpses while the crucified One lives. The women's immediate reaction—fear mingled with great joy—captures the paradoxical emotional fusion characteristic of encounter with the transcendent (Matthew 28:8). Narrative-critical scholars identify this scene as a commissioning pericope, structurally parallel to prophetic calls where divine messengers empower reluctant humans for mission (Isaiah 6:1-8; Jeremiah 1:4-10). Second-Temple angelology viewed angels as custodians of revelation, and their presence at empty tomb aligns with earlier birth narratives where angels announced incarnation, framing resurrection as complementary climactic act. The instruction to "go quickly" embeds urgency within the Gospel's cadence, signaling that resurrection news brooks no procrastination. Patristic sermons often likened the stone rolled away to Scriptures once sealed, now opened by Christ's victory, with angels as exegetes guiding seekers into understanding. Cultural anxieties regarding grave tampering are assuaged by divine testimony, pre-empting anti-resurrection polemics that surfaced in rabbinic circles (Matthew 28:11-15). Liturgically, Easter vigils replicate this angelic proclamation through the Exsultet hymn, inviting congregations to rejoice as the women did. The encounter thus transitions the narrative from lamentation to proclamation, installing the women as official envoys of resurrection. Their acceptance of angelic instruction models epistemological humility, receiving revelation while retaining agency to act. In apologetic dialogue today, this account underscores that Christian proclamation rests on revelation validated by witnesses rather than subjective intuition alone. The angelic moment, therefore, functions as theological hinge upon which the rest of resurrection history swings.

2.3.1 Description of the Angelic Appearance

The Gospel depictions employ vivid sensory metaphors—lightning, snow-white garments—to convey the angel's heavenly origin, aligning with apocalyptic literature where brilliance denotes divine presence (Daniel 10:6; Revelation 10:1). The seismic disturbance accompanying the angel's descent functions not merely as dramatic flourish but as symbol of creation's groan giving way to renewal (Romans 8:22). The angel's posture—seated on the stone—signifies authority over death's domain, visualizing Psalm 110:1 where enemies become a footstool for the Messiah. Comparative studies identify parallels with Greco-Roman epitaph iconography, yet the angel's demeanor diverges by inviting inspection rather than guarding a tomb, reversing funerary symbolism. The ointment-bearing women expected somber stillness yet encountered a locus of eschatological energy, an experiential dissonance scholars term "cognitive shock." Angelic speech pattern follows a triadic structure: reassurance, proclamation, commission—reflecting covenant formulae that combine grace with sending. The use of second-person plural pronouns in Greek underscores collective address, ensuring no woman is marginalized in the directive. Iconographers often depict the angel gesturing toward the vacant slab, reinforcing pedagogical emphasis on forensic evidence. Textual critics note minor variations among Synoptics—single angel in Matthew and Mark, two in Luke—yet harmonization recognizes that Matthew foregrounds primary spokesman while Luke includes full complement, paralleling dual witness requirement in Deuteronomy 19:15. The angel's visage "like lightning" evokes the Transfiguration's radiance (Matthew 17:2), bracketing Jesus' earthly ministry with luminous epiphanies. Rabbinic lore considered lightning a transient manifestation of divine voice, thus readers attuned to Hebrew imagery would perceive the angel's appearance as encoded revelation. The static physicality of the seated angel contrasts the dynamic haste commanded of the women, creating narrative tension that propels the plot. For modern readers, this contrast invites contemplation on divine restfulness alongside human urgency in mission. The angel's unarmed presence, in contrast to Roman soldiers wielding weapons, suggests that resurrection victory operates through proclamation, not force. Psychological anthropology posits that numinous encounters often trigger pro-social behavior; indeed, the women immediately share news rather than hoard privilege. Therefore, the angelic appearance constitutes a performative act, embodying the message it conveys through symbolic posture, luminous attire, and authoritative calm. Such multilayered description strives to evoke reverent awe, integrating sensory detail, theological symbolism, and missional impetus.

2.3.2 The Commission to Go Tell Disciples

The angel's directive initiates the first Gospel mission post-resurrection, charging the women to "go quickly and tell His disciples" (Matthew 28:7), thereby establishing an unbroken chain of verbal witness vital for ecclesial formation. The instruction integrates urgency ("quickly"), audience specificity ("His disciples"), and content ("He has risen... He is going ahead of you to Galilee"), forming a concise communication strategy. Organizational leadership theory highlights clarity, brevity, and actionable steps as hallmarks of effective directives; the angelic commission exemplifies such principles. The message reorients the disciples from retrospective grief to forward-looking rendezvous in Galilee, emphasizing future mission rather than past failure. In rabbinic pedagogy, a messenger's authority derived from fidelity to the sender's words; thus, the women's precise repetition of angelic phrasing later in Luke 24:10 authenticates their role. Theologically, the commission democratizes apostolic function by entrusting women with identical proclamation responsibilities later formalized for the Eleven (Matthew 28:18-20). Missiologists interpret this moment as proto-Great Commission, prefiguring universal evangelism beginning with marginalized voices. Narrative sequencing positions the women between heavenly messenger and apostolic leadership, modeling mediating service akin to deacons who later distribute apostolic teaching (Acts 6). The directive's geographical cue—Galilee—underscores inclusivity, for Galilee of the Gentiles (Matthew 4:15) symbolizes outreach beyond Judean religious epicenter. Angelic assurance "there you will see Him" anchors mission in relational encounter rather than abstract ideology, affirming that proclamation invites people to meeting with Christ, not mere doctrinal assent. Practical theology applies this paradigm by advocating testimonies grounded in personal Christ-encounter that beckon listeners to seek Him. The angel's command implicitly critiques passive spirituality; witness requires movement, speech, and risk. The directive also initiates narrative suspense: will the disciples believe women's words? Their eventual confirmation exhibits the self-correcting nature of communal discernment, illustrating that truth prevails despite biases. Liturgical traditions emulate this commission during Easter liturgies by sending congregants forth with the acclamation "Christ is risen," echoing angelic imperative. Apologetically, the role of women as first commissioned heralds stands as historical criterion unlikely to be manufactured by later patriarchal editors seeking credibility. Finally, the commission embodies divine pedagogy where revelation demands response, ensuring that resurrection remains dynamic event shaping ongoing mission rather than static object of contemplation. Taken together, the angelic commission encapsulates Gospel logic: from heaven through unexpected messengers to the nations.

2.4. The Path from Tomb to City

Leaving the tomb in hurried obedience, the women traversed a brief yet transformative span of perhaps five hundred meters, shifting from sorrow-infused silence to ecstatic proclamation readiness (Matthew 28:8). Topographical studies indicate that Joseph's garden lay near a disused quarry outside the northern wall, requiring the women to navigate rugged terrain before reaching paved streets. The urban threshold they crossed mirrors the internal passage from private revelation to public testimony. Their bodily speed—described as running—contrasts the earlier measured walk toward the tomb, symbolizing resurrection's energizing impact. Hypothalamic-pituitary-adrenal responses to fear typically prompt flight, yet here flight is re-channeled into mission rather than avoidance, illustrating sanctified neurobiological reactivity. The Synoptic notation of "trembling and bewilderment" (Mark 16:8) conveys physiological shaking, integrating human vulnerability with spiritual elation. Passing through the Sheep Gate, they may have encountered early rising priests preparing morning sacrifices, adding ironic resonance: lambs readied for slaughter while the Lamb of God stands risen. Their unladylike haste likely drew curious glances, challenging social decorum that prized measured female demeanor in public. Sociolinguistic theory suggests that such nonverbal signals primed subsequent verbal witness by already disrupting communal expectations, making them catalysts for inquiry once they reached the disciples. The path's auditory landscape—metallic clang of soldier armor, clatter of market carts, distant psalmody from temple courts—formed a sensory backdrop against which their inner transformation unfolded. Archaeological findings of Herodian sewer channels beneath these streets remind modern readers of literal undercurrents of impurity over which resurrection news flowed, symbolizing triumph over decay. The route's brevity underscores that radical spiritual shifts need not require extended timeframes; divine encounters can recalibrate life direction within minutes. Narrative geography functions theologically: movement away from burial site toward living community enacts Exodus pattern of departure from death to life. Practical discipleship gleaning insists that post-encounter believers must not linger in monument-keeping but proceed to mission fields. Luke's emphasis on returning to "tell all these things" highlights the necessity of accurate memory retention amid adrenaline-induced states, perhaps aided by Spirit-prompted recall (John 14:26). Medieval pilgrimage devotions replicate this walk as Stations of the Resurrection, inviting worshipers to embody the women's route. In contemporary homiletics, preachers can leverage the metaphor of transitional spaces—hospital corridors, airport gates—as modern parallels for resurrection carrier pathways. Ultimately, the path from tomb to city epitomizes the liminal passage every Christian must navigate: moving from private faith encounters to public witness, undeterred by social scrutiny.

2.4.1 Geography and Probable Route

Jesus' tomb, hewn out of a garden cliff north-west of the traditional Golgotha, lay within a hundred meters of the modern Church of the Holy Sepulchre site, according to most archaeological consensus. The women likely exited the garden through a service gate leading into the first-century roadway paralleling the city wall before veering south toward the Essene Quarter where many Galilean pilgrims lodged. The topography featured slight elevation changes, requiring careful footing on dew-slicked stone steps carved into bedrock. Street width averaged two and a half meters, barely accommodating carts and pedestrians simultaneously, thereby forcing rapid movers like the women to navigate intermittent bottlenecks. Springtime flora—cyclamen, anemones—bloomed along wall edges, offering sensory contrasts to earlier crucifixion stench. Roman milestones embedded in pavement stones reminded passersby of imperial oversight, yet the women's renewed purpose rendered such symbols impotent before resurrection authority. Spatial theorists argue that transforming events imbue ordinary geography with sacred significance; subsequent pilgrimage routes validate this by memorializing the women's footpath. Proximity to Fortress Antonia meant passing potential detachments of auxiliary troops, heightening risk of interrogation, yet adrenaline likely sustained their courage. Jewish sources describe morning trumpets sounding from the temple at dawn, marking Tamid sacrifice; as these blasts echoed, the women's internal liturgy of joy crescendoed. The route offered vantage glimpses of the Mount of Olives beyond the Kidron, prefiguring Jesus' later ascension locale, hinting at future stages of salvation narrative. Scholars debate alternate tomb sites, yet all plausible routes share common features: compressed urban alleys, multilingual passer-by, and looming temple silhouette. Understanding geography grounds resurrection proclamation in concrete verifiable space, rebutting allegations of mythic detachment. Contemporary Jerusalem guides incorporate these scholarly reconstructions into Holy Week itineraries, ensuring faithful recollection. The route's compactness belies its theological magnitude; a few hundred meters witnessed transition from sealed sorrow to contagious joy. Embodied movement along ancient stones reminds disciples that faith unfolds not merely in intellect but through physical journeys. Such geographical consideration teaches that salvation history intersects real topographies, sanctifying cityscapes as theatres of divine action.

2.4.2 Psychological Transformation Along the Way

Neuropsychological frameworks classify the women's shift from grief to joy as rapid affective reversal, often catalyzed by novel stimuli perceived as life-altering. Exposure to angelic revelation recalibrated their limbic systems, triggering dopamine release associated with reward anticipation—namely reunion with living Lord. Cognitive reappraisal—reinterpreting Jesus' death as necessary prelude to victory—likely emerged as they processed the angel's words while running, exemplifying Romans 12:2's renewal of the mind. Their internal narrative pivoted from tragic closure to open-ended mission, releasing oxytocin that reinforced social bonding and urgency to share news. Trauma studies reveal that positive reinterpretation of traumatic events can mitigate development of PTSD; thus, resurrection encounter preemptively healed crucifixion wounds. Behavioral activation visible in their running counters depressive immobilization, embodying therapeutic principles contemporary psychologists employ. Spiritual direction literature labels such moments as "consolation after desolation," encouraging believers to discern God's hand in emotional uplift. Their psychological shift also included empowerment; previously powerless observers of state violence became fearless proclaimers confronting patriarchal disbelief. This empowerment aligns with Acts 1:8 promise of Spirit-enabled witness, foreshadowed here in anticipatory grace. Philosophers of religion analyze such transformative experiences as evidence of veridical encounter, arguing that fruitfulness of life change supplies pragmatic verification of resurrection claim. The women's experience refutes reductionist theories positing grief-induced hallucination, since group hallucinations with consistent content across individuals are exceedingly rare. Memory consolidation during high arousal states yields vivid recollection, explaining detailed Gospel accounts of early morning sensations. Their transformation underscores Christian anthropology: humans are psychosomatic unities wherein spiritual revelation penetrates emotional and corporeal dimensions. Thus, their psychological journey from tomb to city operates as lived apologetic, illustrating salvation's power to re-script affective landscapes. Pastoral counseling can draw on their narrative to guide mourners toward hope encounters that reframe loss. Ultimately, the women's internal metamorphosis exemplifies resurrection's capacity to transfigure fear into proclamation energy, modeling discipleship's affective trajectory.

2.5. The Sudden Encounter with the Risen Christ

While the women hurried, Scripture records that "Jesus met them" with the greeting "Rejoice!" (Matthew 28:9), a salutation loaded with Isaiahic resonance where Zion is instructed to rejoice at salvation's dawn (Isaiah 62:11). The Greek word χαίρετε functions both as hello and imperative to be joyful, signifying that His presence births joy. Falling at His feet, they grasped them in worship, affirming corporeal reality of His risen body against docetic heresies. Jesus reiterates the angelic commission, adding relational warmth—"my brothers"—thus restoring disciples who had abandoned Him (Matthew 28:10). This personal encounter ratifies angelic testimony, providing experiential redundancy vital for establishing legal certainty under Jewish law. The setting likely occurred along the same urban path, indicating that resurrection does not confine itself to sacred precincts but invades ordinary streets. Literary critics observe inclusio pattern: women depart with joy, confronted by Joy Incarnate, reinforcing thematic coherence. The tactile gesture of holding Jesus' feet echoes the anointing story in Luke 7:38, transforming previous acts of devotion directed toward suffering Messiah into worship of glorified Lord. Comparative resurrection narratives show Thomas later invited to touch wounds (John 20:27), suggesting pedagogical progression from women's foot grasp to disciple's hand probe. Christ's appearance preempts potential rationalizations that angelic vision sufficed; personal encounter is definitive confirmation. Patristic exegesis links women's foot embrace to Isaiah 52:7 about blessed feet heralding good news, making their worship prophetic enactment. Jesus' instruction to proceed to Galilee reaffirms earlier direction, showing divine consistency and urgency. Encounter chronology—angel then Jesus—creates cascading revelation, illustrating God's pedagogical layering. Theological anthropology sees women's prostration as rightful creaturely posture before Creator, uniting familiarity and reverence. Iconography often depicts this scene with Jesus raising His hand in blessing, foot loosely within women's grasp, capturing both transcendence and immanence. Modern gender discourse notes that Jesus entrusts women with mission without paternalistic caveats, demonstrating egalitarian kingdom ethos. The encounter's brevity underscores focus on commission rather than prolonged consolation, signaling that witness supersedes private ecstasy. Joyful greeting balances earlier "do not fear," integrating emotional spectrum of resurrection spirituality. The episode thus anchors women's testimony in dual witness—angelic and Christological—issuing incontrovertible mandate to announce the living Lord.

2.5.1 Recognizing Jesus

Recognition occurred instantaneously, yet underlying cognitive processes drew upon familiarity of voice, posture, and perhaps subtle idiosyncrasies marked during years of discipleship. Post-resurrection appearance narratives often involve initial non-recognition, but here recognition is immediate, suggesting heightened expectancy stirred by angelic news. Visual perception combined with contextual priming—anticipation that they might meet Jesus in Galilee while still near tomb fosters heightened vigilance. Jesus' greeting triggers affective resonance, confirming identity beyond sensory input. Phenomenological philosophy posits recognition as interplay between givenness and interpretive horizon; their horizon expanded moments earlier, enabling rapid identification. The embodiment of Jesus in recognizable form debunks claims of purely spiritual resurrection; physicality is accentuated by women's grasp. Recognition leads swiftly to worship, illustrating that true knowledge of Christ elicits reverence, not mere intellectual assent. Their posture before Jesus juxtaposes earlier lament, highlighting transformation wrought by revelation. Recognition also legitimizes their forthcoming testimony; first-person encounter trumps second-hand report. Church tradition celebrates this moment in Easter liturgies through the troparion "Christ is risen," paralleling women's immediate affirmation. Psychologically, meeting anticipated yet unexpected risen Lord anchors emotional healing, cementing hope. Recognition here differs from Emmaus delayed recognition (Luke 24:31), suggesting diverse pedagogical strategies for varied discipleship readiness. Patristic commentary interprets Jesus choosing to appear first to women as Edenic reversal: Eve listened to Serpent, women now hear Savior, redeeming gender narrative. Their recognition reflects covenant knowledge wherein God knows His people and they know Him (Jeremiah 31:34). For modern disciples, recognition underscores importance of cultivating attentiveness to Christ's presence in ordinary spaces. Therefore, their immediate recognition stands as model of preparatory faith meeting revelatory grace.

2.5.2 Worship and Commission

Prostration represents wholehearted surrender, integrating bodily kinesthetics into spiritual devotion; worship is not confined to liturgies but arises spontaneously in encounter. Grasping feet affirms humility, acknowledging Jesus as rightful sovereign, fulfilling Psalm 2:12's exhortation to "kiss the Son." Jesus' acceptance of worship confirms divinity, contrasting angelic rejection of worship in Revelation 19:10. Commission follows worship, illustrating sequence: adoration fuels mission. Jesus' emphasis on "my brothers" reinstates fractured fellowship, signaling forgiveness precedes commissioning. The directive parallels Exodus 3 where Moses, after removing sandals before burning bush, receives mandate to liberate Israel; here, women clasp feet before sending liberation news. The instruction to go to Galilee underscores mission centrifugal flow—Jerusalem vantage yields global horizons symbolized by Galilean Gentile precincts. Pastoral praxis teaches that authentic worship propels believers outward; static spirituality divorced from mission contradicts resurrection logic. Early Christian art in Roman catacombs depicts this scene, reinforcing message for persecuted believers: worship fuels resilience and proclamation. Commission entrusted to those previously marginalized displays Kingdom upside-down ethic, undermining status hierarchies. The pericope undercuts dichotomy between contemplative and active life; both converge as worship transforms into witness. Jesus' concise phraseology mirrors angel's, ensuring message continuity, critical for apostolic acceptance. Liturgical dismissal "Go in peace to love and serve the Lord" echoes this dynamic, rooting every service within the women's commissioning narrative. Ecclesiology recognizes that church exists primarily as sent community; earliest senders were spice-bearing women turned gospel heralds. The interplay of worship and commission calls modern congregations to evaluate whether adoration produces outward movement or remains insular ritual. Thus, the women's response delineates paradigm for Christ-encountered communities: fall, grasp, rise, go.

2.6. Theological Significance of the Women's Witness

The emergence of women as primary resurrection witnesses constitutes a theological statement about divine sovereignty choosing instruments independent of societal ranking. Their testimony illustrates that revelation disrupts established hierarchies, aligning with Mary's Magnificat where proud are scattered and humble lifted (Luke 1:51-52). Biblical revelation consistently foregrounds unlikely heralds—shepherds at Nativity, Samaritan woman at well, demoniac in Gerasa—culminating in resurrection women. Pauline theology later crystallizes this principle: God chooses what is weak to shame strong (1 Corinthians 1:27). The women's witness also validates embodiment theology; their tactile interaction stresses bodily resurrection integral to Christian hope (Romans 8:23). Soteriologically, their message inaugurates already-not-yet kingdom where new creation dawns yet awaits consummation. Their role exemplifies prevenient grace reaching marginalized before center stage, foreshadowing Gentile inclusion. Ecclesiologically, they prefigure priesthood of all believers, predating clerical structures. Christologically, Jesus' post-resurrection appearance first to women underlines His consistent ministry to outsider groups, reinforcing His identity as inclusive Messiah. Pneumatologically, their immediate empowerment anticipates Pentecostal outpouring across genders (Acts 2:17). Missiologically, they embody Great Commission trajectory: revelation, worship, proclamation. Eschatologically, their journey from grave to city models church as pilgrim people bearing firstfruits of resurrection. Sacramentally, encounter prefigures Eucharistic pattern—meeting Christ, receiving commission, departing in peace—mirrored weekly in liturgy. Ethical implications challenge misogynistic structures in church, calling for retrieval of women's voices. Apologetically, female witness confounds narrative fabrication hypothesis, lending historical credence. Thus, the theological stakes of their testimony permeate multiple doctrinal loci, making their narrative indispensable for holistic resurrection theology.

2.6.1 Gender Dynamics in First-Century Testimony

Roman jurisprudence recognized women's testimony in limited civil matters, yet Jewish halakhah seldom accepted female witness in capital cases, rendering the Gospels' preservation of women's resurrection testimony subversive. Josephus explicitly notes that women are prone to hysteria, a prejudice the evangelists counter by portraying composed, articulate reporting. Feminist scholars argue that retaining such culturally awkward details indicates commitment to truth over social expediency. The women's experience therefore critiques patriarchal gatekeeping of divine revelation. Their narrative encourages hermeneutics from marginalized perspectives, enriching ecclesial exegesis. Historical reception varied: some medieval commentators minimized their role, but reformers like Luther restored emphasis, demonstrating interpretive pendulum swings. Contemporary global church sees women often leading underground movements, echoing first Easter dynamics. Gender dynamics thus reveal ongoing tension between Gospel liberation and societal structures. Recognizing early female witnesses invites churches to repent of silencing women and embrace Spirit's pattern of empowerment. Their testimony reorients authority from institutional certification to Spirit-breathed encounter validated by fruit. Male disciples' initial skepticism substitutes for patriarchal doubts, later reversed by personal encounters, teaching openness to marginalized insights. Gender studies in psychology affirm that mixed-gender collaboration improves group decision quality, exemplified by early church corpus. Therefore, theological engagement with gender dynamics integral to resurrection narrative remains urgent for modern ecclesiology.

2.6.2 Pattern of Discipleship and Proclamation

The women embody a discipleship model marked by attentive presence, sacrificial service, courageous inquiry, receptive faith, transformative encounter, and active proclamation. Attentive presence at cross and tomb contrasts flight of many male disciples, emphasizing perseverance. Sacrificial service manifested in spice procurement demonstrates tangible love. Courageous inquiry surfaces in questioning stone removal logistics. Receptive faith receives angelic word without protest, unlike Zechariah's doubt (Luke 1:18-20). Transformative encounter with risen Christ consummates relational depth. Active proclamation sees them relay news despite anticipated dismissal, mirroring prophets facing unbelief. This pattern aligns with Markan discipleship cycle of call, misunderstanding, restoration. Spiritual formation curricula can employ this template to guide believers through stages of maturing faith. Missional praxis observes that genuine encounter precipitates outward movement; stagnant discipleship signals encounter deficit. Catechetical instruction may highlight women's pattern to inspire youth groups toward courageous witness. Homiletically, each stage offers sermon series scaffold. The pattern affirms holistic discipleship integrating affective, cognitive, volitional dimensions. Neglecting any stage—e.g., service divorced from proclamation—creates truncated spirituality. The women's path thus offers comprehensive discipleship blueprint authenticated by resurrection narrative.

2.7. Harmonizing Gospel Accounts

Apparent divergences—number of angels, sequence of appearances, names listed—often fuel skeptic critiques, yet closer analysis reveals complementary layering consistent with independent eyewitness traditions. Mark ends abruptly at 16:8 in earliest manuscripts, capturing raw astonishment; later ending likely integrates traditions preserved elsewhere. Matthew highlights dual appearance of angel and Jesus on route, Luke records two angels and immediate disciple reporting, John focuses on Mary Magdalene's solo encounter followed by Peter and John visit. Multiple visits, group splitting, and overlapping timelines resolve disparities without forcing artificial conformity. Legal historiography values converging testimony with minor variances as hallmark of authenticity. Early church displayed no discomfort preserving four distinctive narratives, suggesting confidence that truth emerges from polyphonic witness. Harmonization efforts from Tatian's Diatessaron to modern synopses aid devotional reading but should respect each Gospel's theological voice. Narrative criticism reveals each evangelist shaping material to theological aims: Mark centering fear, Matthew highlighting worship, Luke stressing prophetic fulfillment, John accentuating personal relationship. Apologetic discourse benefits from demonstrating that core facts—empty tomb, angelic message, female witness, subsequent appearances—remain constant. Literary devices such as telescoping and spotlighting explain select detail omission without contradiction. Understanding ancient historiography, less preoccupied with strict chronology than thematic arrangement, alleviates modern expectations of journalistic precision. Thus, harmonization affirms rather than undermines confidence in resurrection history.

2.7.1 Differences and Complementary Perspectives

Mark's open-ended silence invites reader response, compelling disciples of later generations to move beyond fear into proclamation, while Matthew supplies resolution via worship encounter, reinforcing liturgical dimension. Luke's emphasis on scriptural fulfillment positions women as bridge between prophetic promises and apostolic preaching. John personalizes narrative to highlight recognition through intimate voice, enriching relational theology. Differences in angel numbers underscore evangelists' theological priorities rather than factual conflict; presence of at least one angel remains common denominator. Variations in women's names reflect different focus groups: Matthew and Mark mention Salome, Luke includes Joanna, demonstrating broader female network. Complementarity extends to location of Jesus' first appearance: Matthew situates it en route, John in garden, emphasizing that Christ meets disciples both in spaces of death and on road of mission. These perspectives collectively portray multidimensional resurrection accessible across contexts—garden solitary grief, road communal mission, upper room fearful seclusion. The evangelists thus weave resilient fabric where threads of difference enhance depth. Discipleship communities today can learn that unified proclamation does not necessitate narrative uniformity; diversity of testimony enriches corporate faith.

2.7.2 Apologetic Value of Multiple Witnesses

Legal analogies note that congruent testimonies with minor variations carry more credibility than rehearsed unanimity. Skeptics alleging collusion must explain why fabricated story retains female witnesses, apparent discrepancies, and embarrassing cowardice of apostles. Historians like E. P. Sanders concede that empty tomb and women witnesses stand among "almost indisputable facts." Resurrection's public defensibility rests partly on multiplicity of witnesses across gender, geography, and temperament. Early preaching in Acts appeals to collective witness, inviting verification (Acts 2:32; 13:31). Paul's summary in 1 Corinthians 15 confirms early creedal reliance on multiple appearances. The variance of narratives guards against mythologizing, anchoring event in messy reality. Apologists can leverage this diversity to build cumulative case: independent attestations, criterion of embarrassment, and transformative outcomes converge. Women's witness particularly subverts conspiracy theories, as forgery would omit socially discounted testimonies. Therefore, multiplicity of accounts functions not as liability but as evidential strength.

2.8. Implications for Contemporary Discipleship and Mission

The women's journey urges modern disciples to embody resurrection proclamation with courage, inclusivity, and joyful urgency. Churches must cultivate spaces where marginalized voices become central heralds, reflecting Kingdom inversion. Spiritual disciplines—early morning prayer walks, acts of compassionate service—rehearse the women's dawn devotion. Missional strategies should prioritize relational credibility earned through persistent presence, echoing women's pre-Easter service. The narrative challenges congregations to balance lament and joy, integrating emotional authenticity within worship. Gender equity in leadership becomes theological imperative grounded in resurrection precedent rather than sociopolitical trend. Evangelists can model testimony on women's concise confession: "We have seen the Lord," thereby stressing encounter over argument. Pastoral care to trauma survivors can employ resurrection journey as template for processing grief toward hope. The episode encourages theological education curricula to highlight female exegetical contributions historically marginalized. Global missions benefit from recognizing that cross-cultural gospel expansion often depends on networks of ordinary believers akin to spice-bearing women. Ethical advocacy emerges from resurrection confidence that death-serving systems are temporary, emboldening church to challenge injustice. Digital evangelism can learn from women's swift dissemination: timely, authentic, relational rather than institutional. Small group discipleship may reenact their path through imaginative prayer, fostering embodied Scripture engagement. The narrative fortifies apologetic confidence, equipping believers to address doubts by pointing to transformed lives. Ultimately, embracing implications of women's witness propels church toward holistic, inclusive, and courageous embodiment of resurrection hope.

2.8.1 Courageous Proclamation

Courage involves action despite fear; the women's trembling yet obedient running models this paradox. Contemporary believers face pluralistic skepticism analogous to first-century patriarchal dismissal. Courageous proclamation necessitates authenticity rooted in personal encounter, not memorized formulas. Practices such as testimony evenings and digital storytelling platforms can amplify lived resurrection experiences. Courage extends to advocating for oppressed, reflecting resurrection's triumph over death-dealing forces.

Church leadership must empower members to speak within vocational spheres, echoing women on public streets. Courageous proclamation resists comfort idol, embracing discomfort for sake of truth. Training in apologetics enhances confidence, but primary impetus remains Spirit-fueled conviction. Women's example encourages believers who lack formal authority to nonetheless testify boldly. Courage also entails vulnerability in sharing past wounds transformed by Christ, mirroring women's journey from trauma to joy. Therefore, courage anchored in resurrection becomes hallmark of authentic discipleship.

2.8.2 Integration of Worship and Witness

Women's posture illustrates inseparability of worship and witness; encounter fuels proclamation, proclamation invites further worship. Contemporary liturgy should culminate in commissioning, not closure. Small groups can structure meetings with upward worship, inward transformation, outward mission, reflecting women's sequence. Worship devoid of witness stagnates; witness devoid of worship burns out. Missional churches balance Sunday adoration with weekday service. Spiritual rhythms of gather-scatter align with women's experience. Song selections celebrating resurrection can segue into testimonies of lived renewal. Witness becomes doxological when it glorifies God through storytelling. Conversely, worship becomes evangelistic when non-believers overhear authentic praise. Integrative practices counter dichotomies crippling church effectiveness. Women's narrative thus provides blueprint for holistic spirituality combining devotion with declaration.

Conclusion

Their pre-dawn trek began with heavy jars and heavier hearts; it ended with light footsteps and lighter spirits singing the first Easter refrain. In the liminal space between tomb and city, "the other women" became the prototype community of resurrection: grounded in historical reality, transformed through divine encounter, and propelled into courageous proclamation. Their story dismantles hierarchies, legitimizes embodied faith, and maps a discipleship journey that marries worship to witness. By tracing their path—through historical context, ritual devotion, angelic instruction, Christ encounter, theological import, and practical mission—this chapter illuminates how ordinary fidelity becomes extraordinary testimony when touched by resurrection power. The church's ongoing vocation, then, is to inherit their rhythm: to rise early in hope, to carry fragrant acts of love into places marked by death, to receive revelation with trembling joy, and to run—yes, run—into the streets announcing, "We have seen the Lord."

Chapter 3. Road to Emmaus – Two Disciples

The Emmaus narrative recorded in Luke 24 : 13-35 is more than a historical anecdote about two distraught disciples; it is a carefully crafted theological drama that turns a seven-mile trek westward from Jerusalem into a mobile classroom on Christology, hermeneutics, psychology, hospitality, sacrament, and mission. Luke deliberately positions the scene on Resurrection Day, yet away from the empty tomb, in order to demonstrate that the risen Lord is not restricted to holy sites or to the company of the Jerusalem leadership. Instead, He seeks out confused disciples on an ordinary Roman road, joins their lament, re-reads Scripture in fresh messianic light, and transforms a simple evening meal into a moment of sacramental revelation.

3.1. Historical and Geographical Setting of the Emmaus Road

Luke specifies that the village called Emmaus lay about sixty stadia—approximately eleven kilometers—from Jerusalem, giving readers a precise spatial framework for the narrative's unfolding (Luke 24 : 13). First-century Roman roads in Judea typically followed ridge routes that balanced security with ease of travel, so the disciples' pathway likely skirted olive groves, vineyard terraces, and sporadic military watchtowers set up to deter brigandage. Archaeological surveys near today's Abu Ghosh, Nicopolis, and Motza reveal milestones and paving stones consistent with a minor arterial road, indicating that the disciples walked a corridor frequented by pilgrims heading home after Passover. The gentle westerly descent from Jerusalem's 760-meter elevation toward the Shephelah provided natural vantage points where travelers could periodically look back toward the city's skyline, a topographical feature that resonates with the disciples' backward-looking conversation about recent events. Springtime climate in Judea—cool morning breezes and warm afternoons—would make an early afternoon departure comfortable, while the lengthening shadows of late day would nudge travelers to secure lodging before nightfall. Roman garrisons stationed at Emmaus after earlier revolts attest to the village's strategic importance as a staging post, yet by the mid-first century the settlement served more as an agrarian market town than a military hub. Cultural geographers note that road networks doubled as information highways, allowing news to spread quickly among Galilean pilgrims, which explains how the disciples could recount crucifixion details to the unrecognized Stranger without delay. Luke's mention of "that very day" roots the narrative in calendar specificity, emphasizing how resurrection revelation intersects ordinary chronology rather than mystical timelessness. By situating the encounter on a publicly accessible route, Luke undermines claims that resurrection appearances occurred only in esoteric visionary spaces; instead, they happen where commerce, politics, and piety mingle. The narrative's geographical concreteness also rebuts allegations of legendary fabrication, for Luke appeals to verifiable distances and identifiable locales known to his first readers. For modern disciples, the Emmaus road represents the everyday spaces—commutes, sidewalks, bus lines—where the risen Christ still meets people in their disillusionment. Mapping the route reinforces the incarnational principle that God's redemptive acts inhabit real soil and stone, not only temple courts or church sanctuaries. The geography of Emmaus thus sets the stage for theological geography: divine presence charting new coordinates in the cartography of human experience. Recognizing this anchors faith in historical reality and invites believers to expect sacred interruptions along their own mundane pathways. The land itself becomes witness that resurrection hope travels well beyond liturgical boundaries, threading through valleys of disappointment into villages of renewed vision.

3.1.1 First-Century Judaean Road Networks and Distance Calculations

Roman engineers measured distances by stadia, with one stadion approximating 185 meters, and they placed inscribed milestones along major routes to facilitate taxation, troop movement, and commercial logistics. The sixty-stadia reference in Luke offers internal evidence of the author's concern for precision, aligning with administrative conventions that would have been familiar to Hellenistic readers accustomed to itineraries like the Antonine Itinerary. Excavations near the modern Jerusalem-Tel Aviv highway have uncovered sections of a Roman road layered with basalt chips and limestone curbs, suggesting a durable surface that allowed travelers to cover eleven kilometers in roughly two and a half hours at moderate pace. Contemporary accounts, such as Josephus' descriptions of troop movements during the Jewish War, corroborate the strategic importance of roads radiating from Jerusalem to coastal plains. The Emmaus road would have intersected ancillary paths leading to Beth-Horon and Lydda, creating a network that channeled both commerce and rumor. Distances mattered for ritual observance; pilgrims needed to calculate Sabbath-day journeys, so Luke's audience would intuit the disciples' freedom to travel that Sunday afternoon without halakhic infringement. The measurement detail also functions rhetorically: it is near enough for the disciples to return the same night yet far enough to symbolize their initial withdrawal from the locus of hope. Lukian scholarship often notes that the Gospel writer uses spatial markers—Nazareth, Capernaum, Jericho—to frame theological motifs; here distance underscores alienation and subsequent re-engagement. Modern pilgrimage ministries retrace the route as spiritual exercise, validating Luke's distance through GPS mapping that mirrors ancient stadia counts. This historical-geographical granularity encourages readers to treat the Emmaus event not as myth but as verifiable occurrence on a known Roman road. The disciples' precise measurement underscores their credibility as witnesses who recall concrete facts even amid emotional turmoil. In homiletical settings, preachers can leverage this logistical accuracy to demonstrate Scripture's rootedness in everyday realities of mileage, terrain, and time management. The Emmaus road's distance therefore serves dual functions: narrative authenticity and theological symbolism of the liminal space between doubt and faith. Appreciating first-century road systems enriches understanding of how the Gospel traveled— literally on foot—across the Mediterranean world. By meditating on stadia markers, believers gain appreciation for the embodied effort embedded in early Christian witness, prompting gratitude for the physical journeys that carried good news from Jerusalem to Rome and beyond.

3.1.2 Socio-Political Atmosphere in Post-Passover Jerusalem

Passover week in AD 30-33 drew hundreds of thousands of pilgrims to Jerusalem, swelling its population four- or five-fold and intensifying Roman surveillance, particularly by procurator Pontius Pilate. Following the festival's conclusion at sundown Saturday, many pilgrims lingered into the first day of the week to settle debts, purchase supplies, and discuss rumors surrounding recent crucifixions. The execution of a Galilean teacher labeled "King of the Jews" (Luke 23 : 38) would have been a flashpoint conversation topic, especially given the Roman penchant for crucifying insurrectionists at public gateways to deter unrest. Political tension remained high because Rome feared that messianic fervor, stoked by prophetic interpretations of Passover's liberation theme, might ignite revolt, as it later did in AD 66. The Sanhedrin leadership, anxious to avoid blame for civil disturbances during festive seasons, collaborated with Roman prefects to ensure rapid removal of bodies and swift suppression of would-be movements. Against this backdrop, the disciples on the Emmaus road embodied the average Galilean pilgrim caught between nationalistic hopes and imperial realities. Their dialogue with Jesus references expectations that He would "redeem Israel," revealing how crucifixion appeared to nullify political aspirations (Luke 24 : 21). Additionally, the report of women claiming an empty tomb circulated as potential security threat; Matthew records bribery of guards to disseminate alternative explanations (Matthew 28 : 11-15). Such rumors would have reached road travelers quickly, heightening confusion and fear. Pilgrims departing Jerusalem that Sunday therefore navigated an atmosphere thick with anxiety about Roman retaliation and religious perplexity about prophetic fulfillment. Social psychologists note that crisis contexts amplify rumor transmission, and Luke depicts this dynamic as the disciples trade fragmented information while traveling. Understanding this socio-political milieu clarifies why the disciples considered it safer to leave Jerusalem and why they displayed downcast faces when interrogated by the Stranger. Their decision to lodge in Emmaus rather than continue to Galilee underscores both travel fatigue and caution about nighttime security patrols. For contemporary readers, recognizing the atmosphere of surveillance and factional suspicion illuminates the courage required later that night when the disciples returned to Jerusalem. The Emmaus episode thus unfolds against a tension-filled canvas where imperial power, religious authority, and eschatological hope collide, making the revelation of the risen Christ not merely a private comfort but a politically charged proclamation.

3.2. Profiles of the Two Disciples

Only one of the walkers is named—Cleopas—while the second remains anonymous, inviting generations of readers to imagine themselves in the narrative. Cleopas may be the same person as Clopas mentioned in John 19 : 25, potentially the husband of Mary of Clopas who stood at the cross, which would situate him within the extended family of Jesus and lend extra poignancy to his dashed hopes. The anonymous companion has been variously identified in patristic and modern scholarship as Cleopas' spouse, possibly Mary, or as Simon (not Simon Peter), whom Luke references obliquely in the summary of resurrection appearances (Luke 24 : 34). While exegetical certainty eludes us, Luke's narrative design benefits from dual focus: a named witness anchors historicity, while an unnamed partner extends interpretive openness, allowing readers—male and female, scholar and layperson— to step into the shoes of a seeker journeying from confusion to illumination. Both disciples had evidently followed Jesus closely enough to know the details of His public ministry, prophetic reputation, and crucifixion, yet they were not part of the Eleven, illustrating how the wider circle of seventy-two (Luke 10 : 1) constituted essential conduits of witness. Their departure from Jerusalem highlights the centrifugal dispersion of disciples before Pentecost regrouping, revealing human vacillation even among committed followers. Luke's inclusion of Cleopas broadens the resurrection witness list beyond apostles and women at the tomb, signaling that Christ's appearances are intentionally democratic. The disciples' rhetorical skills in narrating events to the Stranger imply literacy or oral proficiency, suggesting they were not illiterate peasants but men—or a man and woman—capable of articulating theological disappointment. The narrative thus dispels notions that early Christian faith was predicated on gullible credulity; rather, it shows thoughtful individuals wrestling intellectually with prophetic texts and historical events. Their willingness to extend hospitality despite sorrow reflects Jewish ethical norms of welcoming the traveler, norms that Jesus subtly capitalizes on to reveal Himself. Cleopas and companion thereby model disciples who are honest about disillusionment, open to dialogue, and committed to communal care, traits highly relevant for twenty-first-century believers navigating crises of faith. By profiling these disciples, Luke invites reflection on the diverse makeup of the resurrection community—family members, couples, secondary leaders—whose aggregated testimonies build a multifaceted case for Easter's reality.

3.2.1 Cleopas and Family Connections to the Early Christian Community

The name Cleopas is a Hellenized form of the Aramaic Chalpai, which may correspond to Clopas; many early commentators, including Hegesippus as cited by Eusebius, identify Clopas as Joseph's brother, making Cleopas Jesus' uncle by marriage. If this family linkage holds, Cleopas' shattered expectations acquire deeper resonance, as he would have harbored both patriotic and familial hopes in Jesus' mission. John 19 : 25 lists Mary of Clopas among the women at the cross, which, when combined with Luke's Emmaus account, paints a portrait of a household experiencing both crucifixion anguish and resurrection surprise. Such familial proximity would explain Cleopas' knowledge of the women's tomb report yet accentuate his confusion when confronted with conflicting testimonies about angels. Family networks served as primary conduits for early Christian witness, and Luke's mention of Cleopas underscores how kinship ties propagated resurrection news across Galilee and Judea. Early church historian Papias preserves traditions that offshoot communities in Emmaus traced their origins to Cleopas' witness, indicating the narrative's evangelistic aftereffects. Genealogical speculation aside, Luke's deliberate naming of Cleopas demonstrates historiographical concern; ancient readers valued named sources, akin to footnotes, for verifying oral testimony. The presence of a family member outside the Twelve also safeguards the resurrection tradition from charges of elitist fabrication, showing how broader relational webs corroborated extraordinary claims. For pastoral theology, Cleopas' family connections highlight the role of households in nurturing resilient faith, especially during seasons of corporate grief. Modern small-group ministries can glean insight from familial discipleship patterns that integrate lament, study, and hospitality. Cleopas' probable socioeconomic status as artisan or smallholder, inferred from typical Galilean livelihoods, also underscores the resurrection's reach into working-class environments. In sum, Cleopas personifies the intersection of family loyalty, patriotic yearning, and theological inquiry, making his Emmaus encounter a microcosm of first-century discipleship dynamics. Recognizing his network invites contemporary believers to leverage familial relationships for gospel witness while acknowledging the profound disillusionment that can accompany perceived divine failure within close-knit circles. Cleopas thus functions as both historical anchor and narrative mirror for faith communities navigating the tension between cherished expectations and surprising divine fulfillment.

3.2.2 The Identity of the Second Disciple: Interpretive Possibilities

Luke's narrative silence regarding the second disciple has sparked imaginative exegesis across centuries, each proposal illuminating different facets of the story. Some patristic writers, such as Origen, suggest that the unnamed disciple is Luke himself, thereby positioning the Evangelist as firsthand witness modestly veiling his presence; while intriguing, this view lacks explicit internal evidence. A popular modern hypothesis identifies the companion as Cleopas' wife, Mary, aligning with Luke's inclusive portrayal of women and explaining the household hospitality dynamic at Emmaus; this reading also complements the pattern of paired male-female witnesses in Luke-Acts (e.g., Simeon-Anna, Aquila-Priscilla). Alternatively, several scholars propose Simon, mentioned obliquely in Luke 24 : 34, which would reconcile the Emmaus report with Paul's list of resurrection appearances to Cephas (1 Corinthians 15 : 5); however, the sudden switch from Emmaus to Simon in Jerusalem complicates narrative flow. Other possibilities include one of the seventy-two, perhaps Matthias or Barnabas, reinforcing the theme of widespread resurrection verification before apostolic election. Literary critics argue that Luke purposely withholds the name to invite reader identification: every listener becomes the anonymous pilgrim whom Christ meets on life's road. This open slot in the cast list functions homiletically, enabling preachers to encourage congregants to see themselves as traveling companions awaiting scriptural illumination. The anonymity also emphasizes that resurrection encounters are not privileges reserved for ecclesial elites; the risen Lord engages ordinary disciples on dusty roads. Psychologically, the blank identity encourages projection, allowing believers to insert personal stories of disappointment and renewed faith into the Emmaus framework. Theologically, the unknown disciple represents the church collective, which continually hosts Christ unawares and only recognizes Him in the breaking of bread. While historical curiosity may remain unsatisfied, Luke's deliberate ambiguity broadens application horizons, reminding readers that names are significant but not prerequisite for transformative encounter. In pastoral counseling, the unnamed disciple serves as archetype for believers who feel invisible or secondary, assuring them that the risen Christ draws near regardless of public recognition. Ultimately, the companion's obscurity reinforces the universal reach of resurrection grace, extending the Emmaus invitation to every reader across time and culture.

3.3. Walking in Despair: The Psychological Landscape

Luke's depiction of the disciples' emotional state—"they stood still, looking sad" (Luke 24 : 17)—captures a psychological profile of disenchantment, cognitive dissonance, and grief-induced tunnel vision. Their conversation centers on dashed messianic hopes, demonstrating classic grief processing where individuals rehearse painful events in order to make sense of them. Contemporary bereavement studies affirm that narrative reconstruction is a primary coping mechanism after traumatic loss; the disciples' dialogue exemplifies this phenomenon as they seek a coherent interpretive frame. Cognitive dissonance emerges because their long-cherished expectation that the Messiah would liberate Israel appears irreconcilable with the humiliating death of their teacher. Social identity theory suggests their sense of group belonging eroded at the cross, leading to existential disorientation reflected in their slow gait and downcast demeanor. Luke underscores the irony that their very proximity to the resurrected Christ goes unnoticed, revealing how psychological grief can restrict perceptual awareness. They interpret women's angelic reports as "an idle tale," illustrating how emotional despair biases cognitive evaluation of evidence. Ancient Jewish mourning customs, such as tearing garments and sitting shivah, provided communal structures for processing loss, yet these pilgrims are isolated on a road, amplifying their vulnerability. The Stranger's open-ended question—"What are you discussing?"—functions as pastoral intervention, inviting articulation of sorrow before revelation. Narrative therapists highlight the healing potential of such questioning, which validates emotion while creating space for re-storying. The disciples' willingness to explain events to a perceived stranger demonstrates social trust still partially intact, despite collective trauma. Their summary restates crucifixion events in neutral civic terms—"handed over," "condemned," "crucified"—indicating emotional numbing typical in shock aftermath. Yet they betray lingering hope by referencing "the third day," revealing subconscious recall of resurrection forecasts despite conscious doubt. Jesus responds with gentle reproof, labeling them "slow of heart," thereby diagnosing spiritual sluggishness rooted in misaligned hermeneutics. The psychological landscape thus reveals interplay between cognition, emotion, and theological interpretation, showing that despair often results from reading Scripture through selective lenses that omit suffering servanthood themes. Understanding this dynamic equips modern disciples to recognize how unmet expectations can distort perception, leading to resignation unless confronted by fresh revelatory perspective. The Emmaus journey therefore offers a therapeutic model: honest lament, externalization of pain, cognitive reframing through scriptural exposition, and experiential confirmation in communal meal.

3.3.1 Cognitive Dissonance and Messianic Expectations

First-century Judaism nurtured diverse messianic hopes—royal Davidic deliverer, priestly teacher of righteousness, apocalyptic warrior—derived from texts like 2 Samuel 7, Psalm 2, and Daniel 7. The disciples likely internalized a composite expectation of political liberation and eschatological renewal, reinforced by Jesus' triumphal entry and cleansing of the temple (Luke 19 : 37-46). Cognitive dissonance theory posits that when reality contradicts held beliefs, psychological tension drives either belief revision or information distortion. The crucifixion produced acute dissonance, prompting disciples to reinterpret Jesus as failed prophet rather than adjust their messianic framework. Their selective reading ignored Isaianic suffering servant motifs (Isaiah 53), although Jesus Himself had integrated these themes in passion predictions. The presence of an empty tomb report introduced conflicting data, intensifying dissonance but insufficient to trigger belief change without interpretive scaffolding. Jesus' scriptural exposition serves as cognitive restructuring, aligning their schema with prophetic testimony of necessary suffering preceding glory. Cognitive neuroscience suggests that story-based reframing can rewire neural pathways, enabling new associations between previously incompatible concepts—in this case, crucifixion and victory. The process underscores the importance of theological education that encompasses both triumphant and suffering motifs to immunize believers against disillusionment. For modern readers, recognizing cognitive dissonance invites humility about interpretive blind spots, encouraging ongoing engagement with the full counsel of Scripture. Communities that champion a prosperity-only gospel risk reproducing Emmaus-like despair when suffering intrudes, whereas holistic teaching prepares disciples for paradox of cross-shaped glory. The Emmaus narrative thus serves as cautionary tale and corrective lens, showing that messianic identity must be constructed from comprehensive biblical witness rather than selective proof texts.

3.3.2 Grief Processing in Ancient Jewish Culture

Jewish mourning rituals involved immediate lament upon death, burial before sunset, seven-day intense mourning (shivah), and thirty-day lighter mourning (sheloshim), integrating community support with structured phases of grief. The disciples, however, left Jerusalem prematurely, thereby suspending communal mourning rhythms and exacerbating emotional dislocation. Their discussion en route approximates an informal shivah circle, seeking meaning outside traditional setting. Psalmic laments, especially Psalms 42-43 and 88, provided linguistic templates for grief, and echoes of such psalms resonate in their language of dashed hope. Rabbinic texts counsel mourners to recall God's past faithfulness; ironically, the disciples' memory fails to connect passion events with covenant narrative until Jesus intervenes. Anthropologists note that pilgrimage contexts often disrupt routine mourning, creating liminality where new religious meanings can emerge. The Emmaus road becomes such liminal space, transitioning disciples from rupture to renewal. Jesus' incognito presence honors mourning norms by initially listening rather than preaching, demonstrating pastoral sensitivity to grief. His eventual scriptural exposition aligns with Jewish practice of turning to Torah for comfort, yet His Christocentric reading imbues familiar texts with unanticipated consolation. Modern grief counseling parallels this by integrating patient narratives with meaning-making frameworks, affirming the Emmaus model's psychological validity. The narrative reassures believers that Christ joins them in sorrow, respects process, yet gently guides toward hope anchored in redemptive storylines. Recognizing cultural mourning practices also explains disciples' hospitality reflex—providing meal for traveling teacher aligns with mitzvah of comforting mourners, thus turning roles unexpectedly when comfort is reciprocally bestowed.

3.4. The Stranger's Exposition of Scripture

Luke reports that beginning with Moses and all the prophets, Jesus interpreted the things concerning Himself, delivering perhaps the most comprehensive messianic Bible study never directly quoted in the New Testament (Luke 24 : 27). This sweeping hermeneutical lecture reframed Torah, Prophets, and Writings through the lens of Christ's suffering and glory, establishing authoritative precedent for apostolic preaching in Acts. The method models a typological approach where events, institutions, and figures—Passover lamb, bronze serpent, Davidic king—foreshadow Christ's redemptive work. Jesus' exposition demonstrates that correct reading of Scripture requires recognition of a cruciform trajectory culminating in resurrection, countering interpretive systems that divorce messianic hope from sacrificial atonement. The disciples' later testimony—"Were not our hearts burning within us?"—indicates affective resonance accompanying cognitive illumination, illustrating the dynamic interplay of Spirit-empowered teaching and inner transformation. Modern biblical theology owes much to this Emmaus hermeneutic, which legitimizes Christ-centered reading across canon without allegorical excess. The lecture likely surveyed Genesis 3 : 15, Exodus 12, Leviticus 16, Numbers 21, Deuteronomy 18 : 15-19, Psalm 22, Isaiah 53, Zechariah 12 : 10, and Daniel 7, weaving them into a unified narrative arc. By expounding "all the prophets," Jesus asserts prophetic consensus on messianic suffering, challenging sectarian proof-texting that isolates triumph texts. The disciples, steeped in synagogue lectionary cycles, would have recognized these passages yet misaligned their significance; Jesus pivots their interpretive posture from geopolitical liberation to cosmic redemption. The exposition's timing—during physical journey—embodies the Jewish pedagogical tradition of walking instruction, reminiscent of Deuteronomy 6 : 7 about discussing Torah "along the way." This mobility symbolizes progressive revelation: understanding grows as disciples move forward, both literally and figuratively. The unknown Stranger thus becomes paradigm for Christ as both content and interpreter of Scripture, establishing hermeneutical humility whereby readers rely on risen Lord through Spirit to unlock textual meaning. The Emmaus study also critiques reductionist historical-critical methods that exclude theological teleology, asserting that Scripture's climax is a person, not merely ethical principles. For contemporary teachers, the passage mandates Christocentric exegesis that honors original contexts yet culminates in revelation of crucified-risen Messiah. The Stranger's mastery of Scripture reinforces the unity of Old and New Testaments, dispelling Marcionite tendencies to sever them. Ultimately, Emmaus hermeneutics invites believers to expect that diligent study will ignite hearts, indicating experiential confirmation of doctrinal insight.

3.4.1 Moses and the Prophets as Messianic Witness

Foundational Mosaic narratives—creation, fall, exodus, covenant—frame human predicament and divine rescue, culminating in a promised prophet greater than Moses (Deuteronomy 18 : 15). Jesus likely highlighted typological correspondences: Passover lamb prefiguring sacrificial death, manna foreshadowing bread of life, and the rock struck in wilderness mirroring pierced Savior (1 Corinthians 10 : 4). Prophetic literature advances these motifs: Isaiah portrays a servant pierced for transgressions, while Zechariah envisions a shepherd struck yet leading purified remnant. Jesus may have linked Psalm 22's righteous sufferer with crucifixion details and Psalm 16's promise of God not abandoning His holy one to decay with resurrection. The "all the prophets" phrase signals comprehensive scope, not selective cherry-picking, affirming canonical coherence around messianic suffering-glory sequence. Early apostolic sermons—Peter in Acts 3, Paul in Acts 13—mirror this pattern, demonstrating Emmaus lecture's lasting catechetical influence. Studying Law and Prophets as witness to Christ undermines supersessionist claims that Old Testament is obsolete; rather, it is fulfilled and illuminated. For Jewish-Christian dialogue, Emmaus model encourages respectful engagement with Hebrew Scriptures' integrity while presenting messianic fulfillment. The lecture's structure may have followed Jewish midrashic techniques—stringing texts (pesher), analogical reasoning (heqesh)—showing Jesus' pedagogical accommodation to contemporary interpretive forms. Recognizing Torah-Prophets convergence around Christ balances hermeneutics that over-emphasize either moral law or end-time prophecy, integrating both within redemptive storyline. Thus, Emmaus establishes scriptural continuity that sustains Christian faith against accusations of novelty. Believers today are called to emulate this holistic reading, allowing Law's demand and Prophets' hope to find resolution in crucified-risen Lord.

3.4.2 Hermeneutical Keys Provided by the Risen Christ

Three interpretive keys emerge from Emmaus exposition: necessity, unity, and experiential confirmation. First, necessity—"Was it not necessary that the Messiah suffer?"—frames cross and resurrection as divine must, not tragic accident, aligning with earlier passion predictions and Acts' emphasis on divine determinate plan. Second, unity—the entirety of Scripture converges on Christ, affirming canonical coherence amid literary diversity. Third, experiential confirmation—the disciples' heart-burning testifies that proper interpretation elicits spiritual vitality, indicating hermeneutics is not merely academic but transformational. These keys challenge post-Enlightenment skepticism that views biblical narrative as disjointed anthology and see messianic readings as contrived. Jesus' authoritative exegesis bestows confidence that Scripture, when read through resurrection lens, yields cohesive redemptive message. This does not license eisegesis; rather, it establishes Christ as hermeneutical governor whose life, death, and resurrection set canonical trajectory. For theological education, Emmaus keys call for curricula integrating biblical studies with Christology and spiritual formation, preventing compartmentalization of exegesis and devotion. Pastors can employ these keys to craft sermons that trace gospel threads across diverse texts, fostering congregational literacy shaped by Christ's explanatory framework. Moreover, Emmaus hermeneutic models dialogical pedagogy: questions followed by exposition foster discovery rather than unilateral indoctrination, respecting learners' cognitive process. Hermeneutical humility arises, acknowledging need for divine illumination to perceive Scripture's depth. Therefore, Emmaus keys remain indispensable for robust, life-giving engagement with the Bible in every era.

3.5. Hospitality at Emmaus: Breaking Bread and Recognition

Upon reaching Emmaus near evening, the disciples offer lodging to the Stranger, fulfilling Jewish hospitality ethics that treat travelers as potential bearers of blessing (Genesis 18 : 1-8). Jesus accepts and, in a role reversal, becomes host at table, blessing bread, breaking it, and distributing portions, at which moment their eyes open and recognition dawns (Luke 24 : 30-31). Ancient Near Eastern meals carried covenantal overtones; sharing bread signified mutual acceptance and solidarity, so Jesus' hosting act establishes a new covenantal fellowship with these disciples. Liturgical scholars see in this gesture a proto-Eucharist that links resurrection presence with sacramental meal, prefiguring later Christian liturgy where Word and Table converge. Recognition triggered by familiar table practice underscores that discipleship entails formation through repeated ritual actions embedding theological memory. The verb Luke uses for "recognized" echoes LXX terminology for divine manifestation, implying epiphany. Jesus' immediate disappearance post-recognition shifts focus from physical sight to interpretive insight, teaching that resurrection presence now operates sacramentally and scripturally. Hospitality thus becomes sacrament of encounter: inviting stranger opens door to hosting Christ. Sociologically, table fellowship dismantled social hierarchies; the Emmaus meal inclusive of a formerly unknown traveler heralds church's universal dining table where Jew and Gentile, male and female, united in Christ. The disciples' invitation—"Stay with us"—models spiritual yearning that welcomes revelation, contrasting with earlier reluctance to accept women's tomb report. The chronology—from Scripture exposition on road to sacramental recognition at table—establishes Christian worship pattern of Word followed by Meal. The event also rehabilitates memories of last supper gloom by showing risen Christ now presiding over joyous post-crucifixion feast. Practically, Emmaus invites contemporary believers to cultivate hospitality as context for gospel encounter, expecting Christ to reveal Himself in shared meals, community groups, and household communion. The narrative offers corrective to individualistic spirituality, reminding the church that ecclesial recognition often occurs in collective acts of breaking bread. Furthermore, the story equips sacramental theology against accusations of empty ritualism by demonstrating that when blessed by Christ, ordinary bread mediates extraordinary revelation. The disciples' transformed perception illustrates that faith "sees" differently through ritual enacted memory, tying cognition to embodied practice. Thus, Emmaus table fellowship forms a foundational paradigm for Christian ecclesial identity and mission.

3.5.1 Ancient Near Eastern Hospitality Practices

Hospitality (philoxenia) in first-century Judea functioned as social currency, compensating for limited public inns and reflecting Torah commands to love the stranger (Exodus 22 : 21). Hosts provided water for foot washing, oil for anointing, bread, and secure lodging; failure to offer such care risked communal shame. Emmaus disciples, though grieving, adhere to this cultural norm, demonstrating ethical resilience. Hospitality carried reciprocal expectation: guest reciprocated with blessing, teaching, or news—fulfillment realized dramatically when Jesus opens Scriptures and reveals resurrection. Greco-Roman literature attests similar customs, and archaeological remains of domestic courtyards with shared ovens suggest communal meal preparation aligning with Luke's depiction. Rabbinic sources commend hospitality as greater than receiving Shekinah glory, a sentiment prophetic in Emmaus where welcoming stranger leads to divine manifestation. Inviting traveler at dusk extended risk, as banditry increased after dark, underscoring disciples' sacrificial generosity. Modern missional theology retrieves hospitality as evangelistic praxis, citing Emmaus as biblical warrant for gospel-centered table fellowship. In global south house-church movements, hospitality remains primary vehicle for discipleship, mirroring first-century patterns. Understanding ancient practices enriches appreciation for Emmaus narrative: it is not quaint courtesy but covenantal act that becomes crucible of revelation. Contemporary Western individualism erodes such practices; Emmaus challenges churches to reclaim open homes as sacred space.

3.5.2 Eucharistic Echoes and Sacramental Theology

Luke deliberately employs fourfold liturgical actions—take, bless, break, give—paralleling Last Supper and feeding of five thousand, creating intertextual resonance that signals sacramental significance. Early church fathers such as Irenaeus and Cyril referenced Emmaus when articulating real presence of Christ in Eucharist, noting that eyes opened "in the breaking of bread." The disciples' burning hearts during Scripture exposition culminate in decisive recognition at table, revealing dialectic of Word and Sacrament. Sacramentally, the event confirms post-ascension mode of presence; believers meet Christ in communal meal even when physical appearances cease. The narrative also affirms continuity between cross and table: bread broken symbolizing crucified body now serves risen fellowship. Liturgical traditions incorporate Emmaus imagery in Eastertide Eucharistic prayers, invoking narrative to frame celebrants' expectation of encounter. The story resists reduction of Eucharist to memorial-only view, highlighting transformative recognition through consecrated action. Conversely, it guards against magical objectification by linking sacrament to scriptural illumination and mission. The disappearance of Jesus signals eschatological tension: sacramental presence mediates yet anticipates fuller consummation at messianic banquet (Revelation 19 : 9). The Emmaus pattern also legitimizes lay table leadership—Cleopas, not apostle, experiences Christ's presiding—which informs debates on who may officiate communion. For ecumenical dialogue, the account offers common ground: all traditions affirm breaking bread as privileged moment of meeting the risen Lord. In pastoral formation, Emmaus encourages clergy to balance preaching with sacrament, ensuring both hearts and eyes of congregations are opened. Disciples' immediate missionary impulse post-meal demonstrates Eucharist's missional trajectory; communion fuels proclamation. Thus, Emmaus undergirds sacramental theology with narrative vivacity, situating Eucharist within resurrection reality.

3.6. The Burning Hearts Phenomenon

When the disciples reflect on their experience, they speak of hearts burning within as Jesus opened Scriptures (Luke 24 : 32), describing an affective-cognitive ignition that combines intellectual clarity with spiritual fervor. The phrase evokes prophetic fire imagery—Jeremiah 20 : 9's "burning in my bones"—linking scriptural understanding to vocational passion. Psychologically, such inner warmth aligns with limbic system activation triggered by meaningful insight and relational presence, releasing dopamine associated with reward and motivation. Theologically, burning hearts signal Spirit-enabled illumination, foreshadowing Pentecost tongues of fire that will empower corporate witness. The phenomenon validates emotional response to doctrinal truth, countering dichotomies that pit intellect against affection. Early monastic writers cited Emmaus to describe lectio divina, where meditative reading ignites love for God. In revival history, testimonies of "strangely warmed" hearts echo Emmaus, from Wesley's Aldersgate to modern renewal movements, demonstrating narrative's ongoing resonance. The disciples' bodily metaphor underscores incarnation principle: faith engages whole person, not disembodied reason. Contemporary neuroscience supports this integration—insight without affect seldom motivates behavior; burning hearts propel disciples back to Jerusalem. Worship leaders can glean from Emmaus that songs rich in Scripture catalyze transformative ardor. The narrative also cautions against pursuit of emotional thrills detached from biblical grounding; burning arises from exegesis, not from manipulated atmosphere. Homileticians can pattern sermons after Emmaus dynamic: diagnose despair, expound Scripture, invite response, expecting Spirit to kindle conviction. Disciples' reflection demonstrates metacognition—recognizing internal changes fosters spiritual awareness. The burning also functions apologetically: subjective experience corroborates objective revelation, though never replaces it. Emmaus thus offers integral model where heart and mind, Scripture and Spirit, converge in life-directing warmth.

3.6.1 Phenomenological Analysis of Spiritual Illumination

Phenomenology examines lived experience, and Emmaus provides prototypical account of illumination characterized by sudden coherence, affective heat, and motivational compulsion. Prior confusion gives way to gestalt shift as narrative of suffering Messiah aligns disparate scriptural pieces. Such "aha moments" correlate with anterior superior temporal gyrus activation, yet Luke attributes primary agency to Christ's exposition. The experience includes intersubjective dimension: both disciples share burning sensation, indicating communal validation of spiritual insight. Phenomenological descriptors—warmth, enlightenment, energy—bear resemblance to mystic literature across traditions, yet Emmaus roots them in historical revelation rather than private contemplation. The temporal sequence—burning hearts precede recognition—suggests preparatory function: interior illumination readies perception for sacramental epiphany. The disciples retrospectively recognize burning, showing sometimes awareness of grace is post-event discernment, encouraging believers to reflect on subtle movements of Spirit. Pastoral praxis can incorporate examen prayer to help disciples identify "heartburn" moments. The Emmaus burning contrasts with anxiety-induced heart racing; its quality is peace-infused zeal, distinguishing divine illumination from emotional hype. Recognizing phenomenology aids spiritual directors in accompanying seekers experiencing similar warmth. The account also challenges purely rational apologetics to integrate experiential component, acknowledging God engages imagination and emotion. Phenomenological appreciation thus broadens discipleship to honor subjective aspects within objective faith.

3.6.2 Role of the Holy Spirit in Post-Resurrection Revelation

Although Luke does not mention the Spirit explicitly in Emmaus pericope, subsequent Pentecost narrative imbues earlier events with pneumatological retrospect. The burning hearts anticipate Spirit's ministry of illuminating Scripture (John 16 : 13) and warming affections (Romans 5 : 5). Apostolic preaching in Acts mirrors Emmaus pattern— Spirit-filled exposition of prophecies to interpret Christ events. The Spirit also enables recognition of risen Lord in Eucharistic symbols, bridging bodily absence until parousia. Patristic theologians viewed Emmaus as prefigurement of sacramental epiclesis where Spirit descends upon bread and believers. Pneumatology safeguards against fossilizing Emmaus into past event; same Spirit continues to open Scriptures and hearts today. Charismatic traditions appeal to burning hearts as experiential evidence of Spirit's present work, while sacramental traditions emphasize Spirit's role in consecrating meal. Integrating both yields balanced spirituality that delights in Word, Sacrament, and experiential presence. Emmaus thus teaches that resurrection revelation is Trinitarian: Father's plan, Son's exposition, Spirit's ignition. Contemporary disciples can pray for Spirit-kindled understanding whenever they engage Scripture, expecting transformative warmth that propels mission.

3.7. Return to Jerusalem: From Private Epiphany to Communal Witness

The disciples, though it is late and travel after dark is risky, immediately set out for Jerusalem, demonstrating that authentic encounter overrides self-preservation (Luke 24 : 33). Nighttime travel along unlit roads exposed them to bandits, wild animals, and Roman patrols enforcing curfews, yet burning hearts generate courageous urgency. Their reversal of direction symbolizes conversion—turning back toward community they had abandoned. Upon arrival, they find the Eleven assembled, already receiving separate confirmation of resurrection through Simon's experience, illustrating convergence of independent testimonies. The Emmaus duo recount both road exposition and bread-breaking recognition, supplying church with double assurance: scriptural and sacramental. Their narrative enriches apostolic understanding, weaving broader witness network. Luke's emphasis on immediacy models chain-reaction evangelism: good news cannot be hoarded. The return also fulfills geographic centripetal pull: witness begins in Jerusalem before radiating outward (Acts 1 : 8). Logistically, their trek likely took two hours; they arrive near midnight, yet community remains awake, signaling collective expectant tension. Sociologically, their reintegration into apostolic circle restores relational bonds ruptured by despair, demonstrating resurrection's reconciling power. The Emmaus testimony will shape early kerygma; Peter and John later embed scriptural exposition resembling Emmaus template. For contemporary mission, the return underscores necessity of communal accountability for personal revelations, guarding against idiosyncratic interpretations. It also encourages believers to overcome fatigue and risk in order to share transformative experiences. The narrative affirms that isolated epiphanies reach maturity only within ecclesial conversation, where multiple witnesses cross-verify God's acts.

3.7.1 Night Travel Risks and Narrative Urgency

First-century roads lacked artificial lighting; moon phase around Passover is full, slightly mitigating darkness, yet travelers still relied on torches prone to extinguish in wind. Roman law sometimes restricted civilian movement at night to prevent uprisings, so disciples risked arrest as suspicious wanderers. Banditry in Judea's hinterlands was notorious; Josephus records numerous highway robberies. Yet narrative urgency propels disciples, reflecting prophetic motif of feet running with good news (Isaiah 52 : 7). Their haste contrasts earlier sluggish sadness, evidencing transformation. The risk underscores sincerity; fabricated story benefitting from daylight would not necessitate dangerous nocturnal journey. Literary critics view night travel as liminal motif—transition from ignorance to enlightenment. The urgency also foreshadows missionary journeys facing peril for gospel's sake (2 Corinthians 11 : 26), setting precedent of sacrifice. For modern ministry, Emmaus night run challenges comfort-oriented witness, urging timely sharing even when inconvenient. It also addresses spiritual lethargy: renewed vision re-energizes purpose beyond natural fatigue. Recognizing risks inflames admiration for disciples' zeal and invites imitation in contemporary contexts where testimony may entail social or legal jeopardy.

3.7.2 Integration into the Apostolic Testimony

Upon joining the Eleven, Emmaus disciples contribute unique pieces: scriptural exposition content and Eucharistic recognition pattern, shaping apostolic teaching. Their testimony complements women's tomb report and Peter's appearance, constructing multifaceted evidence for resurrection. Luke's compilation in Acts demonstrates reliance on such eyewitness strands to craft sermons. The integration illustrates ecclesial epistemology: truth emerges in communal pooling under Spirit's guidance. It also models inclusivity: non-apostolic witnesses share platform with core leaders, democratizing proclamation. The Emmaus story likely influenced early liturgical structure—Word and Table— adopted in apostolic communities. The disciples' presence when Jesus later appears to group (Luke 24 : 36-49) validates their earlier report, vindicating their nocturnal risk. For ecclesiology, Emmaus emphasizes necessity of communal discernment; solitary revelation must be tested within body. For ecumenism, narrative underscores complementarity of diverse traditions—scriptural exposition (Protestant), sacramental focus (Catholic), experiential encounter (Charismatic)—within single resurrection testimony. Integration of Emmaus witness thus enriches church's collective memory and reinforces reliability of resurrection claim.

3.8. Theological and Missional Implications

The Emmaus account establishes foundational principles for Christian life and mission. First, Christocentric hermeneutics: all Scripture converges on crucified-risen Christ, guiding preaching, teaching, and personal study. Second, discipleship as journey: faith matures through honest dialogue, shared lament, and progressive revelation along life's pathways. Third, hospitality as sacramental space: welcoming strangers opens avenues for divine encounter and communal recognition. Fourth, Word and Table integration: worship structures should unite scriptural exposition with bread-breaking to facilitate holistic recognition of Christ's presence. Fifth, affective engagement: burning hearts validate emotional resonance as integral to spiritual transformation. Sixth, mission urgency: authentic encounter compels immediate witness, overcoming fear and fatigue. Seventh, communal verification: individual experiences attain maturity and credibility within ecclesial fellowship. Together these implications shape missional churches that study Scripture

Christocentrically, practice generous hospitality, celebrate sacrament meaningfully, cultivate passionate yet discerning spirituality, and mobilize members for courageous proclamation. Emmaus also speaks to postmodern skepticism by demonstrating that doubt can be gateway to deeper understanding when addressed through relational dialogue and scriptural re-reading authored by Christ. It challenges consumer Christianity that seeks private inspiration without communal accountability or costly mission. Finally, Emmaus underscores eschatological hope—journey ends not at Emmaus but in Jerusalem where Spirit will be poured out, signaling ongoing adventure until consummation. Thus, Emmaus vision equips church to navigate pluralistic cultures with confidence that the risen Lord still walks unrecognized beside seekers, ready to ignite scriptures and break bread in surprising places.

3.8.1 Christocentric Hermeneutics for the Church Today

In an age flooded with interpretive methodologies—historical-critical, literary, socio-political—the Emmaus model insists that any faithful reading must ultimately bear witness to Jesus' redemptive work. This does not negate rigorous scholarship; rather, it positions Christ as hermeneutical horizon guiding critical investigation toward theological telos. Seminary curricula can incorporate Emmaus-based courses that train students to trace redemptive themes across canon while honoring textual contexts. Congregational Bible studies can adopt Emmaus questions: How does this passage anticipate Christ? Where do cross and resurrection shed light here? This hermeneutic nurtures worship as apostles model in doxological exegesis (Romans 11 : 33-36). Christocentric reading also safeguards against moralism, showing that Scripture's primary function is to reveal divine rescue, not merely prescribe ethical principles. Such orientation fosters humility, recognizing need for Spirit's illumination rather than human ingenuity alone. Ecumenically, shared Christocentric focus provides unifying interpretive center amid denominational differences. Thus, Emmaus hermeneutic stands as timeless compass for navigating biblical landscape toward the living Christ.

3.8.2 Spiritual Practices of Journeying and Table Fellowship

Emmaus inspires disciplines of pilgrimage—literal or metaphorical—where believers walk, reflect, and converse about Scripture, inviting Christ to join dialogue. Retreat ministries can structure walking meditations punctuated by scriptural reflection, culminating in communal meals. Families can practice "Emmaus dinners," reading passages, discussing disappointments, and sharing bread with expectancy of Christ's presence. House churches replicating Word-Meal rhythm embody early pattern, fostering relational depth and missional readiness. Hospitality teams can view guest reception as potential Emmaus moment, cultivating attentiveness to hidden Christ among visitors. Spiritual directors can guide counselees to identify burning-heart episodes, helping integrate intellect and affection. Urban ministries may organize neighborhood prayer walks, discerning Christ's activity along streets like Emmaus road. These practices translate ancient narrative into contemporary rhythms, ensuring resurrection remains lived reality, not distant story. Emmaus thus shapes vibrant spirituality where journeys and tables become theaters of ongoing revelation.

Conclusion

The road to Emmaus begins in the shadow of shattered dreams and ends in the blaze of communal proclamation, charting a trajectory every disciple must eventually trace. Along that dusty stretch between Jerusalem's political turmoil and Emmaus' humble hearth, the risen but unrecognized Jesus reorients despairing hearts through Scripture, awakens embodied recognition at table, and kindles missionary zeal that refuses night's intimidation. Cleopas and his unnamed companion embody humanity's pilgrimage from interpretive blindness to sacramental sight, showing that Christ meets us not only in sacred precincts but on ordinary roads, at cheap supper tables, and within honest conversations laced with disappointment. Their burning hearts testify that the Spirit still fuses intellect and emotion when Scripture is opened Christocentrically, while their nocturnal sprint back to Jerusalem exemplifies how genuine encounter propels courageous witness. The Emmaus narrative therefore serves as perpetual template for the church's worship and mission: Word interpreted by Christ, bread broken in remembrance, hearts ignited by Spirit, and feet sent to relay integrated testimony. In every era, believers who welcome strangers, listen to Scripture's full story, and share meals in expectancy discover anew that the Lord is risen indeed—and that realization forever redirects their journeys from retreat to proclamation, from solitude to community, and from bewildered sorrow to hope-filled action.

Chapter 4. Private Appearance to Simon Peter

The terse but tantalizing notice that the risen Jesus "has appeared to Simon" (Luke 24 : 34; cf. 1 Cor 15 : 5) opens a window onto one of the most poignant and pastorally charged moments in the resurrection drama. More is left unsaid than said: Luke records no setting, John gives no dialogue, and Paul merely lists the appearance among the foundational events of the Gospel he received. Yet the silence itself invites reverent imagination guided by exegetical, historical, and theological inquiry. Simon Peter—the outspoken disciple who had embraced Messianic hope with audacity, then denied his Lord with oaths—occupies a liminal space between shame and restoration, failure and future leadership. A private meeting with the risen Christ therefore functions not merely as an isolated consolation but as a pivot for the entire apostolic mission.

4.1. Biblical Record and Witnesses of the Private Appearance

4.1.1 Scriptural Evidence in Luke 24 : 34 and 1 Corinthians 15 : 5

Luke's resurrection narrative climaxes with the Emmaus travelers bursting into the Jerusalem gathering and hearing, almost in chorus, "The Lord has risen indeed, and He has appeared to Simon!" (Luke 24 : 34). The Greek perfect ἐγήγερται underscores durable reality rather than fleeting event, positioning Peter's encounter as foundational fact already circulating among disciples before the nightfall appearance in the locked room. Paul, writing two decades later, integrates the same datum into his earliest creedal summary: Christ died according to the Scriptures, was buried, was raised on the third day, and "appeared to Cephas, then to the Twelve" (1 Cor 15 : 5). That Pauline order suggests the Simon meeting pre-dated the collective experience later that evening, placing private restoration ahead of public commissioning. The appearance's double attestation in Luke and Paul meets stringent historical criteria—multiple independent witnesses and early creedal inclusion—indicating that the church never considered Peter's encounter legendary embellishment. Instead, it belonged to the bedrock proclamation transmitted within months of Easter. No verbatim conversations survive, yet the recurring emphasis on sequence reveals narrative logic: Peter, as first among the apostolic band to encounter the risen Lord, becomes credible voice for the Twelve, just as Mary Magdalene had become first witness among the women. The textual lacuna, far from undermining authenticity, aligns with ancient biographical conventions that sometimes veil intimate dialogues yet foreground decisive reversals. Luke's insertion of the Peter appearance between Emmaus and the group epiphany also serves a literary purpose, interlocking individual, paired, and communal testimonies in escalating crescendo. Modern readers attentive to Gospel artistry recognize that Luke's mention functions like a hinge, turning private repentance into collective joy. Historically minded scholars note how Luke's simple sentence anticipates the Pentecost sermon where Peter, now restored, preaches the resurrection with bold clarity (Acts 2 : 14-36). The scriptural evidence therefore allows confident affirmation that a discrete, transformative meeting occurred early on Resurrection Sunday, shaping everything that followed. It simultaneously cautions interpreters against speculative reconstruction beyond the contours the Spirit deemed sufficient. Exegetes thus approach the sparse verses neither to invent details nor to minimize their weight but to trace their theological trajectory. At the intersection of Luke's narrative precision and Paul's apostolic tradition, the appearance to Simon emerges as irreplaceable link in the chain of Easter verification.

4.1.2 Harmonization with Other Resurrection Narratives

Integrating the Peter appearance with the broader synoptic and Johannine witness requires careful sequencing without forcing artificial uniformity. The earliest events of Resurrection Day unfold rapidly: women visit the tomb at dawn (Luke 24 : 1-9; John 20 : 1-2); Peter and the beloved disciple rush to inspect the linens (John 20 : 3-10); Mary Magdalene lingers and converses with Jesus (John 20 : 11-18); other women meet Him on the pathway (Matt 28 : 8-10); and the Emmaus travelers share supper revelation (Luke 24 : 13-32). Within this tapestry, Peter's private encounter fits chronologically after his tomb inspection yet before the Emmaus pair returns, explaining why Cleopas can cite it as established news. The harmonization upholds narrative integrity: Peter, still burdened by denial shame, likely remained in Jerusalem vicinity while others scattered. The women's testimony seeds hope but does not expunge his guilt; personal restoration requires direct conversation. Harmonization also clarifies why Luke omits Peter's role in the John 20 : 19-23 meeting; restoration has already begun privately, allowing Peter to receive communal commission without unresolved breach. John's later Galilean beach reinstatement (John 21 : 15-19) functions not as initial forgiveness but as public ratification of prior reconciliation, consistent with biblical patterns where God often confirms in community what He first addresses in secret (cf. Joseph's private testing of brothers before familial reunion, Gen 44-45). The integrated chronology eliminates perceived contradictions and underscores the multidimensional strategy of the risen Christ: He appears to women, pairs, individuals, and groups, tailoring revelation to each pastoral need while orchestrating corporate witness. Harmonization moreover sketches a psychological timeline: Peter moves from shock at the empty tomb, through isolating remorse, into solitary encounter, and finally toward public leadership. That trajectory resonates with modern disciples who likewise oscillate between communal worship and private wrestling in seasons of restoration. Recognizing narrative flow also bolsters apologetic confidence, for diverse accounts interlock without dependency, displaying patterns typical of truthful eyewitness memories rather than collusion. The linear chart that emerges testifies less to rigid chronology than to Spirit-supervised coherence where every appearance, including the brief mention to Simon, contributes indispensable brushstrokes to the resurrection mosaic. Far from being an incidental note, the harmonized place of Peter's encounter reveals divine intentionality: the very disciple who denied with curses becomes earliest apostolic recipient of grace, ensuring that subsequent proclamation rings with authenticity born of forgiven failure.

4.2. Psychological and Spiritual Landscape of Peter

4.2.1 The Weight of Denial and Shame

Few narratives in Scripture capture catastrophic self-betrayal with Peter's threefold denial by the charcoal fire (Luke 22 : 54-62). Each repudiation escalated in vehemence, culminating in oaths that severed public association with Jesus precisely when solidarity mattered most. Luke's poignant detail—"the Lord turned and looked at Peter"—seals the wound, embedding shame in memory. Shame differs from guilt: guilt laments wrong action; shame internalizes wrongness as identity, chanting "I am a failure" rather than "I failed." In first-century Mediterranean honor culture, public denial before servant girls and temple guards inflicted communal disgrace, jeopardizing Peter's standing among peers and family. Psychological studies on moral injury reveal that transgressing one's core commitments triggers intrusive rumination and social withdrawal—symptoms Scripture hints at when Peter "went out and wept bitterly." Early morning after Passover, Peter likely replayed every syllable of denial, juxtaposing it with cockcrow prophecy he had scorned hours earlier (Mark 14 : 29-31). The arrest context magnified his collapse: swords drawn, disciples scattered, covenant hopes imploding. Shame flourishes in isolation; Peter's earlier bravado now impeded confession to the remaining disciples, reinforcing silence. Luke notes no direct interaction between Peter and the women upon their tomb report, hinting he remained on emotional margin. Neurobiologically, shame activates brain's pain circuitry akin to physical hurt, draining motivation and distorting perception—conditions fertile for despair. Religious shame intensifies anguish because failure violates sacred loyalty, provoking fear of divine rejection. The psalter's dirges echo in such soul states (e.g., Psalm 51). Peter's previous mountaintop moments—walking on water, confessing Jesus as Messiah, witnessing transfiguration—now deepen regret, for he squandered privileged insight. Moreover, he had been singled out for leadership promises (Matt 16 : 18-19), making betrayal appear doubly treacherous. Contemporary leaders mirror Peter when moral lapse fractures vocational identity, prompting hiding. The weight of denial thus sets stage for unique pastoral need: a solitary, grace-laden encounter that speaks specifically to shame's secrecy. Without such meeting, Peter might have remained peripheral, sabotaged by self-condemnation. Luke's laconic reference thus unveils psychological realism: before corporate mission can proceed, the shepherd must mend the tear in his own soul. Jesus' pursuit of Peter recognizes that unsutured shame eventually radiates toxicity into communal leadership. Therefore, understanding denial's weight accentuates the therapeutic brilliance of a private resurrection interview.

4.2.2 Grief, Fear, and Hope in the Aftermath of Crucifixion

Peter's emotional spectrum on Resurrection Day encompassed layers of grief over Jesus' violent death, fear of arrest as disciple accomplice, and flickers of hope ignited by empty tomb evidence. Grief stirred memories of Galilean journeys, healings, and kingdom promises apparently buried with the Master. Lament in Jewish piety allowed questioning God's purposes, and Peter's silence in Gospel narratives suggests internal struggle rather than vocal lament. Fear stemmed from Roman reprisal: crucifixion signaled crackdown on insurrectionist circles, and Peter, identified by accent in courtyard, risked surveillance. Fear also involved spiritual dread; denying publicly might provoke divine reprobation, recalling Jesus' warning that disowning Him before men invites reciprocal disowning (Matt 10 : 33). Amid these dark currents, hope flickered when women declared angelic news; Peter's sprint to the tomb (Luke 24 : 12) displays desperation to verify possibility of reversal. Physical exertion expresses psychic longing; yet the sight of linens without corpse still left puzzle unsolved, feeding cognitive dissonance. Conflicting emotions can paralyze decision making; thus Peter may have retreated to upper-room shadows, waiting for clarity. The Emmaus travelers' account that "some of our companions went to the tomb" but did not see Jesus (Luke 24 : 24) subtly alludes to Peter's unresolved status—eyewitness to emptiness but not to living Lord. That limbo highlights Jesus' initiative in seeking him. From pastoral perspective, many believers inhabit similar liminality—experiences pointing toward hope yet overshadowed by unresolved guilt. Recognizing emotional complexity helps avoid simplistic moralizing when preaching Peter's restoration. The interplay of grief, fear, and hope also heightens dramatic tension: a combustible mix demanding divine intervention lest despair harden into unbelief. Jesus meets Peter precisely within this turbulence, validating emotions while re-anchoring identity. The pattern models how resurrection addresses whole personhood, not merely doctrinal assent. Modern trauma research affirms that recovery accelerates when the injured receive presence of trusted figure before cognitive processing—mirroring Peter's restorative encounter preceding theological explanations given later in public gatherings. Consequently, appreciating Peter's emotional aftermath enriches gratitude for Jesus' pastoral sensitivity and demonstrates resurrection power to reconcile contradictory affections into renewed mission.

4.3. Theological Significance of Jesus Appearing to Peter First Among the Twelve

4.3.1 Restoration of Leadership

Peter's primacy among the Twelve is evident throughout the Gospels: he speaks first, leaps first, and is named first in apostolic lists (Matt 10 : 2; Mark 3 : 16). His denial thus imperiled not only personal integrity but corporate direction. By selecting Peter as first male witness within the apostolic cohort, the risen Christ highlights restorative grace as leadership qualification. Biblical precedent exists: Moses resumes shepherding Israel after murder exile; David reigns after moral collapse. Yet in each case divine encounter marks pivot—burning bush, Nathan's confrontation, respectively. Peter's inclusion continues pattern: leadership emerges not from flawlessness but from forgiven failure that deepens dependence. The appearance communicates to all subsequent church eras that pastoral authority flows from grace experienced, not performance kept. Early Christian communities attested this logic when making Peter's restoration part of baptismal catechesis, assuring new converts that lapses need not disqualify permanently. Theologically, restoration reveals covenant faithfulness: Jesus had prayed that Peter's faith would not fail and commissioned him to strengthen brothers after turning back (Luke 22 : 32). The private appearance fulfills that prophetic intercession, proving that Jesus' prayers prevail over Satan's siftings. It also underscores resurrection as more than victory over death; it inaugurates ministry of reconciliation transforming betrayers into pillars (2 Cor 5 : 18-19; Gal 2 : 9). Some traditions link this meeting to conferral of renewed apostolic authority, viewing it as antecedent to John 21's public recommissioning. Liturgically, the Latin rite celebrates "Sunday of Peter and Paul" near end of June, acknowledging restored apostles as twin foundations, with Peter's earlier appearance signaling precedence of mercy over mission.

Doctrinally, the encounter combats perfectionism and clericalism: leaders remain sinners saved by grace, shepherds who limp. For spiritual formation of pastors today, Peter's restoration challenges cultures that cancel fallen leaders without pathway to recovery; yet it equally warns against cheap grace by highlighting intense personal confrontation preceding reinstatement. Thus, Jesus' choice to meet Peter first among Twelve radiates ecclesial ethos: bold witness emerges only after searing mercy has burned away presumption.

4.3.2 Foreshadowing of Apostolic Ministry

The private meeting anticipates Peter's Pentecost preaching, Cornelius milestone, and martyrdom in Rome by embedding resurrection reality in his consciousness before collective strategy sessions. Apostle in Greek means "sent one"; effective sending demands personal encounter with sender. Unlike later commission to Paul on Damascus Road, Peter's apostolic clarion rings from Jerusalem outward, and the early appearance ensures that ring. Luke's Pentecost speech brims with scriptural exposition echoing Emmaus style, indicating restoration encounter might have included hermeneutic illumination. Peter's later boldness before Sanhedrin (Acts 4 : 8-13) contrasts sharply with courtyard cowardice, signifying that private forgiveness birthed public courage. Theologically, meeting highlights necessity of grace-saturated apostolate: messenger embodies message. Early church art in Roman catacombs depicts rooster and keys flanking Peter, visually juxtaposing denial and authority, reminding viewers of this formative moment. Patristic homilies, such as Chrysostom's, used Peter's restoration to encourage priests to combine humility with zeal. Missiologically, appearance models pattern wherein Christ heals wounds of pioneer leaders to fortify them for expansion into hostile environments. Peter's later vision of sheet in Acts 10 may find roots in paradigm shift begun during private meeting: Messiah's mission includes those Peter once deemed unclean, paralleling how grace embraced him despite defilement. In ecumenical dialogues, Petrine primacy debates often cite John 21, yet underlying authority seeds lie here; understanding private appearance nuances discussion by anchoring primacy in forgiveness rather than hierarchy. For preaching, emphasizing foreshadowing helps congregations see continuity: the rock emerges from rubble only through divine encounter. Modern missionaries likewise experience critical junctures where failure could abort call; Peter's story testifies that Christ restores to advance mission, not merely to soothe conscience. Therefore, the private appearance functions not only as pastoral balm but as strategic investiture of apostolic future.

4.4. Possible Locale and Timing of the Appearance

4.4.1 Jerusalem Setting Hypothesis

Most scholars place the private meeting within Jerusalem's city walls or its immediate environs, arguing from narrative proximity to other resurrection events recorded that day. After Peter and John inspect the empty tomb at dawn, the disciples congregate somewhere in the city—likely the same upper room rented for Passover, given security concerns. The Emmaus pair's evening return finds "the Eleven and those with them gathered together" (Luke 24 : 33), implying limited movement. A Jerusalem locale would allow swift access for Jesus, who appears corporeally yet enters locked spaces later that night (John 20 : 19). The city also bears symbolic resonance: Peter's denial occurred in high priest's courtyard inside Jerusalem; restoration in same urban context epitomizes divine reversal on enemy turf. Archeological studies of first-century homes near Mount Zion reveal multi-room structures capable of hosting medium-sized groups and private conversations; Jesus might have summoned Peter aside to adjacent rooftop or garden courtyard. Rabbinic custom considered rooftops places of prayer, aligning with Jesus' earlier prediction that denials would conclude before cockcrow on rooftops (Matt 10 : 27). A Jerusalem setting situates Peter's encounter amid festival crowds, highlighting God's ability to meet individuals in bustling chaos. Chronologically, scholars propose mid-morning or early afternoon gap between tomb inspection and Emmaus departure—ample window for private dialogue.

This timing coheres with Peter's emotional urgency; he would not endure hours of shame if immediate solace were available. Moreover, a city context ensures that rumor of appearance could spread rapidly, reaching Emmaus travelers before evening. Critics who argue resurrection meetings are hallucinations must account for diverse locations and times; Jerusalem setting demonstrates tangible dimension among familiar surroundings. Pastoral application observes that restoration often occurs closest to the site of failure, teaching disciples not to flee geographical memory points but to receive redemption within them. Therefore, the Jerusalem hypothesis harmonizes narrative flow, psychological plausibility, symbolic richness, and historical feasibility.

4.4.2 Alternative Galilee Hypothesis

A minority of interpreters suggest the appearance happened later in Galilee, based on Matthew's emphasis that Jesus would meet disciples there (Matt 28 : 10) and John 21's beach encounter on Sea of Tiberias. They posit that Paul's listing "to Cephas, then to the Twelve" might reflect Galilean chronology, with private meeting after group arrival north. Proponents argue Galilee, Peter's home turf, would offer secluded setting for intense conversation without temple guard threat. The familiar shoreline and fishing milieu parallel John 21's restorative meal, implying earlier one-to-one talk could precede public commission. Galilee's prophetic significance as land of great light (Isa 9 : 1-2) might further accentuate reversal theme. However, chronological difficulties arise: Emmaus travelers cite Peter's encounter on same day as tomb discovery, and rapid travel from Judea to Galilee within those hours is unlikely. Still, some scholars propose Luke compresses time for narrative effect, not chronology. Galilee hypothesis invites reflection on layered restoration: an initial word of forgiveness in Judea, deepened later amid vocational symbols of boats and nets. Even if private meeting began in city, completion may have unfolded across multiple appearances in Galilee, fitting pattern of progressive healing. The alternate view reminds readers that Scripture sometimes withholds logistic precision to focus on theological import. For spiritual formation, Galilee possibility highlights that restoration journeys may entail returning home landscapes where calling originated, allowing grace to reframe vocation in its birthplace. Ultimately, whether Jerusalem or Galilee, locality underlines incarnational truth: Christ meets disciples in physical coordinates, sanctifying geography of guilt into geography of grace.

4.5. Dynamics of Forgiveness and Reconciliation

4.5.1 Patterns of Repentance in Jewish Tradition

Jewish repentance (teshuvah) comprises recognition of sin, confession, restitution where possible, and commitment to changed behavior, often sealed during Yom Kippur liturgies. Peter's bitter weeping fulfills recognition and emotional contrition but lacks opportunity for confession to offended Master—crucifixion prevents it. Resurrection reopens avenue: private appearance furnishes forum for verbal confession in rabbinic pattern, perhaps echoing Psalm 51's plea for restored joy. Second Temple Judaism emphasized that God receives penitent even after grievous betrayal; Targumic paraphrases of Hosea stress divine yearning for return. Jesus' pre-Passion parables—the Prodigal Son, Lost Sheep—had already sketched Father's posture toward repentant. Peter now lives the parable's sequel. Confession likely includes explicit acknowledgment of denial, aligning with Leviticus 5 : 5 requirement to "confess the sin." Rabbinic sages taught that public sin demands public confession, though God encounters begin privately; thus later Johannine beach scene may serve communal dimension. Restoration also involved symbolic acts—washing, sacrifice—which Jesus fulfills as High Priest offering once-for-all atonement. Peter, steeped in Jewish rhythms, would interpret encounter through lens of teshuvah, recognizing Jesus as mediator who both grants and embodies forgiveness. This cultural framework deepens understanding of scene: it was not casual chat but covenantal rite. For contemporary disciples, Jewish repentance matrix affirms value of specific confession and tangible restitution in leadership restoration processes. Peter's story illustrates that New Covenant grace does not bypass moral accountability; it transforms it into relational dialogue with resurrected Lord who carries scars of betrayal yet returns in peace.

4.5.2 New Covenant Dimensions of Grace

While teshuvah offers template, the private appearance introduces New Covenant distinctives: forgiveness grounded in atoning death and empowered by indwelling Spirit. Jesus' prior pronouncement at Last Supper—"This cup is the new covenant in My blood" (Luke 22 : 20)—frames resurrection meetings as covenant ratification ceremonies. Peter experiences grace not as abstraction but as encounter with glorified bearer of his sins. Isaiah 53's wounded servant now stands before him alive, validating substitutionary suffering. Grace here is proactive: Jesus seeks Peter before confession; initiative belongs to the offended party. This inversion subverts transactional religiosity, depicting divine forgiveness as gift preceding human rectitude. Moreover, grace commissions: Peter will feed sheep, strengthening brothers, signifying reconciliation's missional vector. The private appearance thus epitomizes Pauline theology later articulated: justified by faith, given ministry of reconciliation (Rom 5 : 1; 2 Cor 5 : 18). New Covenant grace also redefines identity: Simon, wavering reed, becomes Peter, stable rock, through encounter. Existential shame yields to vocational destiny. This identity shift foreshadows Spirit baptism empowering obedience beyond self-effort. Grace further establishes community ethos—first leader is trophy of mercy, thus early church must be mercy culture. Contemporary application urges congregations to design restoration pathways reflecting proactive, identity-reframing grace while maintaining seriousness of sin. Private meeting underscores confidentiality before publicity; pastoral confidentiality fosters honest confession essential for genuine change. In sum, New Covenant grace, embodied in risen Jesus appearing to Peter, transforms repentance pattern from law-based obligation to love-based response, ensuring that forgiveness launches rather than merely absolves.

4.6. Implications for Ecclesial Authority and Shepherd Imagery

4.6.1 From Fisherman to Shepherd

Peter's career trajectory pivots from casting nets to tending sheep, symbolizing shift from gathering converts to nurturing community. Although the explicit shepherd language surfaces in John 21, its conceptual seed germinates in private meeting where Jesus forgives under-shepherd dereliction and entrusts future care. Ezekiel 34 condemns shepherds who abandon flock; Peter's denial parallels hireling flight, yet restoration proclaims new covenant shepherding where grace equips faithfulness. The fisherman image emphasized evangelistic harvest; shepherd image balances pastoral oversight, essential for nascent ecclesia. Early church writings, such as 1 Peter 5 : 1-4, demonstrate Peter internalized shepherd motif, exhorting elders to tend God's flock willingly. Private appearance likely imprinted this calling; personal experience of tended soul births capacity to tend others. Linking restoration to shepherd role underscores leadership drawn from vulnerability, countering authoritarian tendencies. Iconography of Peter with keys and shepherd staff illustrates dual authority: doctrinal gatekeeping and compassionate care. Modern leadership training benefits from recovering shepherd imagination—protecting, guiding, healing—rooted in personal grace encounter. Whenever leaders fail today, Peter's story reminds them that restoration reorients purpose toward humble service, not power consolidation. Fisherman-to-shepherd metamorphosis also parallels church's mission expansion: from individual conversion nets to sustained communal pasturing across Mediterranean. Thus, the private appearance serves as hinge between vocation metaphors, forging unified apostolic identity encompassing outreach and nurture.

4.6.2 Petrine Primacy Debates

The singular resurrection appearance to Peter enters ecclesiological discussion on Petrine primacy. Roman

Catholic tradition cites Luke 24 : 34 alongside Matt 16 : 18-19 and John 21 : 15-17 as evidence of Christ conferring unique pastoral jurisdiction. Orthodox voices emphasize honor primacy but resist universal jurisdiction, viewing private appearance as personal restoration not administrative appointment. Protestant reformers highlighted equality of apostles, interpreting Peter's meeting as paradigmatic grace rather than hierarchical endowment. Regardless of confessional stance, historical fact remains: Jesus chose to meet Peter individually before meeting the Twelve, signaling special attention to his leadership health. Primacy therefore originates in mercy, not merit; debate narrows when mercy considered central. The appearance also tempers absolutist claims: if foundational leader could fail egregiously, infallibility must be derivative, contingent on abiding with Christ, not intrinsic. Thus, Peter's restoration both grounds and relativizes authority. Contemporary ecumenical dialogues, such as those by the Catholic–Lutheran commission, recognize Peter's role as witness to unity emerging from forgiven sin. The private meeting offers shared starting point—need for grace. Whether one views Peter as prototype bishop of Rome or first among equals, the resurrection encounter underscores that authentic authority springs from humbled heart responsive to personal call. Ecclesial structures today can draw from this to prioritize spiritual formation over managerial prowess in selecting leaders. The debate, when reframed through resurrection lens, shifts from power distribution to stewardship of reconciled community.

4.7. Lessons for Contemporary Discipleship

4.7.1 Coping with Moral Failure

Peter's experience furnishes a roadmap for believers confronting personal collapse. Step one is honest grief—Peter wept bitterly, resisting denial of denial. Step two involves proximity to community even while ashamed; he remained reachable when women relayed news. Step three welcomes divine initiative: Jesus moves toward the fallen rather than waiting for self-improvement. Step four embraces private dialogue, permitting confession without defensive posturing. Step five receives grace that not only erases guilt but re-commissions purpose. Psychology corroborates these steps: recovery from moral injury requires truth telling, empathetic listening, restorative justice, and positive identity reconstruction. Churches can design care pathways mirroring them—safe spaces for confession, mentors representing Christ's listening ear, structured restitution, and reintegration into ministry roles when appropriate. Peter's story also cautions against self-exclusion: he ran to tomb despite failure, modeling pursuit of evidence rather than hiding. The narrative demolishes fatalism; denial isn't destiny. For leaders specifically, Peter shows that public sin demands private starting point preceding public acknowledgment but culminating in transparent reaffirmation. Failure can refine empathy; Peter later cautions fellow elders against lording over flock, empathy born from own collapse (1 Pet 5 : 3). Disciples struggling with repeated sin find hope in Peter's triple denial matched by triple affirmation, indicating restoration can be as thorough as failure was deep. The private appearance testifies God schedules personal appointments for prodigals, inviting expectancy. Practical disciplines—lament, examen, accountability—help modern Peters perceive Christ's approach. Thus, moral failure, while grievous, becomes crucible for deeper grace when patterned after Peter's resurrection meeting.

4.7.2 Leadership Restoration Processes

Restoring fallen leaders today often provokes polarized reactions: swift reinstatement risking scandal, or permanent banishment fostering despair. Peter's journey charts balanced course. Restoration began quickly but unfolded in phases— private forgiveness, public recommission, communal empowerment at Pentecost. Time elapsed between denial and Pentecost allowed character recalibration without indefinite limbo. Key components included: encounter with living Christ, affirmation of love (John 21), reception of Spirit (Acts 2), and observable fruit in courageous preaching. Modern processes can mirror these four markers: spiritual counseling to facilitate encounter; structured reflection on vocation and love for Christ; equipping experiences fostering Spirit-dependent ministry; and accountability to fruit-measuring community. Peter's reinstatement included re-entrustment of responsibility, signaling trust rebirthed. Yet Jesus also predicted Peter's martyrdom (John 21 : 18-19), reminding leaders that restoration serves self-giving mission, not status recovery. Policies today should combine grace with sober awareness of future suffering inherent in shepherding. Peer support—James, John, later Paul—played role in Peter's ongoing growth; restoration teams today need multi-voice oversight. Ultimately, Peter's story teaches that effective processes move beyond crisis management toward transformative discipleship, producing leaders who lead out of compassionate humility. The private resurrection appearance remains template: confrontation coupled with irrevocable love, followed by experiential empowerment and mission clarity. Churches embracing such blueprint honor both holiness and mercy, reflecting character of the risen Shepherd.

Conclusion

A single, cryptic line—"the Lord has risen and has appeared to Simon"—conceals a universe of divine tenderness, psychological rescue, theological profundity, ecclesial shaping, and missional propulsion. From the agony of courtyard denials to the jubilant chorus of Pentecost, Peter's trajectory is forever bent by a meeting hidden from public eye yet radiant in ecclesial memory. The resurrected Jesus sought out His failed friend not to rehearse the shame, but to transmute it into rock-solid testimony that mercy triumphs over judgment. On that private stage, leadership was restored, Scripture's promises were re-illuminated, and future shepherding ethos was forged. Whether the conversation occurred in a shadowed room of Jerusalem or against Galilean dawn, its echoes reverberate through every age whenever weary disciples—especially leaders—wonder if their collapse is final. It whispers that the Christ who conquered the grave still crosses locked thresholds of self-condemnation, names the failure without flinching, and invites the fallen to rise into a destiny scarred but radiant. For the church, the appearance to Simon Peter stands as perpetual summons to cultivate communities where truth and grace kiss, where hospitality to brokenness births bold proclamation, and where authority rests not on unblemished record but on wounds healed by the Shepherd who first bore them. In tracing the contours of that still-private conversation, we recover a public Gospel: that every denial can find its sunrise when the risen Lord speaks the sinner's name in love.

Chapter 5. First Evening in the Locked Room – Ten Disciples

The first Easter evening—sometimes called the night of the locked room—carries a narrative density out of all proportion to the scant lines in which the evangelists relay it (John 20 : 19-23; Luke 24 : 36-49). Gathered behind barred doors, ten surviving disciples (Judas dead, Thomas absent) huddle in an atmosphere thick with rumor, fear, and fragile expectation. At sunrise they heard women proclaim empty tomb and angelic gospel; by mid-day Cleopas and a companion raced back from Emmaus testifying to a Stranger who broke bread; somewhere in between Simon Peter stumbled in breathless with a private assurance that the Lord had indeed sought him out. Yet none of these second-hand flashes expels terror of temple guards or dissolves the shame curdling within those who fled the garden. Into that chiaroscuro of doubt and dawning faith the risen Jesus suddenly stands, speaks peace, shows scars, commissions a Spirit-empowered mission, and breathes into them the Same Breath that animated Eden.

5.1. The Atmosphere Behind Shut Doors

5.1.1 Fear of External Threat and Internal Failure

The disciples' decision to barricade themselves "for fear of the Jews" (John 20 : 19) reveals a complex interplay of external danger and internal turmoil. Jerusalem's post-Passover streets still bristled with Roman patrols alert for sedition, and temple authorities who engineered Jesus' execution might easily extend their inquisition to His known associates. Every footstep on the pavement below, every flicker of torchlight at dusk, likely jolted adrenal pulses inside the borrowed upper room. Yet fear of arrest masked another dread: what if the women's report was delusion and Peter's story misguided hope? Doubt about their own perceptions fed self-recrimination; after all, each had pledged loyalty then fled Gethsemane. Group psychology records that communal shame amplifies anxiety, creating echo chambers of negativity unless authoritative reassurance intervenes. The disciples' decision to lock a house—perhaps the same where Passover had been eaten—also carried ritual symbolism: they sealed themselves off from contagion of defilement according to purity instincts triggered by contact with executed criminals (cf. Deut 21 : 23). This physical barrier expressed spiritual disconnect—they could not yet imagine fellowship with a crucified-and-risen Lord who had toppled purity codes by bearing curse on tree. First-century homes possessed stout cedar doors reinforced with cross-bars, more than adequate to keep out unwelcome soldiers but also enough to trap residents in claustrophobic darkness once oil lamps gutted low. The same hands that once distributed bread to five thousand now fidgeted with bolts and latches, illustrating how quickly generous ministry contracts into self-protection. Fear inhibits memory; neuroscientists show that stress hormones hamper recall of prior assurances, perhaps explaining why Jesus' clear predictions of resurrection felt remote that evening. Luke notes that some disciples still deemed the women's testimony "nonsense," evidence of how gender bias and fear colluded to suppress hope. Thus the locked room embodied not only architectural but psychological closure:

hearts shuttered by guilt and minds barricaded against cognitive dissonance.

5.1.2 Testimonial Collage: From Emmaus Road to Simon's Report

Despite heavy atmosphere, shards of witness filtered through the cracks. Mary Magdalene's dawn proclamation ignited a first spark, recounting gardener-turned-Rabboni encounter cited in John 20 : 11-18. Subsequent mid-morning verification by Peter and John, who saw linen cloths but no corpse (John 20 : 3-10), added forensic intrigue without resolving absence. Toward afternoon, Simon himself burst in with cryptic certainty that the Lord had shown Himself alive—Luke 24 : 34 preserves this earliest male apostolic claim. Then, close to sundown, Cleopas and partner arrived panting from Emmaus, weaving Scripture exposition and bread-breaking recognition into breathless narrative (Luke 24 : 33-35). These overlapping testimonies formed an emerging collage but lacked cohesive frame; each disciple processed others' experiences through filters of personality and expectation. Cognitive psychologists term this stage "informational disequilibrium"—inputs outpace existing schema, prompting either assimilation (editing facts to fit) or accommodation (reshaping worldview). The locked-room cluster teetered between options. Some aligned with Peter's optimism; others defaulted to skeptical prudence, wary of false consolation. Social dynamics also played out: who carried status to persuade—Mary's vision discounted by gender norms, Peter's by recent failure, Cleopas by secondary role? In this swirl of contested anecdotes, the disciples reenacted courtroom jury deliberations minus presiding judge. Meanwhile the sun set, lamps flickered, and Sabbath ended, intensifying logistical questions about next steps: remain in hiding, sneak out of city, or rendezvous in Galilee? Thus the stage was set for intervention from beyond barred wood—a presence to synthesize collage into singular revelation.

5.2. The Appearance of the Risen Christ

5.2.1 Materialization in a Secure Space

John's wording implies instantaneous placement—Jesus "came and stood among them"—without recorded noise of latch or creak of hinge. Theologically, this signals continuity and transformation: the same crucified body now possesses capacities unhindered by locked wood yet still tangible (Luke 24 : 39). Ancient Mediterranean honor codes prized hospitality; hosts rose to greet guests, so Jesus' sudden centrality reclaims host authority in room He once used for foot-washing. The phenomenon challenges binary categories of materiality and spirit; early heresies either docetized (denied flesh) or crudely physicalized resurrection. Luke counters by stressing that Jesus asked for broiled fish (Luke 24 : 42-43), reaffirming bodily reality even as physics bend. For disciples, the sight bridged cognitive gap between empty tomb and living presence, collapsing speculation into fact. Their startled terror, Luke writes, mistook Him for a ghost—residue of popular Jewish lore where righteous dead sometimes manifested in vision (cf. 1 Sam 28). Jesus addresses this by inviting tactile verification, demonstrating He is not incorporeal spirit. The location—a room associated with Last Supper—layers symbolic resonance: covenant inaugurated therein is now ratified through bodily vindication. Entrance without door use foreshadows Pentecost Spirit breaching human interiors without force, quietly but irresistibly. Apologetically, the event critiques hallucinatory theories: collective hallucinations seldom feature invite-to-touch and shared meals. The disciples' witness hence originated not in mental projection but in multi-sensory confrontation.

5.2.2 Liturgical Posture: Standing Amid the Assembly

Liturgical scholars note that the verb ἔστη ("stood") carries priestly overtones of officiant before worshipers (cf. Heb 8 : 1-2). The risen Jesus positions Himself not at periphery but at center, reclaiming leadership surrendered at arrest. This centerspace reveals ecclesiological blueprint: future Christian gatherings will orient around invisible yet present Christ presiding sacramentally. Visual imagination may picture disciples on low couches, Jesus upright in middle—an inversion of Passover reclining signifying finished labor now replaced by risen readiness. His stance also fulfills Malachi's promise of Lord suddenly coming to His temple; this locked room becomes micro-temple meeting place. By occupying center without opening door, Jesus demonstrates sovereignty over boundaries—spatial, social, political—reassuring church in subsequent centuries when locked prisons cannot exclude Him. Today many persecuted believers read this narrative as guarantee that Christ accompanies them regardless of isolation. Furthermore, His central standing models homiletic posture: Word incarnate in midst of listeners before proclamation of peace and commission. Thus, moment functions liturgically, historically, and eschatologically, anchoring worship around presence, not architecture.

5.3. Gifts of Peace and Joy

5.3.1 "Peace Be With You": Shalom as Covenant Fulfillment

Jesus' first utterance—"Peace to you"—translates Hebrew shalom, pregnant with covenant wholeness, not mere calm. Spoken thrice across two verses (John 20 : 19, 21, 26), the phrase both calms agitation and inaugurates new-creation condition prophesied in Isaiah 52 : 7. In previous ministry, Jesus had commissioned disciples as peace-bearing envoys (Luke 10 : 5-6); now He implants peace as internal reality through His resurrection. Semantically, shalom involves rectified relationship with God, neighbor, and self; thus pronouncement heals vertical breach of denial and horizontal fracture of fear. The timing—at evening ensōpion (in their presence)—echoes priestly benedictions concluding temple worship (Num 6 : 24-26), signifying closure of sacrificial cycle by once-for-all atonement. Peace declaration subverts politics of Pax Romana enforced by sword; here peace arises from wounds willingly borne. The phrase also doubles as lawsuit settlement; ancient Semitic courts pronounced shalom when parties reconciled. Jesus' bodily scars function as evidence that debt is paid, so peace is legally binding. Pastoral application highlights that forgiven disciples need not audition for forgiveness; peace arrives unearned. In trauma therapy, hearing unconditional acceptance lowers amygdala hyper-arousal, facilitating learning; disciples thus become receptive to forthcoming commission. Preachers today should emulate cadence: announce peace before demand, grace before task.

5.3.2 Joy in the Presence of Wounds

Luke records that disciples "disbelieved for joy" (Luke 24 : 41), capturing paradoxical affect where incredulity merges with exultation. Joy emerges as fruit of Spirit (Gal 5 : 22) now grafted into their hearts via encounter. Importantly, joy coexists with visible wounds; scars remain, refusing triumphalism that forgets suffering. This juxtaposition shapes Christian spirituality: resurrection joy is cruciform, not naive exuberance. Anthropologically, communal joy counters fear by releasing oxytocin, strengthening group cohesion—a neurological prelude to corporate mission. Early church liturgies inserted paschal greeting "Peace" and response "He is risen," replicating emotional swing from dread to delight. Joy did not erase realities of Roman occupation, but reframed them within victory horizon. Contemporary worship recovers this tone each Easter vigil, declaring joy amidst global suffering. Moreover, the disciples' joy proves authenticity: second-temple Jews deemed visio Dei worthy of fear; experiencing joy indicates relational intimacy. Thus joy becomes badge of resurrection witnesses, sustaining missions through persecution recounted in Acts. Modern disciples, likewise, gauge authenticity of experiences by joy's presence mingled with reverent awe.

5.4. The Scars That Speak

5.4.1 Physical Evidence and Theological Message

Jesus deliberately shows "hands and side," aligning with piercings from nails and spear (John 19 : 34). Ancient legal testimony required two or three witnesses; His wounds supply internal corroboration between death and resurrection. Scars function apologetically—identifying continuity of identity—and sacramentally—tokens of covenant cut into flesh. Patristic commentators view wounds as everlasting, pledges before Father interceding for humanity (Heb 7 : 25). For disciples, tactile invitation transforms empirical doubt into empirical faith. Luke's mention of "feet" adds footnote of total embodiment. Theologically, scars proclaim that victory does not erase suffering but transfigures it. They silence Gnostic dualism by affirming resurrection meatiness, and deflate prosperity gospels by dignifying redeemed pain. Isaiah's promise that we are healed by His wounds (Isa 53 : 5) echoes in sight of nail prints, turning memory of violence into source of healing. Missionally, scars instruct early martyrs: wounds for witness will shine with glory. Artistically, pierced hands become iconographic shorthand for compassionate Savior. Psychologically, Jesus' self-disclosure invites disciples to integrate their traumas, knowing Master retains His. Modern trauma counseling among believers may invoke Jesus' scars to validate bodies carrying violence memories yet destined for resurrection renewal.

5.4.2 Reversing Adamic Shame

Genesis describes Adam hiding his body after sin; now Second Adam displays wounded body without shame. This reversal rehabilitates human corporeality. In Eden, God's breath animated dust; in locked room, scarred God-man breathes Spirit, signifying renewed humanity capable of standing unashamed. Peter's prior denial occurred near fire warming servants; now wounds that received death's chill kindle new warmth of fellowship. The event also overturns Roman symbolism: crucifixion aimed to stigmatize, but resurrected scars convert stigma to glory, undermining empire's terror apparatus. Sociologists call this "symbolic reversal," where oppressed appropriate sign of defeat as emblem of victory—seen later in Christians wearing cross necklaces. For disciples, recognition of scars parallels earlier Emmaus bread-breaking; both gestures rely on bodily memory to ignite faith. Contemporary applications encourage believers to disclose healed wounds to foster authenticity and hope in community. Thus scars become pedagogical and pastoral, teaching for all ages.

5.5. Breath of the Spirit and Apostolic Commission

5.5.1 Receiving the Spirit: Creation Echoes and New Covenant Breath

John's narrative climaxes: Jesus breathes (ἐνεφύσησεν) on disciples and says, "Receive the Holy Spirit" (John 20 : 22). The verb parallels Septuagint Genesis 2 : 7 where God breathes into Adam; locked room thereby becomes second Eden. Pneumatology here anticipates Pentecost yet distinguishes Johannine perspective: an earnest deposit of Spirit enabling forgiveness ministry immediately; Luke's later outpouring empowers global proclamation. Scholarly debates about "Johannine Pentecost" note complementary not competing chronologies—Spirit's multifaceted role unfolds in stages. The breath indicates personal impartation: unlike wind at Sinai, this is intimate face-to-face exhalation, prefiguring Spirit's indwelling in hearts (Rom 8 : 11). Greek imperative "receive" (λάβετε) addresses all ten; Spirit distribution democratizes authority, preventing hierarchy based on personality. The moment also fulfills Upper-Room discourse promise (John 14 : 16-18) that Another Paraclete would dwell with them. Liturgically, many traditions invoke Holy Spirit in communion prayer by breathing lightly over elements—a gesture echoing this scene. The breath counters earlier atmosphere of stale fear with fresh ruach, symbolically ventilating locked space. Modern spiritual formation emphasizes contemplative prayer akin to receiving breath of Christ, linking pneuma and respiration.

5.5.2 Delegated Authority to Forgive or Retain Sins

Immediately following Spirit impartation, Jesus declares authority: "If you forgive anyone's sins, they are forgiven; if you retain them, they are retained" (John 20 : 23). This statement extends keys-language given to Peter (Matt 16 : 19) to wider apostolic body, ensuring ecclesial governance emerges from collective Spirit-discernment. In Jewish jurisprudence, binding and loosing referred to halakhic rulings; here it maps onto declarative proclamation of gospel forgiveness. The church does not generate forgiveness; it announces heaven's verdict, yet announcement actualizes realization in hearers. Retaining sins implies prophetic refusal when repentance absent—seen in Acts 5 with Ananias. Theologically, commission springs from wounds: those forgiven are authorized to mediate forgiveness, embodying principle "freely received, freely give." Historically, this verse underpins sacramental practice of confession and absolution in Catholic, Orthodox, and Anglican traditions; Reformation interpretations emphasize collective preaching of gospel as absolution. Missiologically, authority fuels evangelistic courage; disciples will stand before Sanhedrin declaring remission through Jesus alone (Acts 4 : 12). Ethically, retention warns church against indiscriminate cheap grace. Practical outworking demands discernment charism; Spirit breathed moments earlier supplies requisite wisdom. For pastoral care, authority invites churches to assure penitent of full pardon, countering shame's grip— application of Peter's experience to others. Thus breath and authority form inseparable duo: Spirit empowers ministry, ministry exercises Spirit-guided discernment.

5.6. Transformation and Future Trajectory

5.6.1 From Lockdown to Public Square

Within days, disciples move from bolted doors to temple courts proclaiming resurrection (Acts 3 : 11-16). The catalyst is locked-room encounter. Fear metabolizes into boldness; Greek term παρρησία used in Acts 4 : 13 traces to Spirit injection. Sociologically, crisis communities often collapse;

here they coalesce around shared mission. Luke lists communal practices—apostles' teaching, fellowship, breaking bread, prayers—emerging blueprint birthed that night. Psychologically, witnessing material resurrection rewires death anxiety; hence martyrdom becomes feasible. Geographic trajectory also shifts: commission "as Father sent Me, I send you" (John 20 : 21) propels disciples beyond Judea, ultimately to Rome. Each step outward traces back to doorway once locked in fear. This pattern encourages contemporary churches emerging from pandemic lockdowns: Christ enters enclosed spaces to re-commission them for external engagement. The narrative also demonstrates divine use of interruptions; fear bars door, Christ repurposes barrier to display transcendence.

5.6.2 Thomas's Absence and Subsequent Inclusion

That first evening lacked Thomas, setting stage for second Sunday reprise (John 20 : 24-29). His absence underscores communal responsibility: witness must be shared, not hoarded. The disciples faithfully relay message—but remains inadequate for Thomas until he experiences identical scar encounter. Jesus condescends to duplicate revelation, showing that corporate testimony invites but does not coerce individual faith. Thomas's later confession "My Lord and my God" crowns Johannine Christology, illustrating how absence can yield deeper Christological insight when met with patient grace. Ecclesiologically, event teaches valuing those who miss initial revival; church must provide inclusive space for skeptical latecomers. Homiletically, locked-room narrative over two Sundays shapes liturgical calendar's Low Sunday highlighting faith of Thomas. Application: doubt processed within community leads to robust confession, not exclusion. Thomas's story completes arc begun by ten disciples, ensuring apostolic corpus unified in scar witness.

Conclusion

The first evening in the locked room begins with bolts drawn tight against hostile powers and ends with hearts flung open to a world they have just been commanded to forgive. In the span of a few breath-stilled minutes, the risen Jesus translates fear into peace, despair into joy, shame into authority, and isolation into sent community. He does so not by erasing evidence of crucifixion but by enthroning scars at center of fellowship, breathing life where dread had stifled, and entrusting former fugitives with keys to eternal liberty. The memory of that room will follow them along dusty roads to Galilee, across bustling agorae of Antioch and Corinth, into prison cells where steel bars cannot thwart the One who once walked through cedar planks. Every subsequent Christian gathering—whether catacomb Eucharist, Gothic cathedral mass, house-church circle, or digital livestream—re-enacts this template: Christ in the midst, wounds visible, peace proclaimed, Spirit bestowed, mission ignited. And every believer wrestling with bolted anxieties may look back to that shuttered space and hear anew the greeting that still pierces padlocks: "Shalom. As the Father sent Me, I send you." The locked room has become the church's open door to the nations, its memory engraved on hearts that know no barrier the Crucified-Risen One cannot cross.

Chapter 6. One Week Later – Thomas Included

One full week—eight days by Jewish inclusive reckoning—has elapsed since the first Easter evening, and the small Jerusalem fellowship has undergone a bruising but fruitful oscillation between wonder and unresolved unease. The risen Jesus has breathed His peace, displayed His scars, and entrusted a Spirit-shaped mission, yet one voice within the apostolic circle remains unconvinced. Thomas the Twin was absent that first night, and the testimonies of his ten colleagues—however excited—have sounded to him no more authoritative than fevered hallucinations. He insists on empirical contact, demanding to press his finger into the nail scars and his hand into the pierced side. Rather than scold this skeptic or sideline him in the communal life, the disciples have left the doors unlocked to his questions while maintaining their newborn rhythm of Sunday gathering. Now, on the first day of a new week, they meet again in the same house, a space still scented with oil lamps and tinged with the memory of surprise peace. The doors are shut, but not out of panic;

something closer to holy anticipation fills the air. They sense—without presuming—that the Lord who overcame locks once may do so again. It is in this pregnant atmosphere that Jesus appears for the benefit of a single soul, answering doubt not with distance but with deliberate accommodation. The ensuing dialogue with Thomas supplies the Gospel of John with its climactic confession and shapes Christian theology's posture toward questions, evidence, and the blessedness of faith born in later generations.

6.1. The Setting Eight Days Later

6.1.1 The Rhythms of Early Christian Gathering

The first generation of believers has not yet abandoned the liturgical cadence of Israel, but a subtle calibration has begun. They still honor the Sabbath from Friday sunset to Saturday sunset, observing prayers at the temple courts and reciting psalms as their forefathers did. Yet the crucifixion and resurrection imprint have shifted the gravitational center of their worship to the first day of the week, the day on which their Master stood victorious over the grave (John 20 : 19). By meeting again on the following Sunday they unwittingly inaugurate what will later be called the Lord's Day. This rhythm is both pragmatic and theological: pragmatic because festival pilgrims, merchants, and ordinary laborers resume duties on Monday, leaving Sunday the lone feasible day when Galilean fishermen staying in Jerusalem can linger long in prayer; theological because each new week now echoes Genesis light emerging on day one but with exponentially brighter new-creation brilliance. The location is likely the same upper-room complex where the Last Supper unfolded—a sizeable dwelling owned by a sympathizer who believes the movement has not ended in catastrophe. Oil lamps bracket the walls, casting amber rings that waver as disciples pace, converse, and sit on reed mats. Bread and dates lie on a low table, evidence of shared hospitality rather than formal Passover replication. The doors remain shut more from custom than terror; caution still feels prudent, yet the previous Sunday has instilled confidence that locks are no impediment to the sovereign Christ. In this embryonic church service there is no printed liturgy, but certain features repeat: recounting of Scripture, prayers in familiar synagogue patterns, sharing of memories from Galilee, and mutual encouragement that what seemed impossible has occurred. Mary Magdalene and the other women are almost certainly present, offering clarifications when retelling the dawn narrative. Everyone present recognizes the absence that matters most is not Thomas's but Jesus' physical visibility; their meeting is a deliberate act of waiting as well as worship. Whispered speculation wonders whether He will come again; paired with that hope is pastoral sensitivity not to shame Thomas for his stance. In this earliest Christian liturgical rhythm, therefore, we glimpse the church-planting instinct already at work: meeting consistently, retelling the story, feeding one another, and expecting encounter with the risen Lord to punctuate ordinary time. The room, so recently a cave of cowardice, has become a womb of anticipation. Even the shut doors, far from suffocating, now function like the veil in the tabernacle—thin, permeable, destined to flutter open at the breath of God.

6.1.2 The Emotional Landscape of the Disciples

A week of reflection has exposed fault lines within the community that require patient tending. Peter has spoken publicly about his private restoration but carries lingering humility that tempers old bravado. John radiates serene confidence, repeatedly emphasizing how the linens lay folded in the tomb as if death itself were tidied away. Matthew and Philip oscillate between evangelistic zeal—plotting how soon they can reach Galilee to fulfill Jesus' promise—and pastoral concern for Jerusalem converts who might need continued care. Mary Magdalene exhibits quiet authority, her firsthand conversation with the Lord empowering bold reminders whenever discouragement surfaces. Amid these diverse responses Thomas's unresolved skepticism hangs like unstruck chord. The community refuses to brand him traitor or traitor-adjacent; they recall their own abandonment in Gethsemane and treat doubt as familiar rather than foreign. Each disciple recognizes that belief arrived for him or her through a distinct path: Peter via empty tomb and singular appearance, the Emmaus pair via Scripture exposition and hospitality, Mary via voice recognition in a garden. Consequently, they intuit that Thomas will require his own customized revelation, and their acceptance cultivates an atmosphere roomy enough for faith-process. Yet tension simmers. Some worry that an unpersuaded apostle could hinder collective mission; others fear persecution more intensely knowing one of their number remains unconvinced. Their prayers are tinged with confession—"Lord, help our brother"—and hope—"Show Yourself again." Emotional energy thus weaves between high worshipful gratitude and quiet intercession for a friend struggling on the threshold. This mosaic of feelings will amplify the shockwave of joy when Jesus materializes. The disciples' psychological terrain also foreshadows modern congregations where certainty and question frequently share pews, illustrating that early community life accommodated ambiguity without fracturing unity. Their week of living with Thomas's doubt sets a precedent for patient accompaniment that will become hallmark of Christian pastoral care. It underscores that the journey from rumor to revelation can stretch longer for some, and that faithful friends do not accelerate the timetable by coercion but by presence. The group's willingness to keep meeting, praying, and remembering in his hearing preserves space for epiphany, demonstrating love's capacity to hold mystery until Christ clarifies.

6.2. The Character of Thomas

6.2.1 Biographical Sketch and Personality Traits

Thomas, also called Didymus—the Twin—appears in the Synoptic lists and features in three notable Johannine episodes. Early church historians surmise he may have had a biological twin whose identity Scripture never reveals, symbolically positioning him as everyman, always paired to an unseen counterpart of future generations who will echo his doubts. In John 11 he rallies fellow disciples with courageous resignation: if Jesus insists on returning to hostile Judea, "let us go and die with Him," a pronouncement blending loyalty and pragmatic pessimism. In John 14 he voices confusion during the Farewell Discourse, asking candidly about the way to the Father, eliciting Jesus' famous self-revelation as the way, truth, and life. Such vignettes paint a portrait of a disciple commendably honest, rational, and oriented toward concrete clarity. Later apocryphal traditions, including the Acts of Thomas, place him as evangelist to India, implying that once convinced he channels skeptical disposition into intrepid proclamation. Psychological profiling might label Thomas an analytic processor: he observes data, measures risk, and resists herd mentality. Unlike impulsive Peter or contemplative John, he seeks corroborated evidence. His absence on Easter evening may stem from errands or even from reluctance to rejoin what seemed failed movement. The fact that he returns at all indicates relational commitment; he does not abandon colleagues but demands integrity of testimony. This blend of loyalty and demand for verification embodies a virtue the later church will call fides quaerens intellectum—faith seeking understanding. Thomas's candor also exposes communal vulnerability; by voicing doubts he ensures that belief is not built on groupthink. Modern disciples indebted to critical thinking find in him a patron saint of inquiry: he loves Jesus enough to ask for personal encounter rather than settling for second-hand narrative. Importantly, Scripture never calls him faithless; Jesus will label him "unbelieving" in moment but with aim to transition him into believing. His temperament, when redeemed, becomes asset for mission fields that prize empirical clarity. Thus, the biography of Thomas illustrates that Jesus assembles a spectrum of personalities into His apostolic cohort, foreseeing that global evangelism will require multifaceted witness. Tenacity in testing claims, once blessed by sight, yields tenacity in defending truth abroad.

6.2.2 The Dynamics of Doubt in Johannine Theology

John's Gospel treats signs as vehicles for belief, but he refuses simplistic endorsement of sign-seeking. Early chapters showcase crowds enamored by miracles yet shallow in commitment (John 2 : 23-25). Against that backdrop Thomas's demand might appear spiritually immature. However, John frames doubt not as terminal but as threshold;

Jesus meets honest inquiry with revelatory abundance. Doubt functions pedagogically, prompting deeper self-disclosure by Christ. Moreover, John is careful to distinguish doubt birthed from stubborn will (exemplified by religious leaders who ignore Lazarus's resurrection, John 12 : 10-11) from doubt arising in absence of evidence. Thomas represents the latter: he does not reject the possibility of resurrection; he requests the same sensory confirmation others received. His criteria—touching wounds—match what Jesus voluntarily showed earlier; thus his conditions are not hostile but consistent. Johannine theology links seeing and believing in a nuanced dance: sight often precedes belief (John 20 : 8), but belief also paves way for future seeing (John 11 : 40). Thomas's journey illustrates a third path where tactile seeing transforms into highest Christological confession. John employs Greek perfect verbs—"I have believed" and "I have seen"—to suggest completed yet enduring states when Thomas finally responds. Doubt, therefore, becomes catalyst for narrative climax, safeguarding the reader from reducing resurrection to private vision. In broader theological discourse, Thomas rescues faith from charge of credulity by embedding empirical invitation at Gospel closure. His skepticism also foreshadows Gentile contexts lacking Jewish messianic expectation, anticipating audiences who will ask for concrete basis. John concludes by addressing those future readers: "These things are written so that you may believe." Thus, Thomas typifies transitional witness bridging apostolic seeing and textual seeing for later believers. Doubt in Johannine tapestry appears not antithetical but instrumental, a loom on which robust faith is woven when answered by living Word.

6.3. The Second Appearance of Jesus

6.3.1 The Repetition of Peace and the Relevance of Scars

As evening shadows lengthen on this eighth day, the disciples again experience the sudden materialization of Jesus in their midst. The same greeting—"Peace be with you"—ripples across the gathering, confirming continuity with prior encounter (John 20 : 26). Repetition underscores reliability:

what happened seven evenings earlier was no hallucination. Yet the greeting is not mere liturgical formula; it addresses Thomas's inner storm and affirms corporate harmony. Jesus turns immediately to the Twin without waiting for introductions, indicating omniscient awareness of conversations during His physical absence. He offers the identical evidence Thomas had specified—hands and side—thereby validating the reasonableness of Thomas's earlier request. The risen Lord neither rebukes the desire for empirical confirmation nor withholds it; He acknowledges that scars are permanent credentials of identity and victory. From a medical perspective the wounds, though healed, have left visible indentation; resurrection life integrates memory of suffering rather than erasing it. Thomas's gaze traces iron-darkened crescents, symbolic of execution, yet they now emit peace rather than horror. Theologically, the repetition of peace and unveiling of scars signals that the gospel can meet each generation in its own texture of doubt without altering essence. Jesus contextualizes His offering: to Mary He spoke her name, to Cleopas He opened Scriptures, to the disciples He breathed Spirit, to Thomas He extends tactile proof. The multi-modal communication strategy underscores that resurrection is adaptable yet consistent, satisfying diverse epistemic appetites. Furthermore, showing scars to Thomas secures communal coherence; now all apostles share common experience of encountering wounds, eliminating hierarchy of revelation. The church is forged not around degrees of mystical vision but around equal exposure to the crucified-risen body. This egalitarian distribution of evidence undergirds apostolic consensus essential for future doctrinal formulation.

6.3.2 The Invitation to Empirical Verification

"Bring your finger here; see My hands. Reach your hand; thrust it into My side," Jesus instructs, using imperatives matching Thomas's conditional phrases (John 20 : 27). The verbs echo forensic procedure: examine, verify, conclude. Ancient Mediterranean culture valued tactile proof—Roman legal documents sometimes required seal impressions pressed by signet ring, and here Jesus offers His flesh as living seal. John does not explicitly state that Thomas carried out the action; patristic commentary wrestles with whether faith sprang prior to touch. Either scenario honors Jesus' generosity: He was willing. The invitation dismantles dualistic philosophies claiming divinity cannot host matter. Moreover, it institutes principle that Christian proclamation welcomes rigorous inquiry; the gospel's confidence lies not in suppressing questions but in inviting engagement. In subsequent centuries apologists appeal to apostolic firsthand tangibility to defend against Gnostic visions and docetic denials. From psychological vantage, the offer recognizes learning modalities—Thomas's kinesthetic bent receives pathway to trust. The invitation also reveals Christ's respect for agency; He does not impose proof but proposes it, allowing Thomas the dignity of decision. Liturgically, Eastern churches on the Sunday after Pascha chant hymns praising "touching the life-giving side," integrating sensory theology into worship. Artistically, Caravaggio's dramatic chiaroscuro captures moment of insertion, reminding viewers that faith and doubt intertwine in luminous tension. Missiologically, the narrative equips missionaries to contextualize evidence for varied cultures—philosophical reasoning for Greeks, fulfilled prophecy for Jews, experiential healing for others—mirroring Jesus' personalized approach. Finally, the invitation models pastoral hospitality leader can embody: inviting congregants to examine evidence—biblical, historical, existential—without fear that truth will crumble under scrutiny.

6.4. The Confession of Thomas

6.4.1 "My Lord and My God" – Christological Implications

Thomas's five-word outcry in Greek—Ho Kyrios mou kai ho Theos mou—stands as the highest divine acknowledgment voiced by any individual in the Four Gospels (John 20 : 28). Where Nathanael had earlier hailed Jesus as Son of God and King of Israel, Thomas now fuses personal surrender ("my") with metaphysical acclamation ("God"), completing Johannine crescendo. Scholars note deliberate inclusio: the Gospel opens with declaration that the Word was God; it closes with disciple confessing the same. The pronouns transform theology into relationship: deity is not abstract but possessed in covenant intimacy. This declaration undergirds Trinitarian development; by worshipping Jesus as God without rebuke, Thomas affirms that monotheistic Jews can embrace high Christology without idolatry. Linguistically, the double vocative intensifies reverence; Septuagint Psalms employ similar form addressing Yahweh. Early church fathers leveraged this text against Arian claims, citing apostolic lips as authoritative. Pastoral reverberations abound: doubter becomes doxologist, skeptic becomes psalmist, illustrating trajectory from analysis to adoration. The confession's spontaneity counters notion that John fabricates late Christology; instead, earliest witnesses and skeptic alike reach same conviction when confronting scars. The phrase also anticipates liturgical Kyrie Eleison and Gloria in Excelsis, where believers acclaim Jesus as Lord God. Integrated within personal discipleship, the statement becomes prayer of surrender: acknowledging authority (Lord) and sufficiency (God). For missionaries, Thomas's confession models contextual language bridging Jewish title "Lord" used for Yahweh in Greek Bible and Hellenistic term "God," enabling cross-cultural proclamation. In spiritual formation, meditating on these five words invites holistic worship—mind, affection, will—aligned in unified exclamation. Importantly, the confession emerges not after extended catechesis but post-encounter, signifying revelation's primacy in birthing orthodoxy.

6.4.2 Blessed Are Those Who Have Not Seen

Jesus responds with gentle commendation that extends horizon beyond locked room: "Because you have seen Me, you have believed; blessed are those who have not seen and yet believe" (John 20 : 29). This beatitude, echoing Sermon on the Mount cadence, transports blessing from empirical category to faith category. It does not scold Thomas but situates his experience within unfolding salvation history where future believers will rely on apostolic testimony rather than personal touch. The statement legitimizes subsequent generations, including Johannine community and present-day church, assuring them that absence of visual contact does not relegate them to second-class citizenship. It also safeguards against perpetual sign-demand, establishing sufficiency of scriptural witness once attested by firsthand observers. The verb tense "have not seen but believe" may imply disciples beyond the room already trusting through preaching; thus, beatitude validates growing mission. From theological angle, the blessing exalts faith as relational trust rather than evidential certainty, yet faith remains anchored in objective reality of resurrection as documented. The verse shapes epistemology: knowledge of God interweaves testimony, Scripture, Spirit inner-witness, and reasonable inference. Pastoral application comforts converts from cultures without visionary phenomena; they are not disadvantaged. The beatitude also motivates evangelism—each time gospel is shared, potential exists for blessed belief absent direct sight. In liturgy, Easter season readings include this verse, reinforcing congregational identity as blessed believers. For theologians like Aquinas and Calvin, the statement supported doctrine of sufficiency of Scripture and witness for salvation. Finally, the beatitude serves as ethical check against spiritual elitism; miraculous encounters do not guarantee superior status over those walking by trust. The risen Christ thus locks the circle: He honors Thomas's journey yet pivots focus outward, ensuring narrative's climax directs gaze to generations reading the Gospel centuries later.

6.5. Theological and Pastoral Implications

6.5.1 Faith, Doubt, and the Patience of the Risen Lord

The Thomas episode offers a nuanced theology of doubt. It separates honest uncertainty rooted in unfulfilled desire for truth from willful disbelief hardened by pride. Jesus accommodates the former, meeting the intellect while summoning the heart. Doubt, when held within community and directed toward the Lord, becomes corridor for deeper revelation. The patience of Christ—waiting eight days, returning with scars—models pastoral stance for church leaders toward skeptics. Patience entails listening, contextualizing evidence, and avoiding shaming language.

The episode also validates multidisciplinary apologetics; Christ provides empirical data (touch), personal presence (relationship), and interpretive context (peace pronouncement). Educational ministries can adopt layered engagement—historical, experiential, communal—to mirror this pattern. Furthermore, Thomas's journey teaches disciples to articulate their doubts clearly; vague apprehension rarely receives tailored answer. Spiritual directors encourage journaling specific obstacles, inviting Jesus to address them. The narrative equally cautions that prolonged postponement—"unless I see, I will never believe"—must remain open to divine proof lest doubt calcify. Christ's gracious invitation is not indefinite license for intellectual procrastination; He grants Thomas evidence but also issues final beatitude foreclosing endless sign-seeking. Communities should thus pair patience with prophetic invitation to decision. The passage also reframes doubt within worship; liturgy can incorporate lament and questioning psalms, creating space where modern "Thomases" feel honored rather than marginal. Mental health practitioners see correlation between acknowledging uncertainty and lowering anxiety; church that welcomes questions fosters holistic wellness. Ultimately, the patience of the risen Lord cultivates mature faith able to shepherd others wrestling with uncertainty.

6.5.2 Forming a Community of Testimony Across Generations

The locked-room reprise underscores that Christian testimony is both historical and ongoing. The first disciples become living bridge between visible Christ and unseen future believers. Apostolic reliability rests on two pillars: personal encounter and communal corroboration. Thomas's integration ensures unanimity; all Eleven have now experienced resurrection, fortifying later missionary declaration. This corporate witness passes into written form—Gospels, letters—creating stable deposit for churches distant in time and geography. The beatitude extends blessing to readers who trust that deposit, illustrating Scripture's sufficiency in absence of new appearances. Yet community remains dynamic; Spirit continues to enliven text and sacrament, making Christ present in non-optical ways. Ecclesiology must therefore balance respect for foundational testimony with openness to Spirit encounters that never contradict but illuminate canon. Catechesis can use Thomas narrative to teach transmission chain: from eyewitness, to oral tradition, to inscripturation, to proclamation. Such pedagogy strengthens confidence against skeptical claims that Christianity relies on blind faith. Intergenerational discipleship likewise draws on story: older believers emulate first disciples sharing proofs and peace with youth navigating digital skepticism. Mission agencies deploying to post-Christian West find Thomas passage resonates with seculars demanding evidence; they harness historical apologetics while inviting experiential engagement through prayer. Worship planners schedule "Doubting Thomas Sunday" to celebrate inquiry and declare blessing over non-seeing believers. The community, following model of upper room, must maintain rhythms of gathering where Jesus may surprise with new insights while grounding identity in completed work. Thus, Thomas narrative shapes church's task: steward testimony, foster belonging for skeptics, and send witnesses to speak scars into every culture.

Conclusion

The second Sunday encounter completes a symmetrical arc begun in darkness of a garden and continued through locked doors: from Mary's tears to Thomas's touch, from solitary gardener recognition to communal confession of deity. By returning for one skeptical disciple, the risen Jesus demonstrates that resurrection grace is neither impatient nor economizing; it lavishes itself on every honest seeker until the last objection melts before wounded love. Thomas's transformation from demand to doxology assures generations that the gospel can withstand scrutiny without forfeiting wonder. His exclamation—"my Lord and my God"—rings across centuries as litmus of authentic faith, uniting personal allegiance to cosmic truth. The beatitude that follows blesses all who will believe through apostolic testimony, wrapping the reader personally into Easter narrative. Locked doors have now become thresholds; scars have become credentials; doubt has become doorway; and communal worship has become weekly rehearsal of peace that shatters fear. As modern disciples gather each Lord's Day—whether in cathedrals, storefronts, or living rooms—they rehearse Thomas's journey: hearing reports, voicing questions, encountering presence, and confessing lordship. The promise stands: Christ still steps across barriers—psychological, cultural, intellectual—to disclose Himself in ways each soul can grasp. The chapter of Thomas is thus always contemporary; it invites churches to hold questions without panic, to present evidence without arrogance, and to anticipate the voice that still speaks peace amid every restless mind. In that patient expectancy the church discovers again and again the blessedness of those who have not seen and yet, by the Spirit's illumination, joyfully believe.

Chapter 7. Dawn on the Shores of Galilee – Seven Disciples and the Miraculous Catch

Not long after the two Jerusalem Sundays that forever recalibrated their understanding of reality, a cluster of weary disciples found themselves back on the familiar waters of the Sea of Tiberias. John reports that seven in all made the journey north—Peter, Thomas, Nathanael of Cana, the sons of Zebedee, and two unnamed companions—an uneven number of fishermen and friends who had tasted resurrection wonder yet still carried vocational muscle memory and lingering uncertainty (John 21 : 1-3). Their decision to fish through the night reads on first glance like a retreat into routine, but the dawn encounter that followed would prove a master class in post-Easter discipleship: how the risen Christ meets His own in ordinary toil, transforms scarcity into abundance, and converts charcoal fire into covenant breakfast. This Galilean page of the resurrection narrative is not only a closed-circle epilogue to John's Gospel; it is a theological map guiding every generation into rhythms of obedient listening, vocational integration, and communal restoration.

7.1. Galilee's Quiet Liminal Space

7.1.1 Geographic Texture and Cultural Memory

The Sea of Tiberias, more commonly called the Sea of Galilee or Lake Kinneret, stretches thirteen miles long and eight miles wide, cradled by undulating slopes that funnel cool night air onto its warm surface and generate sudden squalls—a meteorological quirk that once terrified disciples in a wind-whipped boat (Matt 8 : 23-27). By the first century it served as economic engine for the densely populated Galilean basin: Bethsaida processed salted fish; Magdala hosted dye and textile markets; and the Herodian city of Tiberias, founded only a generation earlier, shimmered with Hellenistic architecture, hot springs, and regional bureaucracy. For Peter, Andrew, James, and John, the lake was neither postcard nor pilgrimage site; it was the office floor, the place where nets tore, taxes loomed, and Roman agents tallied harvests. Returning there after the Jerusalem tumult made practical sense: Passover crowds had dispersed, and family households still required sustenance. Yet geography is never mere backdrop in the Fourth Gospel; water had already served as theater for signs—from Cana's purification jars to Bethesda's pool to the storm-calmed sea. Thus Galilee functions as theological womb where Jesus first called fishermen with promise of people-catching and now will midwife their resurrection vocation. The shoreline at dawn, ringed by basalt rocks still warm from the previous afternoon sun, offers natural amphitheater for voice to carry; a man need only cup his hands to call instructions across one hundred yards. Local lore held that dawn was most reliable window for shoals moving toward surface to feed on plankton, yet seasoned crews also knew the risk of empty nets after twilight trawling. Jewish fishermen followed purity laws—avoiding shellfish, washing nets ceremonially—layering spiritual routines onto economic necessity. All these textures converge that night, turning a mundane shift into sacred stage. Galilean topography thus reminds modern readers that Christ's post-Easter agenda unfolds not in rarified sanctuaries alone but in commerce-saturated coastlines, among tax receipts and market stalls, where disciples wrestle with invoices as surely as intercessions.

7.1.2 The Inner Weather of Seven Disciples

The psychological climate among the seven mirrors the lake's own unpredictability. Peter carries fresh memories of private restoration in Jerusalem yet remains uncertain how forgiveness translates into leadership praxis. Thomas bears the stimulus of tactile faith but has yet to test his newfound conviction beyond locked-room walls. Nathanael—once flabbergasted that anything good could exit Nazareth—now stares at hometown shoreline and wonders how Nazareth's native Son might appear again. James and John balance familial obligations—aged father Zebedee may still depend on their labor—with their mother's earlier aspirations that they sit at Messianic right and left, a request now reframed by cross and resurrection. The two unnamed disciples, perhaps Andrew and Philip or even non-fishermen like Matthew, embody the broader community whose stories remain unscripted yet essential. Collectively they journeyed north obeying Jesus' promise, delivered through the women, that He would rendezvous in Galilee (Matt 28 : 7-10). But promise timing is unspecified; tension mounts between active waiting and survival chores. Peter's proposal "I am going fishing" surfaces not as rebellion but coping strategy—return to muscle memory when providence feels ambiguous. Group dynamics favor action: six others echo, "we are going with you," preferring solidarity over solitary rumination. Unspoken is the shared grief that Judean authorities continue to menace believers; distance grants psychological breathing room. Yet unresolved vocational displacement whispers: Are we now itinerant preachers or family breadwinners? Will resurrection appearances continue or wane? In such liminal head-space, nighttime fishing offers rhythms of hand, rope, and oar that still uncertainty for a time. Their decision models how disciples often oscillate between spiritual high points and mundane tasks, revealing that vocational callings seldom erase original trades but infuse them with new telos pending fresh commission. The seven's interior weather—swirling hope, latent guilt, modest anticipation—sets stage for dawn's revelatory calm.

7.2. A Night of Futile Labor

7.2.1 Vocational Reflex and Spiritual Ambiguity

The shift begins at twilight when Mediterranean dusk dyes sky in lavender bands, and fishing crews customarily launch to exploit nocturnal feeding patterns of tilapia and sardines. Peter's boat—likely a seven-meter craft able to hold half-ton catch—pushes off with rhythmic splash of oars, nets coiled at stern. These nets, linen trammel types composed of three layers, require coordinated choreography: one disciple casts while others pay out line in semicircle sweep. They work silently, seasoned eyes gauging moon reflection and water ripples that betray schooling fish. Hours pass. They haul net after net, only to find algae, stray weeds, perhaps a lone glimmering fish flipping back to black water. Failure stings professional pride; each disciple has read the lake like scripture since boyhood. Peter mutters adjustments—row farther offshore, skirt deeper channel near Hippos, drift near Capernaum inlets—but emptiness persists. In biblical symbolism, night often connotes ignorance or toil apart from divine presence; hereby the narrative dramatizes futility of self-directed effort even post-resurrection. The disciples possess resurrection knowledge yet temporarily operate independent of explicit guidance, illustrating that revelation without ongoing obedience can stall fruitfulness. Their labor, though honest, lacks yield; nets droop heavy with fatigue rather than fish. Spiritual writers parallel this cycle to ministries relying on past anointing: prior encounters celebrated yet present direction absent, leading to diligence devoid of breakthrough. Economic anxiety creeps: families awaiting breakfast will taste disappointment; marketplace vendors record shortage. More subtly, the night surfaces memory of Luke 5, when another fruitless vigil preceded first miraculous catch and Peter's haunting confession of sinfulness. Thus, history rhymes: same lake, similar failure, but deeper narrative now in play. Modern professionals, whether teachers enduring disengaged classrooms or physicians wrestling with treatment inefficacy, may identify with disciples' bodily exhaustion and internal questioning—"Why is my expertise producing no fruit?" This dark-to-dawn tension invites surrender that precedes divine intervention.

7.2.2 Empty Nets as Theological Metaphor

John's laconic statement, "that night they caught nothing," is not journalistic throw-away; it pulses with layered theology (John 21 : 3). First, it exposes limitations of human resourcefulness absent explicit Word. Second, it critiques temptation to retreat to pre-calling identities when new calling feels delayed. Third, it sets up miracle contrast, highlighting that abundance flows not from lake fertility but from obedience to resurrected speech. Patristic commentators see allegory: the night represents era prior to Pentecost when apostolic nets remain empty; dawn anticipates Spirit-illuminated mission drawing multitudes. Others note ecclesial symbolism—net strained yet unbroken later mirrors catholic unity holding diverse converts. Psychologically, empty nets surface disciples' fear that resurrection glory might bypass their everyday work; miracle will prove otherwise, validating vocation. Missionally, story instructs church-planters languishing over scarce converts: dryness may signal strategic repositioning rather than final verdict. Theological ethics emerges too: healthy frustration can detox pride, preparing hearts to attribute ensuing success to grace, not technique. Thus, emptiness is not punitive; it is pedagogical pause. Liturgically, some communities pause within Eastertide to lament unfruitful efforts, allowing story to baptize frustration into expectancy. In contemporary conversations about burnout, the narrative offers template: acknowledge empty nets, listen for shoreline voice, and redeploy nets under new instruction. Hence, a seemingly simple sentence becomes evangelical paradigm.

7.3. The Stranger's Dawn Directive

7.3.1 Recognition Deferred by Distance and Disposition

Just as first rays blush Golan cliffs, a silhouetted figure stands about a hundred yards ashore, far enough that facial features blur yet near enough that voice can traverse water's still morning hush. He calls using a colloquial term, paidia—"children" or "lads"—both affectionate and patronizingly playful. The address jolts fatigued men; such warmth from unknown camper feels odd. He inquires about catch outcome, a typical shoreline banter where merchants might prearrange purchase. The disciples' curt negative response betrays frustration, yet they do not recognize speaker. Why? John hints that "they did not know it was Jesus" (John 21 : 4). Factors include dawn haze, mental categories expecting future rather than present appearance, and preoccupation with failure. Recognition motif threads John's Gospel: Mary mistook Jesus for gardener until name articulation; Emmaus disciples knew Him in bread breaking; here recognition will crescendo via miraculous provision. Intentionally, the risen Christ reveals Himself progressively, training disciples that post-Easter perception relies less on optics and more on discerning work of grace. Modern believers likewise may overlook divine presence in colleagues or crises until fruits manifest. The stranger's initial anonymity preserves authenticity of obedience: will they heed instruction even before recognition? This tests readiness to pivot from expertise to submission. Spiritual directors speak of "indirect encounters" where guidance surfaces through ordinary voices; disciples' experience legitimizes such mediated revelation. Thus, non-recognition sets spiritual stage for faith-prior-to-sight dynamic.

7.3.2 Casting on the Right Side: Obedience Preceding Understanding

The stranger issues perplexing yet simple command: "Cast the net on the right side of the boat, and you will find some" (John 21 : 6). Professional fishermen could easily dismiss landlubber advice; right versus left orientation likely seems arbitrary given currents. Yet something in tone or Spirit-prompt nudges compliance. They angle boat starboard, toss heavy nets, and almost instantly feel tug of thrashing mass. Nets swell, ropes creak, arms strain; water churns silver with flailing fish. Count remains unknown, but density shocks them. This obedience-before-insight paradigm echoes Cana servants filling jars with water before wine transformation. Faith manifests as action under puzzling directive; understanding follows yield, not preceding it. Modern disciples often seek clarity before obedience; story reverses sequence, illustrating kingdom epistemology. The miracle's specifics—net not torn, 153 fish counted later—sustain authenticity: professional note-taking behavior after haul highlight realism. Ethically, Jesus honors labor: He does not conjure fish in baskets; He blesses existing skill submitted to word. Vocational theology resonates: Christ partners with dentists, designers, and taxi drivers, directing their expertise toward kingdom abundance. Missiologically, right-side casting signifies strategic adaptation—slight adjustment under divine guidance yields exponential harvest. Organizations plateauing may need subtle course correction rather than overhaul. This cast redefines success metrics: not toil hours but obedience precise.

7.4. Full Nets and Thundering Hearts

7.4.1 Symbolic Weight of 153 Fish and Unbroken Net

When boat beaches on pebbled shore and disciples haul net ashore, John—ever numerically attentive—records tally of 153 large fish (John 21 : 11). Exegetes across centuries propose meanings: Jerome cites Greco-Roman zoologist Oppian's catalogue of 153 known fish species, positing universal mission inclusion. Augustine sees triangular number of 17 (sum of Ten Commandments and Sevenfold Spirit gifts) triangulated representing law-grace synthesis. Modern scholars treat number as eyewitness detail verifying miracle rather than allegorizing. Whatever interpretation, at least three observations endure. First, the count signals order amid abundance—disciples steward miracle by recording specifics, safeguarding memory against exaggeration. Second, "large fish" acknowledges quality as well as quantity, prefiguring diverse yet robust converts. Third, net's integrity under strain indicates nascent church's unity despite numerical expansion. Peter's labor dragging net alone—contrasting earlier distribution of tasks—foreshadows his emergent leadership in global haul. Ecclesially, number invites imagination of catholic fullness where every ethno-linguistic group enters one undivided net. Additionally, professional fishermen counting catch underscores economic realism; miracle honors livelihoods by gifting marketable bounty ensuring families' provision. Hence, 153 functions at intersection of symbol, history, and practicality.

7.4.2 Work Sanctified by Grace

The episode fuses divine initiative and human effort: Jesus supplies fish location, yet disciples row, cast, haul, and count. This synergy corrects dualisms that pit sacred against secular. In vocational discipleship, grace does not circumvent craft; it invigorates it. Peter's water-soaked tunic and calloused hands testify that resurrected encounters do not exempt labor; they recalibrate telos: work becomes witness. Marketplace theologians derive paradigm: Christian engineers co-create solutions directed by prayerful listening; farmers steward land under providential seasons. Net imagery parallels contemporary supply chains; when integrity maintained by righteousness, abundance blesses many without tearing social fabric. Furthermore, miracle critiques prosperity gospel: disciples still exert; abundance arrives after night of lack, reminding that timing rests with sovereignty. Spiritual disciplines of perseverance, attentiveness, and gratitude guard against entitlement. Feasting on catch soon becomes communal breakfast, subverting individualistic gain; grace flows toward fellowship. Thus, sanctified work evidences not only output but relational fruit.

7.5. Breakfast by Charcoal Fire

7.5.1 Echoes of Denial and Re-creation of Fellowship

Upon landing, disciples glimpse charcoal fire with fish laid and bread prepared (John 21 : 9). Only two charcoal fires appear in Gospels: Peter's denial courtyard (John 18 : 18) and this seaside scene. Parallel invites redemptive reading: where Peter warmed hands while denying, now he is warmed while being restored. Charcoal smoke aroma resurrects memory, but hospitality reframes it under grace. Jesus, who asked earlier for fish, already has fish—signifying self-sufficiency—yet invites disciples to contribute from miraculous haul, modeling cooperative grace. He serves them breakfast, adopting host role reminiscent of feeding five thousand and Last Supper yet distinct in casual simplicity. Breakfast—a mundane meal—teaches sacramental presence in daily sustenance. In Middle Eastern culture, eating together seals reconciliation; thus, community fractured by flight now mends over grilled tilapia. Psychologically, shared meals foster oxytocin bonding, strengthening group identity ahead of mission. Liturgically, early church agape feasts echo this breakfast, preceding Eucharist. The fire also prefigures Pentecost tongues—charcoal embers glowing as pledge of Spirit blaze. Modern small-groups replicating potluck fellowship reenact seaside grace, turning brunch tables into altars of restoration.

7.5.2 Provision as Precursor to Commission

Jesus' "Come and have breakfast" precedes deep conversation with Peter (John 21 : 12-19). Chronology matters: nourishment before probation. This reveals divine pedagogy: hunger addressed, trust reinforced, then challenging call articulated. Missional praxis should likewise feed before preaching, build rapport before discipling. The meal also evidences eschatological foretaste; Isaiah anticipated feast of rich food after death's shroud lifted (Isa 25 : 6-8). Now resurrected Messiah inaugurates modest version, promising ultimate banquet. Provision demonstrates that mission flows from abundance, not scarcity mindset; disciples leave with both nets full and hearts full. Churches fund mission best when rooted in confidence of Christ's ongoing breakfast-making. Finally, invitation extends to seven but radiates symbolically to world; the One who cooked fish invites nations to taste and see. Thus, breakfast is sacrament of sufficiency that secures obedience to forthcoming shepherd charge.

7.6. Re-Commissioning on the Shore

7.6.1 Peter's Threefold Affirmation and Pastoral Mandate

After meal, Jesus addresses Simon son of John with triadic question "Do you love Me?" matching triple denial. Each affirmative unlocks shepherd action: feed lambs, tend sheep, feed sheep (John 21 : 15-17). Greek lexical contrast between agapao and phileo sparks debates but consensus leans toward rhetorical variation rather than rank degrees. Critical is progression from love confession to pastoral vocation; affection for Christ translates into concrete care for people. Restoration occurs publicly before six witnesses, establishing accountability and trust for future leadership. Christ does not dwell on failure details; He reframes identity: not fisherman but shepherd. Prophetic echo of Ezekiel 34 indicting false shepherds lingers; now Peter called to embody antidote. Threefold charge covers developmental spectrum of flock— lambs (new believers), sheep (maturing ones). Leadership matrix emerges: nourishing doctrine, protective oversight, sacrificial giving. For pastors today, criterion remains affectionate intimacy with Christ over charisma. The conversation also models corrective yet gentle restoration: Jesus addresses Peter's past indirectly through parallel structure, sparing shame while ensuring acknowledgment. Psychologically, this fosters healthy integration rather than suppression of failure story. Such method informs counseling techniques aiming to redeem trauma through narrative reframing.

7.6.2 Prophecy of Sacrificial Future and Call to Follow

Jesus concludes by depicting Peter's eventual martyrdom: arms stretched, someone dressing him and carrying where he does not wish (John 21 : 18-19). The imagery likely alludes to crucifixion; early tradition records Peter dying upside-down in Rome. This prophecy tempers restored enthusiasm with sober cost realism. Christian discipleship thus weds reconciliation with suffering expectation. Peter's immediate instinct to compare destiny with John's prompts Jesus' corrective—"What is that to you? You follow Me." Leadership cannot anchor identity in peer trajectories; faithfulness is individual call within communal mission. Missiologically, martyrdom prophecy undergirds courageous witness; Peter's later boldness in Acts flows from foreknowledge that ultimate outcome lies in Christ's sovereignty. For modern believers facing persecution, passage offers perspective: shepherding may entail literal or metaphorical death, but obedience outlives violence. The call "Follow Me" bookends Peter's journey, echoing first summons by same lake (Mark 1 : 17), highlighting discipleship's cyclic nature of recommitment after grace. Thus, re-commissioning integrates past, present, and eschatological future in singular vector of love-manifest obedience.

7.7. Contours for Contemporary Discipleship

7.7.1 Listening for Shoreline Voices in Marketplace Life

The Galilee narrative equips modern professionals to discern Christ amid cubicle or construction site. Like disciples failing to recognize voice across water, employees may overlook divine directives when cloaked in ordinary counsel—a manager's suggestion, a friend's text. Practicing attentiveness involves pausing to ask, "Could this right-side casting insight be Spirit whisper?" Faith communities can host vocational discernment groups where members share "empty-net" frustrations, pray, and compare shore-borne ideas. Obedience might look like incremental pivot—adjusting marketing strategy, altering classroom seating—rather than grand overhaul. When abundance follows, counting fish equates to measuring impact while crediting God. Testimonies of such workplace miracles reinforce that resurrection power is not confined to sanctuary but saturates spreadsheets and service industries. Thus, discipleship curriculum should include modules on hearing Christ in professional feedback channels and integrating prayerful listening into project planning cycles.

7.7.2 Building Communities of Grace-Formed Leaders

Peter's seaside restoration shapes leadership pipelines: churches must design pathways where failure does not preclude future service yet requires transparent healing. Mentoring structures can pair "Peters" emerging from burnout with seasoned "Johns" who recognize Lord first and encourage leap from boat. Feasting together—literal meals—mimics breakfast model, facilitating vulnerability. Pastoral teams should track both net integrity (unity) and fish count (growth), resisting false dichotomy of quantity versus quality. The 153-fish narrative encourages diverse inclusion; congregations may adopt global partnerships acknowledging species beyond local comfort zones. Charcoal fire gatherings—retreats focused on confession and recommission—help leaders recall first love. Finally, Jesus' closing imperative forbidding comparison fosters culture where each servant celebrates others' assignments while stewarding own. Such communities reflect dawn shoreline ethic: dialogic listening, obedience, abundance, fellowship, and mission.

Conclusion

The Galilean morning reveals a risen Christ who cooks breakfast as readily as He conquers death, who sends schooling fish into nets yet asks human partners to drag them ashore, and who converts a charcoal-smoked memory of failure into fragrant sacrament of restoration. By retracing the night of futile labor, the shoreline directive, the bulging nets, and the commissioning meal, we discover a discipleship pathway marked by honest toil, responsive obedience, generous provision, and redemptive leadership. The story assures every weary worker that divine guidance can pierce dawn haze, every skeptic that unseen presence becomes unmistakable in hindsight, and every fallen shepherd that love-driven service still awaits. In a world where many nets return empty and many fires spark shame, the risen Jesus still stands on countless metaphorical beaches, calling communities to cast differently, dine gratefully, and follow sacrificially. May today's disciples, hearing His voice across whatever waters they navigate, leap from their routines, drag their many-colored catches to the table of fellowship, and declare with deeds as well as words that the Lord of life reigns even over spreadsheets, marketplaces, and breakfast tables at dawn.

Chapter 8. Mountain in Galilee – The Great Commission

The Galilean mountain that hosts Matthew's account of the Great Commission rises in Scripture like a summit of culmination and commencement, gathering into its heights every earlier ascent in biblical history while simultaneously opening vistas that stretch toward every subsequent generation of the Church. The patriarch Abraham had once trudged up Moriah ready to surrender his beloved son and learned that God Himself would provide the lamb; Moses scaled Sinai and descended radiant with covenant words etched in stone; Elijah stood on Carmel to expose idols and then journeyed to Horeb to hear the still-small voice. Now, after resurrection dawn has flashed across Judea and the Sea of Tiberias has already echoed with restorative breakfast conversations, the risen Messiah gathers His followers on a Galilean ridge—not only to capstone three years of itinerant instruction but to ignite a global, age-spanning mission. Matthew records the scene in a mere handful of verses (Matthew 28 : 16-20), yet those sentences thrum with theological density and missional consequence unparalleled in the Gospel narrative. The pericope unfurls four colossal pronouncements: an affirmation of Jesus' universal authority, a mandate to make disciples of all nations, a sacramental command to baptize into Trinitarian Name, and a covenant promise of abiding presence until time's consummation. Beneath each clause pulses a symphony of Old Testament echoes, Second-Temple hopes, and eschatological horizons that the evangelist assumes his readers will hear.

8.1. Setting the Scene on the Mountain in Galilee

8.1.1 Geography, Symbolism, and Memory

Galilee, the northern territorial quilt of ancient Israel, is framed by rugged hills, fertile valleys, and the shimmering harp-shaped lake that Romans rechristened the Sea of Tiberias. Within this region an assortment of ridges—Arbel, Tabor, the Horns of Hattin—offer panoramic views that can swallow a pilgrim's breath. Matthew does not name the specific elevation, perhaps intending to keep attention on the speaker rather than the scenery, yet his Jewish-rooted audience would instinctively link "mountain" with moments of decisive revelation. In Israel's collective imagination mountaintops were thin places where heaven bent nearer to earth: Sinai thundered with covenant, Carmel crackled with prophetic fire, Zion sang with enthroned kingship. By staging the Great Commission here, the evangelist frames Jesus not merely as rabbi but as mediator surpassing Moses, prophet transcending Elijah, and king eclipsing David. Geographically, Galilee lies astride caravan arteries that once shuffled Phoenician merchants southward and Mesopotamian envoys westward; thus the locale whispers universality even before Christ utters "all nations." Galilee had been lampooned as "Galilee of the Gentiles" (Isaiah 9 : 1) due to its mosaic of ethnic enclaves, yet Isaiah also foresaw that the region mired in gloom would receive first light of redemptive dawn—a prophecy Matthew already tied to Jesus' inaugural preaching (Matthew 4 : 15-16). Therefore, the mountain emerges as geographic sermon: a mixed-heritage region becomes launchpad for global good news, signaling that ethnic borders no longer fence in covenant blessing. Archaeologically, first-century Galilean hills teemed with terraces where farmers coaxed olives and figs from limestone soil; shepherds grazed flocks on slopes; insurgent zealots once plotted ambushes in caves. The disciples, native sons of this landscape, upon climbing the rendezvous ridge would have inhaled scents of thyme, heard bee hum, and remembered youthful footraces—sensory layers that personalized the monumental moment. Hence, Galilee's geography threads memory, prophecy, and strategic symbolism, preparing disciples' imaginations to receive a commission as wide as horizon. In modern missional reflection, selecting meeting places still matters: Christ's use of a hilltop overlooking multicultural trade routes suggests churches should situate their sending ceremonies where urban skylines or digital networks remind gatherers of enlarged fields ripe for harvest. Thus, before a single verb of mandate is spoken, the physical setting preaches quietly but persuasively: the God who once narrowed His focus to one land now widens His embrace from this vantage to the uttermost parts of the earth.

8.1.2 *The Pilgrimage of Obedience from Jerusalem to Galilee*

The disciples' trek north after Passover evokes both literal mileage—roughly eighty to ninety miles depending on route—and metaphorical transition from confusion to clarified vocation. Jerusalem's upper-room apparitions had breathed peace, restored Peter, and satisfied Thomas, yet Jesus' message through the women—"Tell My brothers to go to Galilee; there they will see Me" (Matthew 28 : 10)—lingered as uncompleted directive. Obedience in post-resurrection life thus begins with travel: feet blister, sandals accumulate dust, and muscle ache accompanies contemplation. This pilgrimage echoes Israel's earlier wilderness marches where movement preceded understanding; disciples internalize that resurrected faith is dynamic, not sedentary. Scholars surmise that the journey may have taken three to six days, assuming stops at Samaritan border villages or Jordan Valley inns. Along the way, discussions likely oscillated between theological reflection—"What does 'all authority' entail?"—and pragmatic wonderings—"Will He appear suddenly or meet us openly?" Luke hints that as many as "more than five hundred brothers and sisters" eventually witnessed a Galilean appearance (1 Corinthians 15 : 6), implying that an ever-growing cohort joined the pilgrims. This enlarging caravan foreshadows church growth mechanics: obedience attracts onlookers; anticipation begets invitation. The road north, lined with spring wildflowers after Judea's rains, also retraced Jesus' earlier southbound routes where He set His face toward crucifixion; now disciples reverse trajectory, signifying victory march. Traveling through Samaria they may have revisited Sychar's well where living-water conversation occurred, reminding them that "fields white for harvest" awaited. Each village offered rehearsal for global mission: engaging strangers, lodging with hospitable hosts, discerning receptivity. By the time they reach designated mountain, obedience has already shaped them—legs strengthened, hearts united, doubts aired and partially resolved. Missional praxis today takes cue here: commissioning rituals gain depth when preceded by journeying experiences—retreats, cross-cultural exposures—so that hearing the Great Commission springs from lived obedience not theoretical assent. Moreover, the disciples' willingness to leave Jerusalem's religious epicenter for rustic Galilee underscores humility: power of gospel is not anchored in temple grandeur but in presence of risen Lord wherever He chooses. Thus, pilgrimage from city to hill seeds posture for task ahead: they will soon traverse continents, crossing far more formidable boundaries in obedience to the One whose directive already walked them home.

8.2. The Declaration of Cosmic Authority

8.2.1 Textual Nuances of "All Authority in Heaven and on Earth"

Jesus' first sentence on the mountain is not command but announcement: "All authority has been given to Me in heaven and on earth" (Matthew 28 : 18). The Greek *exousia* conveys delegated right combined with intrinsic power, contrasting with raw force (dynamis) by emphasizing legitimate rule. The aorist passive "has been given" indicates a completed grant, pointing to Father's bestowal following resurrection vindication, as Paul notes in Philippians 2 : 9-11. By coupling heaven and earth, Jesus claims universal jurisdiction—cosmic bracket that leaves no realm unclaimed; such phrasing evokes Daniel 7 : 14 where Son of Man receives dominion, glory, and a kingdom that shall not pass away. Matthew, who foregrounded kingdom language from genealogy forward, thus bookends Gospel: baby visited by Magi under starry heavens (heavenly realm) now declares governance also of earth—Herod's realm dwarfed. The statement also answers Satan's earlier offer of authority over world kingdoms (Matthew 4 : 8-10): what enemy proposed by shortcut, Father now grants via cross. For Jewish listeners, claim extends beyond Davidic throne to encompass angelic spheres, challenging apocalyptic speculation that divided cosmos into competing powers. In Greco-Roman milieu, emperors styled themselves lord of earth; Jesus' assertion eclipses Caesar's coin-stamped auctoritas by spanning heavens too. Grammatically, "all" (pasa) appears fourfold in Commission (all authority, all nations, all that I commanded, all the days), a rhetorical snowball rolling downhill, gathering momentum of totality. Pastoral implication: disciple can obey mandate amid hostile contexts because no sector—political, educational, digital—lies outside Christ's remit. Systematic theology extracts high Christology: enthroned Christ mediates creation's coherence (Colossians 1 : 17). Ethically, authority grounds discipleship's radical demands; they flow not from charismatic leader's whim but from cosmic sovereign's decree. Worshipfully, doxology becomes logical response: hymns that ascribe universal lordship align with mountain pronouncement. Thus, Christ's preface functions as legal warrant, emotional reassurance, and theological thesis for everything that follows.

8.2.2 Early Church Reception and Canonical Echoes

Acts portrays apostles acting under this claimed authority: Peter confronts Sanhedrin, Paul disputes Roman governors, Philip baptizes Ethiopian official—all convinced that risen Lord outranks religious council and empire alike. The book's programmatic verse—"You will be My witnesses… to the ends of the earth" (Acts 1 : 8)—mirrors mountain horizon, showing Luke's complement rather than contradiction to Matthew. Epistles echo same authority: Ephesians speaks of Christ seated above every rule, authority, power, and dominion, his name invoked in every age. Hebrews presents enthroned Son sustaining universe by His word. Revelation depicts Lamb receiving worship from multitudes in heaven (angelic) and on earth (nations), fulfilling dual-realm claim. Patristic fathers leveraged text against imperial cult: Ignatius calls believers "Christ bearers" because their loyalty belongs to One possessing all authority, not Caesar. Nicene Creed crystallizes this by asserting His kingdom will have no end. Liturgically, baptismal rites integrate authority clause before triple immersion, reminding catechumens that entry into church means transfer of allegiance. Even Christian art picks motif: domes of ancient basilicas show Pantokrator—Christ the almighty—hovering over earthly scenes. Politically, medieval investiture controversies pitted papal and monarchical powers; both sides cited Matthew 28, yet deeper reading cautions against conflating Christ's cosmic rule with human hierarchies. Modern missiology draws confidence: translation work in unreached tribes rests on conviction that language barriers fall under Christ's jurisdiction. In sum, early and ongoing reception of authority statement shapes worship, mission, and courage, ensuring that Great Commission never reduces to human aspiration but remains response to enthroned King.

8.3. The Mandate to Make Disciples of All Nations

8.3.1 Parsing the Missional Triad: Go, Baptize, Teach

Grammatically, the lone imperative in Greek is "make disciples" (mathēteusate), flanked by three participles—going, baptizing, teaching—that delineate how discipling unfolds. First, "going" implies movement, whether across street or sea; it presumes disciples will not wait for nations to arrive but will cross cultural, linguistic, and socio-economic chasms.

Matthew's earlier mission discourse limited reach to lost sheep of Israel (Matthew 10 : 5-6); resurrection broadens vector to ethne, all people groups, fulfilling Abrahamic blessing promise (Genesis 12 : 3). Second, baptizing "into the name of the Father, and of the Son, and of the Holy Spirit" incorporates converts into Trinitarian life. Name (singular) yet threefold persons encapsulates mystery early church would later defend at Nicaea and Constantinople. Baptism serves identity marker supplanting ethnic, familial, or civic loyalties with primary allegiance to Godhead community. Third, teaching "to obey everything I have commanded" safeguards against truncated gospel of decision without discipleship. The curriculum is not selective; the adjective "all" again surfaces, covering Sermon on the Mount ethics, parable-shaped imagination, and cross-shaped love. The triad forms pedagogical loop: going introduces gospel, baptism initiates into community, teaching matures believers who in turn go. Mission agencies craft strategies aligning with this syntax—pre-evangelism, sacramental incorporation, formative catechesis. Pastoral praxis notes that baptism and teaching are communal acts; thus disciple-making cannot occur in isolation. Moreover, baptizing before exhaustive teaching underscores grace precedence: belonging precedes perfect understanding, yet teaching ensures lifelong growth. In pluralistic contexts, emphasis on teaching obedience counters relativism; disciples submit intellect, desires, and habits under lordship. Thus, the missional triad balances outreach and nurture, sacrament and instruction, conversion and sanctification.

8.3.2 "All Nations": Cultural Engagement and Inclusion

"All nations" (panta ta ethnē) signifies more than geopolitical states; in biblical usage ethne includes clans, tribes, language groups. Hence, the mandate anticipates ethnolinguistic diversity later cataloged in Revelation 7 : 9. The phrase demolishes ethnocentric privilege; Jewish disciples must embrace Samaritans, Romans, Ethiopians. It also invalidates modern racism within church; any exclusionary stance contradicts original charter. Historically, early Christians obeyed intuitively: Antioch church emerged cross-cultural,

Syrian missionaries reached Sasanian empire, Thomas tradition to India persists. Culturally, engaging nations requires translation—linguistic (Scriptures into native tongue) and cultural (gospel contextualized without compromise). The incarnation model—Word becoming flesh—guides missionaries to respect local art, music, customs, filtering through biblical lens. Missiologists like Andrew Walls describe "pilgrim principle" (gospel travels light across cultures) and "indigenizing principle" (gospel at home in culture); both derive from "all nations" clause. Ethical dimension arises: evangelism divorced from justice becomes hollow; addressing poverty, oppression, and disease demonstrates gospel relevance. In interfaith dialogue, commission motivates respectful witness, not coercion, trusting Spirit to convince hearts. Digital age expands ethne to online affinity groups; cyber-mission sees gamers, influencers, refugees on social media as nations needing discipleship. Ecologically, nations include future generations; stewardship of creation ensures commission's longevity. Thus, "all nations" is clarion for borderless compassion, innovative strategy, and humble learning posture before cultures that will contribute fresh melodies to global doxology.

8.4. The Promise of Perpetual Presence

8.4.1 *"Always, to the End of the Age" – Chronology of Assurance*

Jesus seals mandate with eschatological bracket: "and surely, I am with you all the days, until the consummation of the age" (Matthew 28 : 20). The adverb idou ("behold" or "surely") commands attention, linking presence to previous authority statement—authority yields presence. "All the days" (pasas tas hēmeras) suggests daily companionship, not sporadic visitation; disciples embarking on perilous voyages can bank on continuous Emmanuel reality promised at Nativity (Matthew 1 : 23). "End of the age" frames mission within temporal horizon; the Great Commission is not interim task but remains until parousia when gospel proclamation gives way to worshipful consummation. Therefore, presence is both temporal (all days) and eschatological (until end), granting durability under persecution, plague, or cultural shifts. Theologically, this presence is mediated by Holy Spirit, as Acts and John 14 clarify; pneumatological indwelling ensures that Jesus' departure in ascension does not nullify promise. Pastorally, verse comforts missionaries isolated in remote outposts; mothers discipling children at kitchen tables; students witnessing in hostile campuses. Liturgically, church calendar embodies presence: each Sunday memorializes resurrection companionship; sacraments materialize pledge—bread and wine as tasted presence, baptism water as enveloping presence. In spiritual disciplines, practicing presence of God (Brother Lawrence) extrapolates from mountain promise to mundane pots and pans. Apologetically, promise challenges deism; Christian God is immanent within mission. Conversely, triumphalism is checked: presence is gracious gift, not disciples' achievement. Thus, chronological assurance fortifies perseverance.

8.4.2 Pneumatological Fulfillment in Acts and Church History

Acts opens with ascension, yet disciples soon experience Pentecost—visible tongues of fire and audible wind—assuring them that Jesus' unseen presence now operates through Spirit. Peter attributes crippled man's healing at temple gate to "faith in Jesus' name," evidence of ongoing power. Stephen, while stoned, sees Son of Man standing—vision confirms presence in martyrdom. Paul in Corinth hears night vision: "Do not be afraid…I am with you," echoing mountain words. Across centuries, missionary accounts recount similar assurance: Patrick's breastplate hymn, Francis Xavier's letters from Asia, Harriet Tubman's underground railroad guidance—each cites Christ's nearness. Institutionally, presence shapes ecclesiology; absence of physical head means Spirit equips body with gifts. Sacramentally, Eastern Orthodoxy speaks of "real presence" in Eucharist; Reformation traditions highlight Word-mediated presence—both trace to promise. Charismatic renewal emphasizes manifest presence through gifts; contemplative traditions emphasize interior indwelling presence—diversity of experience under one guarantee. The promise also motivates communal discernment: Christ among gathered two or three empowers church discipline (Matthew 18 : 20) and prayer. Eschatologically, assurance does not wane; Revelation frames consummation as dwelling of God with people (Rev 21 : 3)—presence escalated from pledge to permanent dwelling. Therefore, pneumatological fulfillment is dynamic, contextual, yet consistently faithful, validating mountain utterance through every epoch and geography.

8.5. The Great Commission in Canonical and Covenantal Context

8.5.1 From Abrahamic Blessing to Isaianic Servant

The Commission is not divine afterthought but culmination of missional thread spanning Genesis to Matthew. God's call to Abram promised global blessing through one family; Mosaic law positioned Israel as priestly nation; Wisdom literature anticipated Gentile kings streaming to Zion. Isaiah's Servant songs speak of light to nations; Jonah dramatizes reluctant prophet to foreign city; Daniel dreams of kingdom filling whole earth. In Second-Temple period, Jewish sects debated how Gentiles might share covenant—proselyte circumcision vs. eschatological pilgrimage. Jesus' mountain words resolve ambiguity: universal inclusion flows through allegiance to Messiah, sealed by baptism into Triune name. Scholars view Commission as new-covenant counterpart to Sinai: Moses received tablets; disciples receive mandate; both preceded by divine declaration of authority ("I am the Lord" vs. "All authority has been given"). Chronologically, Commission aligns with Jubilee themes—liberation proclaimed. The connection also reframes violent conquest narratives: where Joshua ascended similar hills to survey Canaan for warfare, Jesus commissions for spiritual conquest via disciple-making, not swords. Thus, canonical context reveals continuity and escalation: God always intended cosmic redemption; resurrection empowers actualization.

8.5.2 Harmony with Other Evangelists' Commission Scenes

Each Gospel preserves commission nuance: Mark's longer ending includes signs accompanying proclamation; Luke's version frames repentance and forgiveness preached to all nations beginning at Jerusalem; John encapsulates commission in locked room, breathing Spirit; acts 1 depicts Spirit empowerment for geographic concentric circles. Rather than contradiction, these facets form multifaceted gem: Matthew emphasizes authority and teaching; Mark highlights miraculous attestation; Luke underscores Scripture fulfillment and Spirit; John foregrounds relational sending "as Father sent Me." When harmonized, commissions produce holistic missiology—word and deed, cross and resurrection, Spirit and Scripture. Early church wove these threads: apostolic preaching joined miracles (Acts), catechesis (Didache), and ethical transformation (Epistle to Diognetus). Modern missional frameworks—Lausanne Covenant—echo multi-angle commission, resisting reductionist evangelism divorced from discipleship or justice. Therefore, Matthew's mountain is indispensable yet not exhaustive; the panorama broadens through fourfold Gospel lens, each vantage enriching mission symphony.

8.6. Contemporary Implications: Theology, Mission, and Ethics

8.6.1 Discipleship Pathways and Ecclesial Structures

In current ministry landscape, the Great Commission challenges churches to evaluate programs: Are converts being taught "all" Jesus commanded? Curriculum must integrate doctrinal orthodoxy, spiritual disciplines, emotional health, and missional practice. Small groups function as micro-classrooms; catechumenate revival addresses baptismal preparation. Leadership pipelines must mirror apprentice model—Paul to Timothy pattern—ensuring reproduction of disciple-makers. Ecclesial polity also engages: Episcopalian hierarchy, Presbyterian connection, Baptist congregationalism—all appeal to Commission for legitimizing governance; each must ensure authority of Christ, not tradition, directs structures. Digital discipleship rises: online courses, podcasts, and mentoring apps extend teaching to "all nations." Yet digital divides caution inclusion efforts; Commission pushes equitable access. Urban church-plants apply Commission by contextual exegesis of city demographics; rural parishes partner globally through prayer and short-term teams, proving locality no barrier. Marketplace discipleship recognizes workplace as primary mission field; companies become arenas for ethical modeling and gospel witness. Metrics shift from attendance to apprenticeship replication. Therefore, Commission shapes ecclesial DNA across technologies, geographies, and vocations.

8.6.2 Holistic Mission: Justice, Mercy, and Environmental Stewardship

"All that I commanded" includes love of neighbor, care for marginalized, and prophetic challenge to unjust systems, as Sermon on Mount and Matthew 25 clarify. Thus, Commission underwrites holistic mission—evangelism intertwined with justice advocacy. William Carey's Serampore mission established schools, combatted sati; his inspiration traced to Commission authority over Hindu caste injustices. Modern movements like International Justice Mission view rescue of trafficking victims as obedient disciple-making, freeing potential worshippers. Creation care emerges as ethic under Christ's universal lordship; if authority spans earth, environmental degradation defies Commission spirit. Youth climate activism within church sees stewardship as evangelistic credibility among "nations" suspicious of religious hypocrisy. Public health initiatives—hospitals started by missionaries—continue baptism-teaching symbiosis. Economic discipleship combats consumerism; fair-trade practices align commerce with kingdom. Peacemaking in conflict zones lives out ethic of enemy love, demonstrating gospel plausibility. Hence, Commission's ethical horizon stretches beyond pulpit to policy, beyond conversion to shalom, ensuring church embodies good news it proclaims.

Conclusion

Atop an unnamed Galilean summit the resurrected Jesus compressed eternity's agenda into four staccato declarations—comprehensive authority, global disciple-making, Trinitarian baptism, lifelong presence—etching them not on stone but on beating hearts that still ignite across continents and centuries. That moment, born from the convergence of Abrahamic promise, Mosaic covenant, prophetic longing, and incarnational triumph, continues to reverberate wherever believers lace shoes for cross-cultural ventures, fill baptismal fonts for new believers, craft sermons that teach hard obedience, or whisper prayers in oppressive prisons confident of Emmanuel's nearness. Its expansive "all" vocabulary refuses partial allegiances: every realm of knowledge, every people cluster, every command of Jesus, and every tick of the clock falls under this commission's purview. The mountain scene thereby dismantles dichotomies—sacred versus secular, evangelism versus compassion, local versus global—by unveiling a King whose reign brooks no territorial or thematic fragmenting. For modern disciples hemmed by digital distractions, political tribalism, or vocational fatigue, the Great Commission offers orientation: look up to enthroned Sovereign, look out to un-reached neighbor, look in to teaching archive of Christ, and look ahead to assured companionship until history bows. Churches that embrace this charter will cultivate communities fluent in many tongues, hospitable to skeptics, bold in justice, and resilient under pressure because they know authority backing. Conversely, neglect of any clause—authority, nations, teaching, presence—dilutes potency. Therefore, each generation must ascend afresh through Scripture and Spirit to that Galilean ridge, hear again the accent of universal Lordship, and descend with sandals dusty but hearts ablaze, ready to disciple neighborhoods, networks, and nations until the eastern sky glows with the return of the One who first said, "Behold, I am with you all the days."

Chapter 9. Appearance to "More Than Five Hundred" Believers at Once

Evening shadows lengthened across Jerusalem on the first day of the week while a shaken circle of Galilean disciples huddled behind barred doors, their breath shallow, their imaginations crowded with fear, their future suddenly opaque. The women had brought astounding news at dawn—an empty tomb and angelic testimonies of resurrection (Luke 24 : 1-9), Mary Magdalene had insisted she had spoken with the Lord Himself (John 20 : 11-18), the pair returning from Emmaus claimed that the Stranger who opened Scripture on the road was unmistakably Jesus once He broke bread (Luke 24 : 30-35), and Peter had divulged a private meeting in which grace eclipsed denial (Luke 24 : 34). Yet awe mingled with skepticism, and dread of arrest by temple authorities remained visceral; after all, Rome's presence still loomed in every torchlit alley, and the Sanhedrin, embarrassed by rumors of a missing corpse, might be combing the city for scapegoats. The ten present—the band minus Judas, lost to despair, and

Thomas, absent for reasons unknown—found their common mind trapped between contradictory emotions: a drive to believe and a pulsating instinct for self-preservation. Doors were bolted, windows cinched, lamplight kept low. Into that sealed space Jesus suddenly stood, eclipsing the architecture of caution and rewriting the disciples' interior geography with a single word of peace.

9.1. Historical and Cultural Coordinates of the Locked-Room Gathering

9.1.1 Physical Setting and Security Concerns

Within the dense urban fabric of first-century Jerusalem, affluent homes near the western hill or the upper city boasted multi-room plans that included an elevated guest chamber accessible by external stairs; the Passover meal just three nights earlier had almost certainly unfolded in such an upper-room space (Mark 14 : 12-16). That location, obtained through pre-arranged hospitality, would have represented the safest immediate refuge for disciples still reeling from their Rabbi's public execution. The residences' wooden doors swung inward and could be secured by a heavy beam dropped into iron brackets, while small slit-windows admitted only minimal airflow, making the interior both tenable for secrecy and stifling for nerves. Roman practice permitted armed patrols after dark during festival weeks to quell sedition, and Jewish temple police, embarrassed by the missing body, would be under pressure from chief priests to trace disciples before rumors metastasized into riot (Matt 28 : 12-14). Fear of capture was rational; association with a crucified claimant to kingship was de facto complicity in treason against Caesar, punishable by the same humiliating death. Halakhic tradition allowed the carrying of keys on a Sabbath that bordered festival days if sewn into garments as accessories, so one disciple likely bore responsibility for bolting the door from within, a detail implied by John's explicit note that the doors were "shut for fear of the Judeans" (John 20 : 19). Lower levels of Jerusalem homes often housed animals or storerooms, so muffled sounds from the street would reach the disciples irregularly, heightening their skittishness whenever a clatter echoed through the stone stairwell. Oil lamps burned olive oil in clay dishes, producing smoke that darkened ceiling beams; the dim light accentuated an atmosphere of hushed vigilance, ready for abrupt extinguishing should a knock jar the night. The disciples undoubtedly kept voices low, mindful that sound traveled through thin plaster walls; neighbors sympathetic to the authorities might eavesdrop and betray them for favor. Thus the geography of the room mirrored the state of their souls—closed, guarded, constricted—awaiting some catalyst capable of releasing compressed anxieties. Cultural codes around hospitality mandated that any after-hours visitor identify himself before entry, yet Jesus' miracle bypassed the threshold mechanics entirely, appearing in their midst without jarring hinges or footsteps on stairs. Such instantaneous presence not only demonstrated the transformed capacities of His resurrection body but also dramatized divine sovereignty over human strategies of containment. Ironically, the very precautions meant to seal the disciples off from danger inexorably prepared the perfect stage for Jesus to authenticate His triumph over barriers both physical and psychological. That same paradox persists whenever modern believers bolt emotional doors against perceived threats only to discover Christ already occupying the locked interior, illuminating dread with resurrected calm. Pilgrimage to today's Cenacle on Mount Zion attempts to honor this memory, yet the real holy ground remains any context where fear-fortified walls collapse under a breath of peace.

9.1.2 Sabbath to First Day—Chronological and Liturgical Markers

The appearance occurred "on the evening of that first day of the week" (John 20 : 19), placing it at the tail end of Nisan 17 by Jewish sunset-to-sunset reckoning, roughly between 7:00 PM and 9:00 PM in early spring. The earlier Sabbath had been singularly heavy: disciples had refrained from travel per Torah and mourned in silence while Roman soldiers guarded a sealed tomb (Luke 23 : 56). Transition from Sabbath rest to first-day activity marked a seismic shift in salvation history, inaugurating new-creation symbolism that early Christians would encode by gathering "on the first day" for breaking bread (Acts 20 : 7). Passover week also included the Feast of Firstfruits on that very Sunday, when priests waved the sheaf of barley before Yahweh (Lev 23 : 10-14), a ritual Paul would later interpret as typological prophecy that Christ is "firstfruits of those who sleep" (1 Cor 15 : 20). Thus, while the disciples cowered, temple liturgy unwittingly dramatized resurrection reality, a convergence Jesus would soon explicate in breath and mission. The chronology further underscores narrative tempo: within approximately twelve hours of the empty tomb discovery, the risen Christ chalks up appearances to Mary, to other women, to Peter, to two disciples on the road, and now to the ten—compressed scheduling that preempts theories of extended hallucination cycles or legend-accretion. Liturgically, the arrival of darkness after festival day normally involved recitation of Psalm 113–118 (the Hallel), songs of praise echoing deliverance from Egypt; poignantly, some of those laments about rejected stones becoming cornerstones (Psalm 118 : 22) were fulfilled before the lyrics left pilgrim lips. Concurrently, households would recline for the traditional festival supper in candlelit rooms, filling the neighborhood with piety-tinged conviviality, while one upstairs chamber throbbed with confused whispers instead of songs. John's timestamp thus situates Jesus' visitation within the ordinary cadence of Jewish festal evenings, accentuating the ordinariness of the hour against the extraordinariness of the event. Early Christian adoption of Sunday worship was not arbitrary but rooted in this anchored memory: the first collective experience of the risen Lord with His apostolic core took place at the very onset of a new week, permanently stamping that chronological slot with eschatological significance. Modern believers who struggle to perceive value in weekly rhythm may recollect that God inaugurated new creation at sundown on the Lord's Day, sanctifying the remaining hours of history by meeting a petrified circle in real time. The intersection of festival calendar and resurrection timeline invites theological reflection: divine revelation does not abolish sacred rhythms but recalibrates them, converting Sabbaths into resurrection rehearsals, and consecrating first-day evenings as perpetual blasts of hope into darkness.

9.2. Interior States: Fearful Hearts and Flickering Faith

9.2.1 Fear, Grief, and Cognitive Dissonance

Fear dominated the atmosphere, its texture thickened by memories of bloodied crossbeams and shrieking crowds only three days earlier (John 19 : 15-20). Psychologically, the disciples displayed classic post-traumatic symptoms: hypervigilance toward noises, intrusive flashbacks of arrest scenes, and avoidance of public exposure. Socio-political fear interlaced with personal remorse; several, particularly Peter, carried recent failures like chains rattling every time conscience stirred. Jewish civic codes allowed authorities to arrest associates of executed criminals, freeze assets, or expel families from synagogues (John 9 : 22), institutional levers that squeezed communal belonging. Cognitive dissonance churned: they had invested three years in a teacher whose kingdom proclamations seemed irreversibly nullified by crucifixion, yet contradictory sensory data—vacant graveclothes, angelic reports—refused to align neatly with despair. Luke's wording captures mental turbulence: "startled and frightened, thinking they saw a spirit" (Luke 24 : 37). Fear is not merely emotion but interpretive lens, causing innocuous stimuli to appear threatening; a creaking beam might echo hammered nails in the auditory memory. Within this swirl, group dynamics can magnify anxious contagion; each disciple scanning the others' faces for reassurance found only mirrored panic, a feedback loop intensifying stress. Simultaneously, glimpses of hope strived to intrude: John, who outran Peter to the tomb and "believed" though not yet understanding Scripture (John 20 : 8-9), likely radiated smoldering expectancy. Yet human groups often default to emotional average, and the more pessimistic voices may have suppressed John's quiet conviction. Absence of Thomas removed one potential lynchpin of solidarity, and Judas' suicide cast spectral gloom, a reminder of catastrophic despair. All these internal currents conspired to create a crucible of tension awaiting a catalytic visitation to re-order affections. Contemporary disciples reading this episode can recall seasons when theological knowledge collides with visceral dread, revealing that earliest believers were not paragons of stoic faith but embodied humans undergoing neurochemical storms. The significance of Jesus' forthcoming greeting, therefore, lies not only in its doctrinal content but in its capacity to fluoroscopically re-wire hearts hijacked by fear. The narrative demonstrates that resurrection faith seldom germinates in calm laboratories; it sprouts in locked rooms where panic breath fogs windows and hope is an unlit wick.

9.2.2 Signals of Hope and the Unsteady Embryo of Belief

Even within fear-saturated walls, rumors of life crackled like distant thunder. Mary's proclamation, "I have seen the Lord" (John 20 : 18), reverberated among them; the Emmaus walkers insisted that Scripture's mosaic now fit only if Messiah suffered and entered glory (Luke 24 : 26-27); Peter's tear-streaked eyes shone with something resembling awe after his private encounter (Luke 24 : 34). Yet secondhand testimonies seldom uproot entrenched skepticism; some present perhaps echoed Nathanael's earlier cynicism: "Can anything good come out of Nazareth?" (John 1 : 46). The mind wants coherence, and early hints of resurrection clashed with empirical realism drilled by Roman crucifixion's finality. The concept of resurrection existed in Pharisaic eschatology (Acts 23 : 6-8) but as distant horizon, not immediate Sunday surprise. Hope, therefore, remained embryonic, fragile, requiring direct experiential confirmation. Grief psychologists describe "anticipatory hope" that surfaces in trauma aftermath when survivors cling to improbable rescue scenarios; this hope is easily dismissed as denial, and disciples likely feared embarrassing gullibility. Yet hope persisted because memory of Jesus' own predictions—"after three days I will rise" (Mark 9 : 31)—nagged at their intellectual honesty. The folded graveclothes provided forensic clue contradicting grave robbery narrative (John 20 : 7), and angelic messages referencing Galilee rendezvous (Matt 28 : 7) hinted at purposeful orchestration. Thus, the room hosted an ambivalent congregation: faith seeds sprouted in some hearts, remained dormant in others, and faced suffocating pressure from communal fear. This complexity sets context for Jesus' approach; His methodology would not merely present new facts but address the psychosocial organism of the group, knitting individual confidence into collective conviction. The dynamic resembles early church gatherings today where testimonies of deliverance stir pockets of trust yet await corporate encounter with the risen Lord through Word and sacrament. The narrative thus normalizes hesitating belief, teaching that mature faith often emerges from a skein of conflicting perceptions gradually harmonized by divine self-disclosure. The presence of hope, however weak, remained crucial; without some ember of expectancy, the disciples might have dispersed permanently. Jesus would soon fan that ember into unquenchable flame, but first He would step across the threshold that no door could hold.

9.3. Actions and Words of the Risen Christ

9.3.1 Pronouncement of Peace and Display of Wounds

Without sound of latch or sweep of curtain, Jesus "came and stood among them" (John 20 : 19). His first utterance, "Peace be with you," echoed customary Jewish greeting *Shalom aleichem* yet carried eschatological depth, for He had promised during the Farewell Discourse, "My peace I leave with you" (John 14 : 27). Shalom in Hebrew thought denotes wholeness, relational harmony, covenant fulfillment; uttering it into a vortex of anxiety signaled immediate reversal of emotional entropy. The statement also enacted priestly benediction from Numbers 6 : 26, positioning Jesus as mediator bestowing Yahweh's face of favor after atonement accomplished. Yet words alone could be misconstrued as ghostly phenomenon, so He showed them His hands and side (John 20 : 20), tangible evidence linking crucifixion trauma with resurrection identity. Luke adds that He invited touch and requested broiled fish to eat, proving corporeal reality, not docetic apparition (Luke 24 : 39-43). The display of wounds held theological symbolism: scars transformed into badges of victory, confirming prophecies of the pierced servant (Isa 53 : 5; Zech 12 : 10). The disciples, seeing and hearing, transitioned "from fear to joy" (John 20 : 20), fulfilling Jesus' prophecy that their sorrow would turn into rejoicing like labor pains birthing new life (John 16 : 20-22). The Greek perfect of "showed" (ἔδειξεν) implies sustained presentation, perhaps allowing each disciple to inspect cruciform evidence, rewriting memory of blood-soaked beams with dignity of healed flesh. His capacity to penetrate locked chambers without breaking physical continuity of body hinted at ontological novelty: a glorified embodiment capable of transcending ordinary spatial limitations yet maintaining continuity sufficient for recognition. Early Christian creeds would parse this mystery, affirming *resurrectio carnis*—the resurrection of the flesh—while acknowledging transformed properties. Liturgically, the sign of peace in Eucharistic assemblies traces to this episode: believers exchange greeting to manifest participation in the peace Christ spoke in the locked room. Pastoral care likewise follows His model: speak peace, then offer embodied reassurance, meeting psychological need for tangible signs. Modern trauma therapy employs similar sequencing—verbal assurance paired with grounding stimuli—to calm dysregulated nervous systems, illustrating timeless wisdom in Jesus' approach. The pronouncement of peace thus initiated multi-layered healing: spiritual reconciliation, communal cohesion, somatic regulation, and doctrinal foundation for later Trinitarian pronouncements.

9.3.2 Breathing the Spirit and Commissioning for Mission

After joy replaced terror, Jesus repeated the salutation of peace, linking it to a missional mandate: "As the Father has sent Me, I also send you" (John 20 : 21). The sentence functions as hinge between incarnation and ecclesial continuation; the disciples are drafted into the Son's own apostolic trajectory, not a novel endeavor. To equip them, He "breathed on them and said, 'Receive the Holy Spirit'" (John 20 : 22). The verb ἐνεφύσησεν deliberately echoes Genesis 2 : 7 where God breathes life into Adam, signaling new creation. Ezekiel 37's vision of Spirit breath animating dry bones also resonates, indicating resurrection community birthed from breath-infused corpses of despair. Scholars debate relation between this Johannine pneumatophany and the Pentecost outpouring in Acts 2; consensus generally views them as complementary, with locked-room breath as prototypical impartation inaugurating regeneration and Pentecost as empowerment for public witness. The Johannine scene emphasizes intimacy: Jesus' breath, warm and proximate, becomes sacramental conduit of divine life, a moment foreshadowing later sacramental practices where physical elements mediate spiritual grace. Immediately He ties Spirit reception to authority: "If you forgive anyone's sins, they are forgiven; if you retain them, they are retained" (John 20 : 23). The statement entrusts church with declarative power to announce or withhold forgiveness in alignment with Gospel proclamation, a juridical function echoing Isaiah 22 : 22's key-bearing steward. Luke's parallel highlights additional commission: "repentance for the forgiveness of sins will be preached in His name to all nations, beginning at Jerusalem" (Luke 24 : 47), situating authority within evangelistic task. The breath, therefore, is not private solace but missional empowerment. Theologically, the passage lays groundwork for Trinitarian mission theology: the Father sends the Son; the Son sends Spirit-indwelt church. Sacramentally, breath evokes Spirit's role in baptismal new birth (John 3 : 5-8) and Eucharistic epiclesis. Ecclesially, it underpins practices of reconciliation, whether in liturgical absolution or restorative church discipline, underscoring that forgiveness remains Christ's prerogative delegated to community. Pastoral counseling draws on this scene for trauma survivors: safe relational presence, breath regulation, and commission into purposeful action integrate healing. The disciples' own bodies now carry breath-encoded mission; their previous lungs exhaled denial and cowardice, now they will exhale Gospel and courage. Contemporary believers receiving Spirit through faith participate in same continuum, reminding church that every locked room visited by Christ becomes a sending station, never a static sanctuary.

9.4. Doctrinal and Practical Reverberations

9.4.1 Authority to Forgive Sins and Apostolic Foundations

The grant of penitential authority in John 20 : 23 stands as one of Scripture's most debated ecclesiological statements, intersecting doctrines of priesthood, sacramental confession, and communal boundaries. The perfect passive verbs— ἀφέωνται ("are forgiven") and κεκράτηνται ("are retained")— imply heavenly ratification of earthly declarations, an echo of "binding and loosing" language earlier entrusted to Peter (Matt 16 : 19) and the wider disciple group (Matt 18 : 18). Patristic writers such as Tertullian viewed the verse as charter for baptismal absolution and post-baptismal reconciliation rites; Augustine linked it to pastoral oversight ensuring ecclesial purity; Aquinas elaborated theological mechanics of sacramental penance. Reformers, wary of abuse, re-situated authority in proclamation of the Word, yet maintained corporate discipline based on this text. Whichever tradition one inhabits, the locked-room commission affirms that forgiveness is not an abstract vertical transaction but mediated through Spirit-inhabited community. The disciples, formerly paralyzed by guilt, become agents of liberation for others, a poetic inversion of their own deliverance. The clause on retaining sins cautions that church also holds responsibility to confront unrepentant wrongdoing, safeguarding holiness. Contemporary application spans public pastoral pronouncement of absolution in liturgies, one-on-one confession practices, and restorative justice processes addressing systemic sin. The text challenges hyper-individualism: salvation experienced privately must be affirmed corporately. Psychologically, hearing forgiveness voiced by another human bridges cognitive acceptance and emotional internalization, proven in studies on confession therapy. The apostolic foundation laid here also legitimizes global mission structures: emissaries carry not only message but authority to enact Gospel implications within new cultures, baptizing and teaching with confidence rooted in this first commission. Ecumenical dialogues have found common ground in seeing John 20 and Matt 18 as mandating mutual recognition of baptized believers across denominations, since forgiveness authority extends beyond parochial borders. Thus, the locked-room empowerment forms cornerstone of church's reconciliatory identity, inviting every generation to steward the keys with humility and courage derived from their crucified-risen Giver.

9.4.2 Prototype of Christian Worship and Missional Community

The evening assembly embodies critical liturgical elements that later solidify into Christian worship patterns. Gathering on the first day anchors weekly rhythm; invocation of peace parallels greeting rites; exposition of Scripture unfolds when Jesus opens minds "to understand the Scriptures" (Luke 24 : 45); table fellowship, implied by fish sharing in Luke, prefigures Eucharistic meal; Spirit bestowal anticipates epiclesis; and benedictory commission mirrors dismissal formulas. Thus, embryonic liturgy arises organically from resurrection presence, not later institutional invention. Moreover, the locked room is both sanctuary and launchpad, correcting dichotomy between worship and mission. The community experiences inclusion, instruction, sacrament, and empowerment in a single event. House-church movements today, often meeting behind literal closed doors in hostile contexts, replicate this prototype: clandestine yet Christ-centered, Spirit-filled yet outward-focused. The narrative also models intergenerational catechesis: Jesus recalls earlier prophecies ("Moses, Prophets, and Psalms," Luke 24 : 44), embedding hermeneutical framework for future preaching cycles. Joy, fruit of encounter, becomes communal hallmark (John 20 : 20), seeding doxological hymnody that will spill into Acts' temple praises (Acts 2 : 46-47). Practical dimensions emerge: locked-room fellowship counters rugged individual spirituality, reminding believers that fear dissipates in presence of embodied community and risen Christ. Digital-age Christians isolating behind glowing screens can revisit this scene to see that physical proximity and shared breath still matter for fullest experience of shalom and mission. The gathering also challenges churches addicted to program expansion: core DNA is simple—peace, wounds, breath, commission. Everything else is scaffolding. Spiritual formation curricula can use this passage to train believers in fourfold rhythm: encounter, formation, empowerment, sending. Thus, the locked-room event functions as theological blueprint and pastoral compass, orienting every congregation toward Christ-centered worship that inevitably births outward witness.

Conclusion

On a spring night in a city tense with rumors and fortified with Roman steel, ten cowering disciples discovered that their most impregnable barricade was no match for a resurrected body shimmering with scars of love. The room designed for hiding became a sanctuary of peace, a classroom of Scripture, a seminary of pneumatology, and a commissioning hall for global mission, all because Jesus refused to let fear have the final word. Every aspect of the encounter—the bolted doors, the greeting of shalom, the tangible wounds, the Spirit-laden breath, the entrustment of forgiveness—converged to transfigure panic into purpose and disarray into apostolic unity. Subsequent Christian centuries would imitate this pattern whenever persecuted believers whispered hymns in catacombs, when reformers risked sword and stake to proclaim justification, and when underground house-churches today gather under curfews to break bread and clutch Bibles. The locked room still exists wherever disciples nurse anxieties about political hostility, personal shame, or cultural marginalization; the risen Christ still appears, bypassing security systems of cynicism, to breathe resilient peace and assign kingdom errands. Thus the evening visitation stands not merely as historical waypoint but as perpetual promise: no fortress of fear can contain the One who conquered the grave, and no servant once crippled by dread will fail to find empowerment when He arrives, breathes, and sends. In remembering that first post-resurrection assembly of ten, the church rediscovers the architecture of its own vocation—walls melted by peace, hearts ignited by wounds transfigured, lungs filled with Spirit for a forgiveness-bearing mission that can never again be locked in.

Chapter 10. Appearance to James (the Lord's Brother)

In the tapestry of post-resurrection appearances, few threads are as weighty—and as often overlooked—as the brief yet pivotal notice that Jesus "appeared to more than five hundred of the brothers at one time, most of whom are still living, though some have fallen asleep" (1 Corinthians 15 : 6). This sweeping glimpse into a mass manifestation stands in narrative tension with the more intimate, dramatic one-on-one revelations recorded elsewhere, demanding fresh attention to its scale, context, and implications. Whereas Mary Magdalene's garden encounter, the Emmaus road dialogue, and the locked-room epiphanies teach us about personal recognition, communal restoration, and leadership commissioning respectively, the appearance to a crowd of believers provides the most expansive canvas of resurrection witness. It underscores the event's public nature, counters charges of isolated hallucination, and inaugurates the church's corporate testimony. Moreover, it situates resurrection not merely as private consolation but as cosmic demonstration—an event that gathered together into a single moment a vast network of disciples in Galilee, Judea, and beyond.

10.1. Scriptural Attestation and Early Witness Tradition

10.1.1 Paul's Credal Statement in 1 Corinthians 15 : 6

Paul's first letter to the Corinthians represents one of the earliest surviving Christian documents, penned within two to three decades of Jesus' crucifixion and resurrection. In chapter 15, Paul provides what scholars widely regard as a pre-existing creed or kerygmatic formula, summarizing core apostolic convictions. Verses 3 – 5 outline the basic sequence: Christ died for our sins, was buried, and was raised on the third day, appearing first to Cephas (Peter), then the Twelve. The subsequent verse, often overlooked in preaching, reads: "Then He appeared to more than five hundred brothers at one time, most of whom are still alive, though some have fallen asleep" (1 Cor 15 : 6). This offhand yet precise reference to a large group occurrence serves multiple functions in Paul's argument. First, it invokes the historical criterion of multiple attestation: unlike private visions or subjective experiences, over five hundred witnesses places resurrection appearance within collective memory. Second, by noting that "most of whom are still alive," Paul challenges his readers to verify the claim directly—an implicit invitation to cross-examination akin to legal practice in Hellenistic courts. Third, situating the mass appearance after individual encounters emphasizes crescendo of revelation from intimate to universal dimension. Fourth, the brief wording without detail harmonizes with Paul's pastoral aim: he needs to demonstrate the reality of resurrection appearances quickly, without digression into narrative elaboration. Finally, his use of archaic verb tenses and shared language suggests that he is quoting a liturgical or catechetical statement rather than crafting original prose. The result is a towering pillar in early Christian apologetics: if Christ's resurrection was matter of fleeting illusion to a few, it would scarcely warrant mention of hundreds of witnesses ready to testify. Instead, Paul presents resurrection as public spectacle, uttering an element so robust that centuries later, skeptics still find it difficult to dismiss wholesale hallucination theory in light of such a claim. Thus, Paul's inclusion of the "more than five hundred" appearance anchors the resurrection in communal bones, not solitary visions, underpinning doctrine with collective verifiability.

10.1.2 Implications of Mass Witness for Historicity

The fact that Jesus appeared to a large gathering carries profound implications for the historical credibility of the resurrection narrative. Firstly, mass sightings resist reduction to subjective visionary experience; group hallucinations are extraordinarily rare and, when they do occur—usually in the context of deep grief—tend to be limited to close associates in intense emotional crisis, not sprawling networks of former followers scattered across regions. Secondly, unlike personal visions that can be dismissed as private psychological phenomena, a collective appearance presents logistical challenges: hundreds of individuals would need to converge in specified time and place, a feat unlikely to be invented by early Christian forgers. Thirdly, the widespread publicity of such an event would draw attention from Jewish authorities and Roman officials; absence of any competing narrative claiming the body had been stolen en masse or denouncing a communal deception underscores the event's plausibility. Fourthly, ancient polemical sources that criticize Christian claims rarely engage specifics of the "five hundred" story, suggesting critics found no convincing counter-claim, perhaps because public gatherings of that scale would have left substantial documentary or oral records. Fifthly, early Christian apologists such as Justin Martyr and Tertullian reference mass witness to defend against charges of mass delusion, indicating that within decades of Paul's writing the memory of "five hundred" circulated as foundational apologetic datum. Sixthly, criterion of embarrassment—if one accepts that boasting of large numbers strengthens credibility—supports historicity: it would be counterproductive for early believers to invent a narrative so easily refutable by opponents. Seventhly, the geographic distribution implied by "brothers" suggests inclusion of believers from both Jewish and Gentile contexts, reinforcing universal scope. Eighthly, the mention serves ecclesiological function: if multiple witnesses attest resurrection, local congregations feel connected to broader early church, grounding unity in shared encounter. Ninthly, the mass appearance underwrites apostolic authority: leaders appointed by Christ himself in visible gathering carry unimpeachable credential for teaching and governance. Tenthly, historiographical parallels—such as Roman accounts of mass sightings of emperors' ghosts—pale compared to the rigor here, where invitation to verify by living witnesses raises the bar for historical acceptance. Collectively, these dimensions demonstrate that mass witness functions both as arrow of apologetic fortitude and as mosaic tile cementing the early church's claims in the bedrock of collective history.

10.2. Historical Context and Sociological Dynamics

10.2.1 Assemblies of Early Believers

To appreciate the "five hundred" gathering, one must reconstruct how early Christian assemblies formed in the volatile landscape of first-century Judea and Syria. The Jewish festival seasons—Passover chief among them—drew pilgrims from across the empire to Jerusalem, swelling the city's population tenfold. Some pilgrims returned home immediately, but others lingered, lodging with families or in proselyte houses where discipleship movements thrived. In the wake of resurrection appearances in Jerusalem, a network of believers coalesced, bound by common memory of crucifixion, empty tomb, and subsequent epiphanies. Philip the evangelist's expansion into Samaria (Acts 8) and Peter's mission to the Gentile centurion Cornelius (Acts 10) hint at broadening relational circles extending from Judean core into coastal cities. By the time of Paul's writing—around AD 55—Christian communities in Antioch of Syria, Ephesus, Corinth, and Rome numbered in the hundreds, implying that at least some of the "five hundred" may have resided outside Jerusalem. Oral communication channels—synagogues, marketplaces, aristocratic patronage networks—carried news swiftly. Regular household meetings, often in one disciple's home (e.g., Priscilla and Aquila's house in Rome), provided venues for teaching and worship, but major gatherings would assemble when apostles or itinerant teachers announced presence. In this milieu, a large meeting of over five hundred disciples may have concerted in a public setting—perhaps an upper court of a wealthy patron's villa, an open field on a Sabbath lunch break, or a private grove—yet inviting sufficient numbers required robust organization and deep relational trust. Sociologically, the fabric of kinship ties and patron-client relationships facilitated such mobilization, as gentile sympathizers and Jewish families housed pilgrims. Furthermore, the commission to assemble in Galilee may have served both strategic and reconciliatory purposes: strategic, to regroup apostles for mission planning away from hostile Jerusalem; reconciliatory, to bind scattered believers into visible unity under risen leader. Thus, the mass appearance did not happen in isolation but emerged from seams of fellowship, hospitality, and shared purpose that early Christians had woven in the years following Easter. Modern churches planning large-scale gatherings—conferences, revivals—can learn from this context: authentic relational networks and missional clarity underpin impactful assembly, not mere marketing or event production.

10.2.2 Sociopolitical Implications of Mass Gathering

In the tightly controlled society of Roman Palestine, any assembly of hundreds risked suspicion as potential insurrectionist meeting. Authorities were vigilant: Passover commemorated national liberation, and memories of rebellion spurred centurions to patrol city gates and countryside. Gathering large numbers could trigger Roman alarm, yet the "five hundred" audience transpired without recorded crackdown, suggesting either discreet negotiation with local officials or rapid dispersal upon conclusion. Jewish council leaders in Sanhedrin would have eyed such meetings warily, recalling Jesus' own warning that the kingdom of God would spread like yeast (Luke 13 : 20-21). The sheer size of gathering undercut any notion that early Christians were a secret society; rather, they were a visible movement claiming Jesus' lordship over imperial rule. This public demonstration underpinned Christian claim that resurrection inaugurates new world order transcending political regimes. Insurrectionist readings of resurrection—some early Jewish sects expected militant Messiah—fizzled in light of communal proclamation urging peace and baptism rather than sword. Sociopolitically, the disciples' mass appearance signaled a radical reorientation: authority is vested not in Rome or Jerusalem but in risen Christ. Modern observers see parallels in movements that begin quietly within homes and burgeon into societies challenging entrenched powers—civil rights marches, anti-corruption campaigns—where shared testimony ignites collective action. The "five hundred" event thus presaged church's calling to be both holy alternative society and prophetic voice, challenging injustices while embodying new-creation ethics. The absence of violent suppression also hints at early protective dynamics—perhaps Angelic interventions or tacit toleration by local authorities accustomed to accommodating pilgrims—reinforcing sense that resurrection event overran usual political logics. For sociologists of religion, the episode furnishes case study in how charismatic movement can achieve rapid diffusion and mass mobilization while navigating authoritarian constraints.

10.3. Psychological Phenomena in Group Revelation

10.3.1 Collective Perception and Memory

When a large group witnesses the same extraordinary event, psychologists warn of conformity bias, shared delusion, and memory blending. Yet studies of collective trauma and joyful gatherings demonstrate that communal emotions enhance, rather than undermine, accurate recall under certain conditions—particularly when observers cross-verify details soon thereafter. In the case of the five-hundred gathering, we can reasonably infer that witnesses compared notes immediately, solidifying core elements in communal memory while purging outliers. Social identity theory illuminates how strong in-group bonds amplify collective acceptance of extraordinary claims, but equally how the presence of numerous in-group members ensures that outlying skeptic voices find public airing and correction. The rapid circulation of resurrection testimony among early churches suggests robust group reinforcement of key facts—empty tomb, bodily appearances, specific interactions. Moreover, cognitive psychology notes that extraordinary events create "flashbulb memories"—vivid, enduring recollections encoded with emotional intensity. Touching glimpses of risen Christ, shared in jubilant assembly, would render such memory balms against later skepticism. Additionally, the practice of reciting the creed in worship services—Paul's own formula included—provided mnemonic scaffolding protecting against decay. Neurological studies reveal that emotional arousal, paired with repeated communal retelling, strengthens neural pathways consolidating memory. Hence, the five-hundred mass appearance likely generated composite narrative that, while varying in minor details, remained stable on essential points. Group perception dynamics thus favored testimonial reliability rather than uniform mindless conformity.

10.3.2 Dynamics of Group Conversion and Communion

Engagement in significant group revelations often sparks catalytic conversion phenomena: individuals move beyond private belief into public allegiance, ready to endure social costs. In the five-hundred case, we can surmise that some attendees were initially tentative—perhaps visitors to Jerusalem from distant regions—yet the communal experience propelled them into committed discipleship. Social influence theory describes how persons surrounded by fervent believers feel normative pressure to align own beliefs, but the unique aspect here is that the object of belief—resurrected Jesus—demonstrably intersects with everyday reality, nullifying mere conformity concerns. The mass gathering thus functioned as both sign and seal: group confessed Christ as alive and commercially viable faith multiplied. Communal eating traditions that followed (breaking of bread on first day of week) likely wove the appearance into sacramental practice, solidifying unity. Group conversion often entails shift in identity and expectations; in this case, attendees instantly reframed their life stories around the resurrection horizon. Social psychologists note that communal stressors—fear, loss, uncertainty—enhance cohesion when a shared hope emerges, paralleling early disciples' terrors after Good Friday. The mass appearance thus doused communal anxieties and sparked collective joy, creating a high-trust group identity instrumental for mission beyond Jerusalem. This dynamic undergirds later Pentecostal effusions where mass audiences, upon hearing Peter's sermon, "were cut to the heart" and baptized (Acts 2 : 37-41). Therefore, psychological mechanisms of group conversion and communion, when harnessed by Spirit-empowered proclamation, yield robust church planting dynamics.

10.4. Theological Significance of Large-Scale Manifestation

10.4.1 Demonstration of Universal Restoration

That Jesus chose to reveal Himself to a vast throng affirms that salvation is not elitarian but expansive. Individual appearances underscore personal reconciliation; the mass appearance underscores corporate restoration. In scriptural typology, communal manifestations of divine glory—Sinai's thunder, Shekinah at temple dedication—signal covenantal identity for entire people. Likewise, Jesus' resurrection appearance to broad assembly inaugurates new covenant community inclusive of Jews and Gentiles, male and female, slave and free. The number "five hundred" itself, far exceeding symbolic multiples in biblical numerology, hints at overflow uncontainable by temple precincts. This demonstration shatters divisions—between inner-circle apostles and outer-circle disciples—and testifies to eschatological vision where every tribe sees salvation. Theologically, it envisions church not as private spiritual enclave but as public, tangible organism brimming with resurrected life. For ecclesiology, this shapes understanding of baptismal unity: the same body experienced risen presence together, making interdependence theological necessity. The vast audience also prefigures future eschatological gathering described in Revelation 7 : 9—a countless multitude from every nation standing before throne. Thus, mass appearance becomes both archetype and down-payment, assuring that final harvest will eclipse even five hundred.

10.4.2 Foreshadowing of Pentecost and Future Missions

The Great Commission and the later Pentecost event share narrative logic: both involve gathering of disciples, an outpouring of divine presence, and emboldened witness. The mass appearance to five hundred forecast Spirit's later descent among 120 gathered in upper room (Acts 2 : 1-4), echoing communal experience. Just as resurrection presence manifested bodily before assembly, so Spirit's presence manifested audibly and visibly before crowd of Jews from many nations. Early church connected these dots, interpreting Pentecost as both empowering fulfillment of Commission and cosmic inauguration of global mission. The "five hundred" narrative thus enfolds into broader missional arc: demonstration of risen Christ leads to infilling of Spirit leads to global sending empowered by tongues. Moreover, the sheer scale of initial appearance models how power unleashed in relatively small group can cascade outward to transform entire Mediterranean world. Contemporary mission movements draw on this template: local church prayer gatherings anticipate Spirit-wind for cross-cultural outreach, building momentum from dozens to thousands. The "five hundred" appearance hence functions theologically as antecedent to universal mission: Christ's victory over death was personal, but its display to a crowd situates mission in corporate context, preparing church for Pentecostal outpouring that will send them worldwide.

10.5. Pastoral and Ecclesial Applications

10.5.1 Nurturing Communal Faith Foundations

Church leaders today encounter individuals whose faith formation emphasizes private devotion over communal experience, sometimes leaving them vulnerable to isolation and doubt. The "five hundred" narrative underscores the importance of collective faith milestones—corporate Bible reading, group testimonies, shared celebrations of resurrection. Pastoral strategies should include communal retreats, small-group Bible studies focused on resurrection appearances, and testimonies where multiple voices recount personal encounters, mirroring ancient pattern. Intergenerational events can facilitate passing memory of Christ's presence from elders to youth, addressing modern rupture where historical memory is easily lost. Liturgical calendar anchoring—Easter vigil, Pentecost services—provides cyclic communal reaffirmation of resurrection realities. Equally, baptismal classes emphasizing communal welcome integrate new believers into responsive context, rather than isolating them in individualistic journey. Pastoral theology must reclaim public, collective dimensions of faith: adversity trials, shared lament, and corporate discernment. In hospitable churches, one finds "five hundred" solidarity in living rooms, sanctuary back pews, and digital gatherings. This communal embedding fortifies disciples to weather storms, as collective memory counters individual forgetfulness. Therefore, church leaders craft environments where collective witnessing loops into personal conviction, advancing communal faith foundations that echo apostolic assembly.

10.5.2 Challenges of Sustaining Mass Conversion

While large-scale revivals or charismatic movements can ignite zeal, sustaining conversion clusters beyond initial excitement remains daunting. The "five hundred" story does not end with appearance; subsequent chapters in Acts reveal tensions—Ananias and Sapphira scandal, Hellenist conflict, apostolic imprisonment—exposing that large numbers yield both potential and pitfalls. Pastoral leaders must plan for ongoing discipleship infrastructure: training new converts in doctrine, ethics, and community life to prevent attrition. Administrative challenges—facility space, resource allocation, volunteer coordination—parallel early church's logistics of house gatherings, communal meals, and financial sharing

(Acts 2 : 44-45; 4 : 32). Cross-cultural dynamics within mass gatherings require sensitivity to socioeconomic, linguistic, and educational disparities among converts. Theological instruction should temper enthusiasm with depth—catechesis on perseverance, suffering, and spiritual warfare. Leadership development pipelines must identify gifted individuals among large crowds to share shepherding duties and prevent burnout among founding figures. Mechanisms for conflict resolution, discipleship pathways, and doctrinal accountability guard against fragmentation. In modern megachurch contexts, leaders translate apostolic principles—house church cells, relational small groups, discipling teams—into scalable models that preserve intimacy within mass conversion. The biblical caution that some of the "five hundred...have fallen asleep" reminds churches of natural attrition through death and desertion, calling for sustainable evangelism pipelines that anticipate ongoing renewal rather than one-time surge. Thus, sustaining mass conversion involves replicating apostolic ethos: abundant grace gluing community together, rigorous teaching embedding truth, and vigilant pastoral care honoring both the collective and the individual.

Conclusion

The fleeting mention of Jesus appearing to more than five hundred brothers at one time unlocks vast dimensions of resurrection theology, historical credibility, communal dynamics, and missional impetus that resonate through two millennia of church life. In that one reference, Paul anchors the Gospel in collective attestation, counters narrow illusions of private visions, and issues timeless invitation to verify hope against the testimony of living witnesses. Historically, the gathering emerges from networks of festival pilgrims, house churches, and relational patronage, illustrating how fledgling movement marshaled resources to convene mass proclamation. Psychologically, the event navigates group perception, memory consolidation, and conversion dynamics that render the resurrection an abiding communal reality rather than an introspective oddity. Theologically, the mass appearance underscores universal restoration ordained by cosmic authority, foreshadowing Pentecost's global outpouring of Spirit and shaping ecclesiological self-understanding as people of the resurrection. Pastoral applications beckon modern churches to cultivate communal faith foundations through intentional gatherings, to respect mass conversion's remarkable surge while prudently investing in sustainable discipleship structures, and to anchor evangelistic zeal in both individual encounter and corporate experience. As believers continue to gather—whether under steepled roofs, in living rooms, or across digital platforms—they stand on the shoulders of that five-hundred-strong chorus that first saw the risen Christ at once. May every assembly, large or small, heed the apostolic example by proclaiming the risen Lord with unified voice and by living into the reality that "where two or three are gathered in My name, there I am among them" (Matthew 18 : 20)—for the echo of that greater gathering still shapes the contours of Christian witness today.

Chapter 11. Final Instructions on the Mount of Olives – Immediately before the Ascension

James, identified explicitly in Scripture as "the brother of the Lord" (Galatians 1 : 19), moves through the New Testament like a figure shrouded in early misunderstanding but ultimately ablaze with pastoral authority. Before the resurrection he is counted among those family members who questioned Jesus' public ministry (John 7 : 3-5); after the resurrection he emerges as moderator of the Jerusalem Council (Acts 15 : 13-21), principal author of the letter that bears his name (James 1 : 1), and eventual martyr who left an indelible imprint on the first-century church. What catalyzed such a drastic change? Paul gives the lone explicit clue when he lists the Lord's post-resurrection appearances, noting that after revealing Himself to more than five hundred at one time, Jesus "was seen by James, then by all the apostles" (1 Corinthians

15 : 7). A single sentence in Paul's earliest surviving letter implies an encounter of monumental consequence—one that transformed a previously skeptical sibling into a steady pillar (Galatians 2 : 9). Because Scripture offers only that tantalizing mention, biblical theologians, historians, and pastoral practitioners have long examined ancillary texts, historical analogs, and psychosocial dynamics to flesh out what the appearance might have entailed and why it mattered so profoundly.

11.1. Historical Profile of James Prior to the Resurrection

11.1.1 Family Lineage, Cultural Milieu, and Social Responsibilities

James grew up in a pious Jewish household in Nazareth where Scripture reading, synagogue attendance, and festival pilgrimage were woven into weekly rhythm. His mother, Mary, and father, Joseph, adhered to Torah prescriptions, evident when they offered the purification sacrifices for a firstborn son (Luke 2 : 22-24). As the eldest male child born after Jesus' virgin birth, James shared carpentry responsibilities in the family workshop, likely shaping beams and plows for Galilean farmers who spoke Aramaic at home and Greek or Hebrew in commerce. Nazareth's proximity to the Hellenistic town of Sepphoris exposed James to Greco-Roman architecture and bilingual marketplaces, sharpening both his linguistic facility and cultural adaptability. The strong honor-shame matrix of first-century Jewish society obligated him to protect household reputation; thus Jesus' itinerant ministry, punctuated by controversy, probably threatened familial standing in local eyes (see Mark 6 : 3). Contemporary rabbinic instruction emphasized respect for older siblings, yet Jesus' claims to messianic authority inverted ordinary primogeniture, creating latent tension in the sibling group. When Jesus remained behind in the temple at age twelve (Luke 2 : 41-49), James, who may have been five or six at the time, would already have witnessed the strain that extraordinary spiritual destiny placed on domestic routine. Later, as Jesus attracted large crowds and scribal antagonism, James presumably continued craft commitments, hearing reports that his older brother healed on Sabbaths, confounded Pharisees, and declared forgiveness of sins—statements that overlapped dangerously with prerogatives assigned to God alone. Jewish tradition required older brothers to intervene if a sibling endangered the family's covenant status; therefore it is unsurprising that, together with other brothers, James attempted to restrain Jesus, concluding He was "out of His mind" (Mark 3 : 21). The Gospel narratives' candor about family misunderstanding buttresses historical plausibility; early Christians would hardly invent skepticism from Jesus' own household if the fact were not well known. Throughout these pre-resurrection years, James inhabited a liminal space between affectionate familial loyalty and guarding ancestral orthodoxy. He negotiated artisan labor, synagogue study, and festival obligations while processing incremental rumors that his carpenter-rabbi brother was provoking both awe and alarm across Galilee and Judea. Each successive incident—conflict at Capernaum, reproof at Nazareth, mounting plots in Jerusalem—deepened James's cognitive dissonance, compelling him to monitor Jesus' actions for any sign of either vindication or disgrace. In this cultural milieu, a private appearance of the resurrected Lord held the potential not only to rescue fraternal relationships but to realign an entire household's social trajectory within the emergent Jesus-movement.

11.1.2 Recorded Skepticism and Signs of Emerging Curiosity

John narrates that Jesus' brothers encouraged Him to showcase miracles at the Feast of Booths precisely because "even His brothers did not believe in Him" (John 7 : 3-5). The verb "believe" in Johannine usage connotes more than intellectual assent; it involves trusting allegiance—which James had not yet rendered. This skepticism manifested earlier at Capernaum when the family attempted a protective intervention (Mark 3 : 31-35), prompting Jesus to redefine kinship around obedience to God's will rather than bloodline alone. That redefinition likely stung James, raising questions about his place in the new messianic family Jesus was forming. Despite doubt, whispers of Lazarus's resurrection, rumors of Jairus's daughter restored, and testimony of cleansed lepers must have unsettled James's initial dismissal. Sociologists refer to cognitive thresholds where cumulative evidence forces reevaluation of bias; James hovered near such a threshold by Passion Week. The Triumphal Entry, overshadowed by Hosanna shouts and prophetic symbolism (Zechariah 9 : 9), might have pinged childhood memories of Jesus' youthful wisdom, prying open curiosity. Yet the abrupt collapse of those hopes at Golgotha cemented earlier fears—that his brother's mission would end in shameful death and perhaps implicate the family with Roman suspicion. Jewish law regarded crucifixion as Deuteronomic curse (Deut 21 : 23), adding theological scandal to political peril. In grief, James nevertheless confronted contradictory data: Jesus died between two criminals but uttered Psalmic trust—"Into Your hands I commit My spirit" (Luke 23 : 46). Such details, when recounted by witnesses, may have triggered nascent wonder. Still, the Sabbath silence that followed entombment seemed final, pressing any lingering curiosity beneath the weight of funeral finality. By dawn of the third day, however, reports of an empty grave and angelic proclamation reached James indirectly through female disciples who braved cultural norms to testify. Women's credibility in male courts was limited; yet James, having matured within Jesus' ethos of upended hierarchies, could scarcely ignore their insistence. These conflicting stimuli—public stigma of crucifixion, private memory of prophetic foreshadowings, secondhand resurrection claims—set the psychological stage for an encounter powerful enough to vault skepticism into robust faith. The appearance to James would not occur in an epistemological vacuum; it answered a restless undercurrent of questions that familial loyalty and Torah devotion could neither suppress nor satisfy.

11.2. Scriptural Witness to the Appearance and Intertextual Echoes

11.2.1 Paul's Creedal Citation and Early Transmission Reliability

Paul's first letter to the Corinthians preserves what scholars widely deem a pre-Pauline creed embedded within 1 Corinthians 15 : 3-7. Chronological analysis positions this formula within five to eight years of Easter, making it one of Christianity's oldest extant confessions. Amid the chain of appearances—Cephas, the Twelve, five hundred, James, all the apostles—James's inclusion signifies independent significance distinct from broader apostolic clusters. The deliberate naming underscores eyewitness reliability: in honor-shame cultures, public appeal to living witnesses invited contradiction if the claim were false. Critics might question why Paul, addressing Gentile believers in Corinth, highlights a Jerusalem leader they scarcely knew; the answer lies in bolstering historical veracity through cross-cultural corroboration. James, as Jesus' brother, served as unimpeachable reference because family members could attest identity beyond doubt. The creedal sequence places James after the mass appearance but before the final group manifestation, perhaps to emphasize incremental widening of resurrection proof—from individual leader, to collective laity, to central governing body. That ordering also reveals oral tradition priority: Cephas anchors Petrine leadership, James anchors kinship leadership, together framing a united testimony bridging Galilean fishermen and Jerusalem clergy. This careful structuring rebuts theories that resurrection faith evolved gradually; instead, earliest preaching already featured multiple intersecting eyewitnesses. The creed's tight syntax—"He was raised on the third day according to the Scriptures"—implies that James's meeting echoed scriptural fulfillment motifs, perhaps referencing Psalm 22's vindication or Isaiah 53's seeing offspring after crushing. Paul, himself reluctant believer turned missionary, knew value of citing another former skeptic now converted—James's story mirrored his own and thus reinforced grace's transformative power.

Consequently, Paul's inclusion of James is no incidental flourish but strategic historical anchor ensuring Gentile congregations appreciate the breadth of Jewish verification underlying gospel proclamation.

11.2.2 Echoes in the Synoptic and Johannine Narratives

Although none of the four canonical Gospels explicitly detail the James appearance, subtle textual signals create resonance. Mark's enigmatic "young man" at the tomb instructs the women to keep Peter and the disciples informed that Jesus will go ahead to Galilee (Mark 16 : 7). Some scholars propose that "and Peter" hints at broader individual appearances eventually including James. Luke's note that "He has appeared to Simon" (Luke 24 : 34) demonstrates authorial awareness of personal meetings beyond the public domain, suggesting Luke could have known of James's encounter but chose thematic economy. John's portrayal of skeptical Thomas satisfied by wounds (John 20 : 24-29) implicitly validates the motif of personal doubts overcome by direct evidence—again gesturing toward a James trajectory. Acts depicts James stepping into leadership effortlessly by Acts 12 : 17, implying a decisive experience post-Passion that elevated his authority. Moreover, when the resurrected Jesus entrusts Mother Mary to the Beloved Disciple (John 19 : 26-27), He bypasses biological brothers, reflecting their pre-Easter disbelief; the Gospels' honesty about this disbelief sets narrative tension resolved only if subsequent resurrection appearances addressed familial skepticism. Such intertextual pointers encourage readers to fill narrative gaps with Paul's confirmation, stitching a canonical tapestry where James's transformation forms essential color thread. By allowing silence where particulars are not essential for faith, the evangelists invite ecclesial imagination bounded by apostolic memory—an approach that safeguards mystery while honoring history. The James appearance thus occupies an interstitial space: absent from Gospel pages yet echoing within them like a refrain unvoiced but perceptible, harmonizing explicitly when Paul finally sings the verse. This canonical kaleidoscope attests to early Christian sensitivity in preserving both public testimony and discreet personal redemption stories, acknowledging that not every sacred conversation requires full transcript to be authoritative.

11.3. Chronology, Locale, and Context of the Appearance

11.3.1 Jerusalem Timing Hypothesis and Festival Backdrop

Most scholars place the appearance to James within the forty-day window Acts 1 : 3 assigns to post-resurrection instruction. Jerusalem, swollen with pilgrims for Passover and the impending Feast of Weeks (Pentecost), remained nerve center for both rumor and revelation. Locating the encounter there fits logistical realities: James, as resident of the city where Jesus' crucifixion occurred, would naturally be present, and Jesus' other appearances cluster around Judea before Galilean epiphanies. John's Gospel records Jesus instructing Mary Magdalene not to cling because He had "not yet ascended" (John 20 : 17), implying ongoing presence around Jerusalem in initial days. James, engaged in family mourning rituals—seven-day shivah period per Jewish custom—would be accessible for a visit at the family's lodging, possibly near Bethany where extended relatives lived. The climatic context of early April offers mild evenings conducive to rooftop prayers, a setting noted later in Acts 10. During this post-Passover period, fervent discussion of resurrection rumors circulated in temple courts; a private, familial meeting would afford discretion amid volatile atmosphere. By appearing in Jerusalem, Jesus also sanctified the city that had executed Him, transforming it into launch site for gospel momentum, with James positioned as home-grown witness. Festival backdrop heightened prophetic fulfillment: as firstfruits sheaves were waved (Leviticus 23 : 10-11), the risen Messiah presented Himself to a brother who would become firstfruits of family faith. The Jerusalem hypothesis coheres with subsequent leadership trajectory: James quickly emerges in Acts as authoritative voice where ecclesial disputes are adjudicated, indicating residence and spiritual stature established soon after Pentecost. Chronological placement also underscores urgency—Jesus addresses familial skepticism before global Great Commission instructions finalize, ensuring internal circle unity. Modern readers glean that Christ often prioritizes reconciliation of closest relationships before broader ministry expansion, modeling concentric strategy of gospel peace.

11.3.2 Alternative Galilean Setting and Pilgrimage Logistics

A minority of interpreters envisage the James appearance transpiring in Galilee, aligning with angelic directive that disciples would meet Jesus there (Matthew 28 : 7). Given that Jesus' family hailed from Nazareth and maintained ties to surrounding villages, a return north for agricultural responsibilities between Passover and Pentecost is plausible. Galilean hills, dotted with terraces and olive groves, offered secluded walking paths where an intimate brotherly encounter could unfold away from Jerusalem surveillance. Some traditions locate James's later ascetic practices—including constant prayer on Mount Olivet—within countryside settings, supporting comfort with rural solitude. Pilgrimage logistics also matter: families often traveled together for festivals; with father Joseph likely deceased, James may have accompanied Mary back home following Passover, thus encountering Jesus en route or upon arrival. Galilee's symbolic resonance as prophetic dawn of messianic light (Isaiah 9 : 1-2) further bolsters theological significance of a northern appearance reaffirming covenant promises. Yet practical challenges arise: Paul's creed suggests sequential logic—James, then all apostles—which most naturally fits Jerusalem chronology because apostolic group reconvenes there before Ascension. Additionally, Acts' portrayal of disciples remaining in Jerusalem from Easter to Pentecost suggests minimal northern travel in that interval. Scholars advocating Galilee must posit dual travel loops or compress timeline into strenuous journeys uncommon in ancient norms. While not impossible—Galilee lay roughly four days' walk north—this scenario requires explanatory layers absent from narrative trajectory. The Galilean hypothesis nonetheless enriches imaginative contemplation, emphasizing that Jesus might meet individuals in familiar vocational contexts: James glimpsing resurrected brother within fields where they once harvested grain, thereby blending memory and revelation. Whatever location, appearance underscores Christ's ability to bridge sacred epicenters and humble hometowns, validating that resurrection presence is not geographically restricted. The ongoing scholarly dialogue reminds disciples to hold curiosity with humility, acknowledging that Scripture preserves essentials while leaving room for sanctified speculation.

11.4. Psychological and Spiritual Transformation of James

11.4.1 From Familial Skepticism to Apostolic Conviction

Psychologists recognize that worldview overhaul often requires disconfirming evidence experienced firsthand, especially for individuals embedded in close relationships with disputed figures. James's skepticism, rooted in shared upbringing and protective caution, shattered the moment he confronted the living Jesus bearing crucifixion scars yet speaking shalom. The encounter likely unfolded through recognition signals—voice tone, gesture patterns, familial humor—combined with unmistakable resurrection reality. Neuroscience notes that intense emotional experiences rewire neural pathways rapidly; James's limbic response to seeing his executed brother alive would surge norepinephrine and dopamine priming memory consolidation. Spiritual transformation followed cognition: Hebrew Scriptures long recited in synagogue began to refract through new Christocentric prism. Passages about suffering servant, rejected cornerstone, and righteous sufferer rose from liturgical familiarity into living fulfillment. James's internal narrative shifted from protecting family honor to proclaiming divine vindication; shame metamorphosed into boast in the cross. This cognitive-affective shift catalyzed behavioral change: he joined incessant prayer gatherings with apostles (Acts 1 : 14), absorbed Pentecost's Spirit, and accepted emerging leadership responsibilities. The speed of transformation evidences authenticity—deeply resistant people rarely flip allegiance to movements they deem delusional unless confronted by overwhelming reality.

Sociologists studying conversion typically observe gradual shifts; James's near-instant pivot stands out, underlining the existential shock of resurrection verified through personal encounter. His subsequent pastoral letter, steeped in wisdom literature and prophetic imperatives, reflects mature synthesis of Jewish piety and Christ-centered ethics, confirming enduring integration rather than temporary elation. Thus, James's transformation offers case study of how resurrection encounters catalyze holistic conversion—mind, heart, and communal direction pivoting around incontrovertible grace.

11.4.2 Emergence of Ascetic Lifestyle and Reputation for Righteousness

Early church historian Hegesippus, quoted by Eusebius, describes James as "Oblias," meaning "Bulwark of the People," and recounts that his knees grew calloused like a camel's from constant intercessory prayer in the temple. Such ascetic devotion signals radical reorientation of daily habits post-appearance. Jewish pietistic movements like the Essenes prized voluntary austerity; James's embodiment of similar disciplines within mainstream church framed him as bridge between rigorist currents and grace-centered gospel. His vow to avoid wine and meat mirrors Nazirite features (Numbers 6 : 1-5), demonstrating consecration to God's service. Asceticism in James did not veer into dualistic disdain for body; rather, it sought solidarity with poor laborers he later championed (James 2 : 1-7). The epistle's emphasis on bridling tongue, resisting lust, and prioritizing mercy reflects leader whose personal holiness derived from continual awareness of resurrected sibling's scrutiny and empowerment. Reputation for righteousness amplified his witness: even Pharisaic and Sadducean segments respected his integrity, delaying persecution of the church until Stephen's trial. When famine threatened Judean believers, Paul's Gentile collection referenced "the poor among the saints in Jerusalem" (Romans 15 : 26), likely managed by James, illustrating trust in his equitable distribution. Ascetic credibility extended influence across theological spectra: Peter, Paul, and Barnabas deferred to James's judgment at the Jerusalem Council (Acts 15 : 13-21), signifying moral authority rooted in disciplined life. The appearance's impact on lifestyle thus radiated beyond personal piety, shaping communal ethos of justice, prayer, and self-restraint. Modern leaders glean that authentic encounter with risen Christ yields not only doctrinal affirmation but embodied holiness that confers lasting credibility in diverse constituencies.

11.5. Theological Ramifications of the James Appearance

11.5.1 Resurrection Validity and Sibling Verification Principle

Apologetically, Jesus' appearance to a biological brother reduces likelihood of mistaken identity, a hypothesis sometimes advanced by critics to explain other sightings. Siblings share developmental memories, facial familiarity, and idiosyncrasies unobservable to casual acquaintances; misidentifying a twin-brother-like impostor becomes virtually impossible. The "sibling verification principle" enhances evidential weight of resurrection because family testimony could not be easily dismissed as wishful thinking—their earlier skepticism undercuts charges of predisposition. Furthermore, Jewish legal standards valued two or three witnesses; sibling corroboration supplements apostolic witness, meeting Deuteronomic criteria for establishing truth (Deuteronomy 19 : 15). Theologically, Jesus' personal initiative toward family underscores Incarnation's sanctification of domestic bonds, illustrating salvation that reverberates through kinship networks. It fulfills prophetic hints that Messiah would restore household integrity—"He will turn the hearts of fathers to their children" (Malachi 4 : 6). Paul's inclusion of James in the appearance roster also links resurrection with ecclesial institutional memory; apostolic preaching anchored in community recognized for rigorous Torah observance. Thus, the James appearance undergirds doctrine that resurrection stands historically public yet intimately relational, capable of converting hardened relatives into heralds. In modern apologetics, referencing James counters psychological hallucination theories; group hallucinations are rare, and transformation of a skeptic sibling into martyr demands explanatory force matching resurrection claim. Consequently, James's testimony persists as linchpin bridging experiential faith and empirical inquiry, verifying that Easter proclamation rests on rock-solid relational evidence.

11.5.2 Christology and the Identity of Jesus as Divine Savior

James's subsequent confession of Jesus as "the Lord of glory" (James 2 : 1) and exhortation to invoke "the name of the Lord" for healing (James 5 : 14) declare elevated Christology unexpected from devout monotheistic Jew unless convinced of divine revelation. His use of "Lord" (Kyrios) aligns with Septuagint rendering of Yahweh, implying identification of Jesus with covenant God. The resurrected appearance revealed Jesus not merely as vindicated human but as glorified Son sharing divine prerogatives, reshaping James's Shema-honed monotheism into Christological monotheism. This theological shift informs James's epistle where wisdom descending from above (James 3 : 17) and implanted word able to save (James 1 : 21) reflect Johannine Logos resonance. By endorsing Jesus' divine identity, a figure once intimately familiar with His human upbringing validates early high Christology as authentic response rather than Hellenistic accretion. The James appearance thereby confirms that worship of Jesus within Jewish Christian circles arose from firsthand conviction, not Gentile syncretism. Trinitarian theology later formalized relies implicitly on such testimonies: divine identity revealed to original monotheists provides continuity between Old Testament revelation and New Testament fulfillment. For pastoral theology, James's acknowledgment offers assurance that close knowledge of Jesus' humanity need not obstruct recognition of His divinity; rather, resurrection glorifies filial relationship and invites believers into similar intimacy.

11.6. James's Post-Appearance Leadership and Martyrdom

11.6.1 Role in the Jerusalem Council and Guardianship of Unity

Acts 15 records a pivotal moment when circumcision controversy threatened Gentile mission. Amid apostolic dispute, "James answered," offering synthesis drawn from Amos 9 : 11-12 and Spirit's Gentile outpouring evidence, recommending minimal covenant markers for inclusion. His speech, marked by balanced concession and scriptural authority, secured unanimous consent, illustrating diplomatic acumen rooted in humility learned at resurrection encounter. His leadership style—listening, referencing Scripture, prioritizing communal witness—mirrors Jesus' patient engagement with disciples post-Easter. Paul later refers to "James, Cephas, and John, reputed pillars" (Galatians 2 : 9), acknowledging triadic governance. James's presence grounded unity between Jewish tradition and Gentile expansion, illustrating that personal transformation fosters corporate bridge-building. Some scholars view his decision as earliest model of conciliar authority guiding doctrine via Spirit-led deliberation—a precedent for later ecumenical councils. James's equitable treatment of socioeconomic classes, emphasized in his letter, shaped Jerusalem church's reputation for caring for the poor, prompting Paul's famine relief efforts (2 Corinthians 8-9). His authority, though robust, remained servant-oriented; he encouraged elders to shepherd rather than dominate (James 5 : 14). Such leadership flow traces directly to resurrection meeting: a forgiven skeptic leads with empathy, weaving grace into institutional fabric.

11.6.2 Final Witness and Death under High Priest Ananus II

Eusebius, citing Hegesippus and Josephus, records that around AD 62, High Priest Ananus II convened a hastily assembled Sanhedrin and accused James of breaking Torah, leading to his stoning near the temple. Josephus notes that many Jews considered the execution illegal and opposed

Ananus, resulting in his removal by Roman procurator Albinus. James's martyrdom occurred in Passover season, echoing his brother's timing and underscoring ongoing tension between Jesus-followers and temple hierarchy. Tradition holds James prayed for his executioners, paralleling Jesus' forgiveness on the cross, further validating inner transformation. His death fortified church resolve, galvanizing believers as far as Damascus to persevere amid hostility. Liturgical calendars commemorate James on October 23 in Eastern Orthodoxy, highlighting his enduring inspiration. Martyrdom sealed his testimony: a brother who'd once doubted now embraced death for conviction that Jesus is risen Lord. Apologetically, willingness to die substantiates sincerity; people seldom endure stoning for what they know to be false. James's final witness demonstrates resurrection's power to generate unflinching courage, challenging contemporary disciples to evaluate the stakes of their own commitments.

11.7. Pastoral and Missional Lessons for Contemporary Faith Communities

11.7.1 Family Evangelism and the Hope of Personal Encounter

James's journey from skepticism to faith offers blueprint for believers praying for unbelieving relatives. Argumentative persuasion alone proved insufficient; transformative encounter with Christ, mediated through Spirit and community witness, ultimately convinced James. Families today can glean hope that patient integrity, coupled with prayerful expectation, prepares soil for divine breakthrough. Mary's steadfast faith, which treasured events in her heart, likely influenced eventual openness; similarly, consistent witness without coercion fosters relational safety. Disciples should avoid despair when kin resist gospel, remembering James's initial opposition. Churches may create spaces for honest questioning, mirroring Jesus' willingness to address familial doubt privately yet directly. Testimonies of siblings or spouses encountering Christ can encourage intercessors. Additionally, James illustrates that sometimes God approaches skeptics outside formal evangelistic programs, using personal grief, cultural rituals, or solitary reflections as meeting ground. Therefore, believers maintain hopeful vigilance, trusting resurrection power to penetrate hardened perceptions.

11.7.2 Leadership Formation Rooted in Grace and Holiness

James embodies leadership forged in crucible of self-awareness and divine mercy. Modern ministers can emulate his blend of piety, justice, and doctrinal fidelity. Leadership training programs might examine his epistle's emphasis on listening, impartiality, and tongue control as competencies shaped by resurrection ethics. His prayer discipline models spiritual resilience; leaders cultivate knee-callouses through intercession before assuming platform. James's deference to Scripture at the Jerusalem Council underscores necessity of biblical anchoring amid cultural disputes. Furthermore, his willingness to shepherd rather than monopolize authority speaks against celebrity pastor syndrome. Contemporary churches can incorporate rhythms of confession and communion reminiscent of James's initial encounter, ensuring leaders minister from overflow of experienced forgiveness. Finally, martyrdom confronts utilitarian calculus infecting leadership ambitions; authenticity may cost reputation or life, but resurrection hope sustains. By studying James, communities learn that the most compelling shepherds are once-skeptical relatives transformed into servants who gladly die rather than deny the risen Christ.

Conclusion

The resurrected Jesus' appearance to James—recorded in Scripture by a solitary verse yet reverberating through apostolic history—transformed an unbelieving brother into a steadfast pillar, harmonizing family loyalty with messianic devotion, and bending skepticism into sacrificial leadership. Historians trace how that private meeting positioned James to guide the Jerusalem church, arbitrate doctrinal crises, model ascetic compassion, and seal his convictions in martyr's blood. Theologically, the encounter supplies unique sibling verification of resurrection, fortifies high Christology emerging from Jewish monotheism, and underpins ecclesial authority rooted in experienced grace. Practically, James's story emboldens believers who intercede for resistant relatives and challenges leaders to cultivate holiness born of personal encounter rather than institutional status. In every era, households wrestle with divided faith commitments, congregations seek balanced guidance amid diversity, and skeptics demand credible evidence; the narrative of James answers each need with quiet potency. It testifies that the risen Lord pursues even those who share His roof yet doubt His call, that He converts private skepticism into public service, and that He entrenches His church's foundation not on sanitized heroes but on relatives once scandalized by the carpenter-Messiah who now rules as Lord of glory. By contemplating James's appearance, modern disciples rediscover Easter's domestic dimension: resurrection power walking through family corridors, speaking peace into sibling rivalries, and raising unlikely saints whose knees bruise in prayer so that communities might stand in joy.

Chapter 12. Post-Ascension Conversations - To Saul of Tarsus

The extraordinary narrative of Saul of Tarsus—later revered across the Christian world as Paul the Apostle—stands as the single most detailed post-ascension conversation preserved in Scripture, and it is foundational for understanding how the risen and exalted Christ continues to call, correct, and commission His people in real time. Luke devotes an extended treatment to the Damascus-road event in Acts 9 : 1-19 and then revisits the story twice more in Acts 22 : 3-21 and Acts 26 : 9-20, while Paul himself alludes to it and its aftermath in letters such as Galatians 1 : 11-24 and 1 Timothy 1 : 12-17. These multiple attestations reveal an early church that considered the conversation between Heaven and the persecutor-turned-preacher to be paradigmatic for grace, mission, and ecclesial credibility. In Saul's journey we witness theologically pregnant themes: the collision of violent zeal with divine compassion, the re-calibration of vocational identity under the voice of Jesus, the indispensability of community mediation through an obedient disciple named Ananias, and the long trajectory of sanctified suffering that testifies to authentic apostleship.

12.1. Historico-Cultural Profile of Saul of Tarsus Before the Encounter

12.1.1 Jewish Pedigree, Hellenistic Exposure, and Rabbinic Ambition

Saul's childhood in Tarsus of Cilicia placed him within one of the most vibrant intellectual centers of the eastern Mediterranean, rivaling Alexandria and Athens for rhetorical training and philosophical discourse (Acts 21 : 39). As a Roman citizen by birth (Acts 22 : 28), he possessed civic privileges unusual for provincials, enabling unhindered travel across imperial provinces without fear of flogging or summary trial. Yet Saul's deepest identity markers were Jewish and Pharisaic; he proudly traced lineage to the tribe of Benjamin, circumcised on the eighth day, nurtured in strict adherence to Torah (Philippians 3 : 4-6). His parents, likely affluent tent-makers or leather-workers, apprenticed him in the same trade, ensuring economic independence that would later fund missionary journeys (Acts 18 : 3). Early schooling included memorization of the Law, Prophets, and Writings, participation in synagogue liturgy, and cultivated fluency in Hebrew or Aramaic alongside the Koine Greek of commercial life. Adolescent Saul traveled to Jerusalem to study under Gamaliel (Acts 22 : 3), a respected Pharisaic sage whose pedagogical reputation blended rigorous exegesis with measured engagement toward Hellenism. Under Gamaliel, Saul honed skills in midrash, typology, and halakhic reasoning, equipping him to expound Scripture with forensic precision—a skill set later redeployed for gospel proclamation. The intellectual ferment of the Second-Temple period exposed him to debates over resurrection, messianic expectations, and the boundaries of Jewish identity vis-à-vis Gentile inclusion, energizing a zeal that would eventually turn militant. Intra-Jewish factionalism between Sadducees (who denied bodily resurrection, Acts 23 : 8), Essenes (who retreated to Qumran enclaves), and Pharisees sharpened partisan passions; Saul aligned with the Pharisees' purity agenda, convinced that rigorous obedience to Torah would hasten covenantal blessing and perhaps precipitate messianic deliverance from Rome. Thus, when followers of "the Way" proclaimed a crucified carpenter as Davidic king and claimed his resurrection as first-fruits of a new age, Saul interpreted such assertions as blasphemous threats to Israel's holiness and national hopes. Hellenistic synagogues in Jerusalem, where Greek-speaking Jews debated diaspora customs, became hotbeds for clashes over Jesus' messiahship, and Saul, well-versed in both language spheres, likely spearheaded disputations that culminated in Stephen's martyrdom (Acts 6 : 8 – 7 : 60). Indeed, Luke depicts Saul as guardian of garments for stone-throwers, suggesting his official sanction and internal fervor (Acts 7 : 58). Early rabbinic ambition merged with eschatological urgency: Saul aimed to purge the covenant community of perceived heresy to secure divine favor. This mixture of cultural sophistication, legal meticulousness, and apocalyptic hope created the combustible context necessary for a spectacular intervention by the exalted Christ.

12.1.2 Psychological Zeal and Persecution Networks Prior to Damascus

Luke summarizes Saul's pre-conversion posture with stark brevity: he "breathed out threats and murder against the disciples of the Lord" (Acts 9 : 1). The Greek present participle ἐμπνέων conveys continuous exhalation, as if zeal were the very oxygen animating Saul's lungs. Cognitive anthropology underscores that such zeal often arises when tightly bounded identity groups perceive existential threat; for Saul, the Way's cross-centered theology undermined Pharisaic purity by decentering temple sacrifices and welcoming sinners without circumcision. He therefore secured letters from the high priest authorizing extradition of Jesus-followers from Damascus synagogues (Acts 9 : 2), indicating institutional collaboration between Pharisaic activists and Sadducean authorities—an alliance otherwise rare given theological rifts. Damascus, lying roughly 240 kilometers northeast of Jerusalem along Roman roads, housed a significant Jewish population and acted as gateway to further diaspora centers; stamping out the movement there would blunt its regional spread. Saul likely organized a cohort of temple police or volunteers; persecution in Jerusalem had scattered believers (Acts 8 : 3-4), so replicating intimidation abroad required logistical planning, financial resources, and intelligence networks in diasporic synagogues. His psychological state mingled righteous indignation with rising reputation among elders, cementing self-esteem in accolades for orthodoxy. Yet deep inside, cognitive dissonance simmered: he had heard Stephen's eloquent survey of Israel's resistant history (Acts 7), watched the man pray for enemies amid stoning, and perhaps glimpsed the face "like an angel" (Acts 6 : 15). Modern trauma studies note that persecutors confronting victims' non-retaliatory endurance sometimes experience moral injury, seeding seeds of doubt. Saul's escalating aggression may partially reflect subconscious flight from those seeds. Neuroscientists describe how ideologically driven violence can generate dopamine surges, reinforcing fervor but also heightening vulnerability to disconfirming epiphanies. In God's providence, the road to Damascus would become the corridor where such vulnerability met revelatory light, toppling Saul's psychological fortress. Consequently, examining Saul's pre-Damascus zeal reveals a portrait of a man both terrifyingly committed and paradoxically ripe for divine disruption—the very sort of person Christ delights to convert into a trophy of radical grace (1 Timothy 1 : 15-16).

12.2. The Damascus-Road Encounter: Narrative Anatomy and Theological Symbolism

12.2.1 Blinding Light, Divine Voice, and Angelic Direction (Acts 9 : 3-9)

Approaching Damascus near midday—a moment when Syrian sun already flooded the limestone landscape—Saul suddenly found himself engulfed by a light "brighter than the sun" (Acts 26 : 13). The motif echoes Old Testament theophanies where dazzling brilliance signifies Yahweh's presence, whether atop Sinai (Exodus 19 : 16-19) or enthroned in Ezekiel's chariot vision (Ezekiel 1 : 26-28). Unlike Moses, who perceived glory indirectly, Saul endured direct radiance that overwhelmed ocular capacity, driving him to the ground—posture of prostration common in reverence yet here induced by incapacitating surprise. Luke records a voice in Aramaic—"Saul, Saul, why are you persecuting Me?" (Acts 26 : 14)—employing double name repetition found in Abrahamic, Mosaic, and prophetic call narratives, thus framing Saul within covenantal continuity. The piercing interrogation underscores corporate identity between Christ and church: harming disciples equals persecuting the risen Lord. When Saul inquires, "Who are You, Lord?" the voice self-discloses: "I am Jesus whom you are persecuting" (Acts 9 : 5). This revelatory declaration fuses crucified scandal with resurrected vindication; the one Saul deemed cursed by Deuteronomy now speaks from heavenly authority. Commands follow: "Get up and enter the city, and you will be told what you must do" (Acts 9 : 6). The imperative reorients Saul's agency—from autonomous persecutor to dependent petitioner awaiting instruction. Accompanying men hear sound but see no one (Acts 9 : 7), paralleling Sinai episodes where thunderous voice confounded bystanders, emphasizing Saul's unique commissioning. Temporarily blinded, Saul rises and is led by hand—a potent reversal of earlier self-assured leadership—into Damascus, where he fasts three days, recalling Jonah's tri-nights in fish and Jesus' own burial span. The blindness operates both literally and metaphorically; physical darkness externalizes spiritual disorientation, preparing him for light of baptismal sight. Theologically, the episode dramatizes conversion as both sudden rupture and progressive unfolding: decisive epiphany on road, interpretive clarification through prophetic mediation, and sacramental incorporation via water and Spirit. Scholars note that Acts' triple recounting adds nuance: Acts 9 offers Luke's narration, Acts 22 emphasizes Jewish context for temple audience, Acts 26 highlights Gentile vocation before Agrippa—demonstrating the event's multiplanar significance for diverse listeners. For devotional readers, the Damascus light functions as icon of prevenient grace—God intercepting human agendas with unmerited revelation, inviting surrender and transformation.

12.2.2 Christological Titles and Covenant Echoes in the Encounter

Jesus identifies Himself not merely by personal designation but through a united identity with His ekklēsia; "Me" and "My" collapse distinction between head and body, revealing high Christology wherein the Messiah continues covenant oversight as cosmic Lord (Colossians 1 : 18). The address "Lord" on Saul's lips signals dawning recognition of divine status—even before he grasps full Trinitarian implications, he instinctively adopts Kyrios, the Septuagint's rendering of YHWH. Later, Paul's soteriology will hinge on confession "Jesus is Lord" (Romans 10 : 9), rooted in this primal utterance. The call's grammar evokes prophetic vocations: "rise and stand" (Acts 26 : 16) parallels Ezekiel 2 : 1 and Daniel 10 : 11, situating Saul among covenant emissaries bearing Yahweh's words to rebellious people. Furthermore, Jesus' statement that Saul will be "a witness... of what you have seen and in what I will appear to you" implies ongoing revelatory dialogue, prefiguring later visions in Corinth (Acts 18 : 9-10) and Jerusalem (Acts 23 : 11). The covenant motif deepens when Jesus adds, "I'm sending you to open their eyes" (Acts 26 : 17-18), mirroring Isaiah's Servant commission (Isaiah 42 : 6-7) and signaling eschatological fulfillment. Thus, the Damascus conversation fuses Abrahamic promise of worldwide blessing with Isaianic servant mission, authorizing Saul's Gentile vocation. The double naming "Saul, Saul" also alludes to 1 Samuel 15 : 10-11 where Yahweh addresses King Saul's disobedience; here, new Saul meets true King, effecting reversal from rebellion to obedience. In sum, every phrase of the encounter layers covenant, prophecy, and Christological identity, transforming persecutor into participant in God's redemptive storyline. For contemporary theology, the episode anchors experiential revelation within canonical echoes, validating charismatic encounter while tethering it to Scripture's metanarrative.

12.3. Mediation Through Ananias and Early Community Reception

12.3.1 Prophetic Vision to Ananias: Obedience Amid Risk (Acts 9 : 10-16)

In Damascus resided a disciple named Ananias, a devout observer of the Law with good reputation among local Jews (Acts 22 : 12). The Lord addresses him in vision, "Ananias," to which he replies, "Here I am, Lord," resurrecting the Isaianic servanthood formula (Isaiah 6 : 8). Christ instructs him to visit Straight Street—archaeologically identified thoroughfare still extant in Damascus—and lay hands on Saul. Ananias' reservations surface: reports of Saul's brutality have reached Damascus, and letters of extradition threaten believers. The vision answers fear with heavenly intel: Saul "is a chosen instrument to carry My name before Gentiles, kings, and Israel" (Acts 9 : 15). This triadic audience foreshadows Paul's eventual hearings before Agrippa, Caesar's household, and synagogue debates, demonstrating divine foreknowledge. Ananias obeys, becoming model of courageous pastoral ministry: he walks into potential arrest scenario yet believes Christ's assurance. The narrative underscores ecclesial necessity of human mediation in conversion; even spectacular encounters require community embrace for completion. Ananias greets Saul with familial term "Brother," preemptively extending forgiveness and inclusion. This act re-humanizes persecutor, reducing shame barrier and facilitating readiness for Spirit reception. Thus, the conversation between Jesus and Ananias forms indispensable subplot: it instructs church that prophetic obedience often involves risking safety to embrace God's unexpected choices.

12.3.2 Baptism, Spirit Filling, and Immediate Preaching (Acts 9 : 17-22)

Upon laying hands, Ananias announces dual purpose: Saul will regain sight and be filled with the Holy Spirit. Scales fall from Saul's eyes—literal healing symbolizing spiritual enlightenment—echoing Isaiah 35 : 5 promise that the eyes of the blind shall be opened. Baptism follows, perhaps in the courtyard mikveh of a Damascus home, marking covenant union with Christ and washing away sins (Acts 22 : 16). Unlike typical catechesis period, Saul transitions rapidly from candidate to proclaimer; "immediately he proclaimed Jesus in the synagogues" as Son of God (Acts 9 : 20). This accelerated deployment testifies to Spirit empowerment and Saul's existing scriptural mastery now refracted through Christological lens. Eyewitnesses marvel at reversal: the one who ravaged Jerusalem now confesses deity of Jesus. Luke notes that Saul "confounded the Jews... proving that Jesus was the Christ" (Acts 9 : 22). The Greek symbibazō (prove) implies stitching together arguments—Saul integrates Messianic prophecies with resurrection testimony. Community acceptance, however, remains cautious; some disciples in Jerusalem later fear him until Barnabas advocates (Acts 9 : 26-27). The Damascus baptism therefore initiates not only personal regeneration but a prolonged process of trust-building within churches traumatized by persecution. Modern missiology gleans from this sequence that radical converts need supportive mentors who both testify to authenticity and facilitate integration, showcasing holistic transformation rather than impulsive enthusiasm alone.

12.4. Early Formation, Desert Solitude, and Apostolic Confirmation

12.4.1 Retreat to Arabia and Reflection on Revelation (Galatians 1 : 15-17)

Paul's autobiographical note that he "did not immediately consult with flesh and blood... but went away into Arabia" intrigues commentators. Arabia likely refers to Nabataean territories south or east of Damascus; there, isolation among rugged valleys provided contemplative space akin to Elijah's Horeb retreat (1 Kings 19 : 8-18). Three years elapsed before Saul visited Jerusalem, suggesting extended theological reconfiguration. Desert solitude allowed reconciliation of revelation with Scripture, framing typological connections between Abrahamic promise, Mosaic law, and messianic fulfillment, later expounded in letters to Romans and Galatians. It also afforded respite from Damascus plots when persecutors conspired with city governor under ethnarch of Aretas (2 Corinthians 11 : 32-33). The pattern of encounter-withdrawal-return mirrors Christ's own ministry rhythms and Moses' forty-day Sinai immersion. Psychological studies indicate that transformational experiences require liminal phases for identity integration; Saul's Arabian sojourn fits such a model, enabling internalization of new calling before public ministry expansion. Spiritually, desert motifs evoke purification, dependence, and revelation; Pauline mysticism—visions of paradise (2 Corinthians 12 : 2-4)—may trace origins to this interval. Thus, the Damascus conversation initiates a process, not a one-time event, demonstrating that apostolic authority matures through seasons of hidden formation.

12.4.2 Jerusalem Visit, Barnabas Mediation, and Antioch Commissioning

After three years, Saul journeyed to Jerusalem to meet Peter and James, remaining fifteen days (Galatians 1 : 18-19). Barnabas, "son of encouragement," bridges fear gap, narrating Saul's conversion to skeptical apostles (Acts 9 : 27). This meeting validates Paul's gospel as congruent with Jerusalem leadership, cementing unity. Intense public debates with Hellenists reignite murder plots, prompting brothers to send Paul to Tarsus (Acts 9 : 30), where he ministers in Cilicia and Syria for nearly a decade (Galatians 1 : 21). During that hidden season, churches throughout Judea hear report, "He who once persecuted us now preaches the faith he once tried to destroy" (Galatians 1 : 23). Barnabas later seeks Paul for Antioch ministry, where for a full year they teach Gentile believers, and disciples first receive the name Christian (Acts 11 : 25-26). The Antioch episode culminates in Spirit-directed commissioning for missionary journeys (Acts 13 : 2-3), fulfilling Jesus' Damascus promise of Gentile witness. This timeline illustrates compounding layers of affirmation: divine encounter, prophetic mediation, desert refinement, apostolic endorsement, and Spirit-led sending. Each phase transforms Saul into Paul, apostle to nations.

Contemporary leadership development paradigms can mirror these progressive confirmations, emphasizing interior call, communal discernment, and Spirit sanction.

12.5. Doctrinal Contributions Rooted in the Damascus Revelation

12.5.1 Justification by Faith and the Righteousness of God

Paul's magisterial exposition of justification in Romans 3 : 21-26 and Galatians 2 : 15-21 flows directly from Damascus epiphany. Realizing he had been opposing God's Messiah despite meticulous law-keeping shattered the works-based righteousness paradigm, compelling embrace of gift righteousness "apart from the law." The phrase "faith in Jesus Christ" (or "faithfulness of Jesus Christ," pistis Christou debate) springs from personal revelation that Messiah's fidelity inaugurates new covenant. Paul's autobiographical argument—"whatever was gain, I counted loss" (Philippians 3 : 7-9)—references Damascus recalibration of value. His polemic against circumcision confidence arises from memory of pre-conversion zeal. Thus, key Reformation motifs, later championed by Luther and Calvin, anchor historically in the conversation between risen Christ and persecutor. The message that God justifies the ungodly (Saul personifying ungodliness) embodies lived exegesis, not abstract theory. Therefore, doctrinal orthodoxy and experiential testimony intertwine, cautioning theologians to ground propositions in transformational encounter.

12.5.2 Union with Christ, Suffering, and Eschatological Hope

Paul repeatedly avers that he is "crucified with Christ" (Galatians 2 : 20) and that believers participate in Christ's death and resurrection through Spirit baptism (Romans 6 : 3-5). These union motifs trace to Damascus identification text: Jesus merges Himself with church ("Me"). Realization that disciples' suffering equals Christ's suffering shaped Paul's theology of co-crucifixion, encouraging believers confronted with persecution. Moreover, Jesus' promise of future revelation of things Saul "will yet see" (Acts 26 : 16) fuels Paul's eschatological confidence; he teaches that present trials are "light afflictions" compared to eternal glory (2 Corinthians 4 : 17). Personal enumeration of hardships—beatings, shipwrecks, imprisonments (2 Corinthians 11 : 23-28)—demonstrates fidelity to Jesus' initial forecast: "I will show him how much he must suffer for My name" (Acts 9 : 16). This theology rejects triumphalism, asserting that union with Christ encompasses both power and pain. Contemporary disciples glean that conversion does not immunize from hardship; rather, it reframes suffering within resurrection horizon. Pastoral application invites communities to accompany new believers through trials, reminding them of Paul's pattern: initial vision leads into lifelong cross-shaped faithfulness.

12.6. Missional Legacy and Contemporary Resonances

12.6.1 Cross-Cultural Strategy and Letter-Writing Innovation

Paul's missionary methodology—urban center targeting, bivocational support, synagogue-to-agora preaching, contextualization of gospel idioms—springs from bicultural upbringing and Damascus call to Gentiles. He crafts epistles as portable sermons, pioneering trans-Mediterranean discipleship through parchment. Scholars credit him with adapting Greco-Roman letter conventions—thanksgiving, exhortation, paraenesis—and infusing them with theological weight. The Damascus conversation thus indirectly empowers global communication networks of the church. Modern digital ministry parallels Paul's letter strategy: using available technology to extend apostolic presence beyond physical reach. Additionally, cross-cultural sensitivity in Acts 17 speeches—quoting Greek poets—reflects Damascus mandate to "open their eyes… turn them from darkness to light" (Acts 26 : 18). Missiologists derive principles of redemptive analogy and cultural bridge-building from Paul's example.

12.6.2 De-Radicalization and Hope for Violent Extremists

Saul's metamorphosis offers case study for contemporary challenges of ideological extremism. Agencies combating religious violence examine factors in his transformation: encounter with dissonant evidence, empathetic inclusion by former targets, and re-channeling of zeal into constructive mission. Ananias's embrace models counter-radical measures of relationship and dignity. Post-Damascus Paul redirects rhetorical prowess toward peaceable persuasion rather than coercion, showcasing capacity of grace to reshape identity without erasing passion. Pastoral counselors working with radicalized individuals might leverage Saul's story, illustrating possibility of new allegiance and communal acceptance. Churches in conflict zones sustain hope that persecutors may become protectors, undergirded by Jesus' ongoing power to break into hostile ideologies with revelatory light.

Conclusion

From the blinding radiance that halted Saul's murderous march to the gentle voice that called him "brother" through Ananias, the post-ascension conversation with Saul of Tarsus reveals that Jesus' resurrection life extends far beyond empty tomb and Galilean breakfast fires. It thunders along dusty Syrian roads, slips into prophetic visions, saturates desert solitude, and echoes in letters addressed to Corinthian dockworkers and Roman aristocrats alike. Saul's encounter teaches that no personal history—however violent, bigoted, or self-righteous—can outmuscle an unveiling of the risen Lord's glory. It demonstrates that divine call involves both vertical revelation and horizontal reconciliation, demanding community participation to nurture new identity. Doctrine of justification, theology of suffering, and global missiology all trace tributaries back to that midday collision outside Damascus, when light eclipsed credentials and grace baptized a persecutor in tears. For modern readers navigating polarized cultures, Paul's transformation embodies undying hope that Christ still interrupts journeys, still asks pointed questions, still grants sight to the blind, and still retools zeal for kingdom service. As Part 1 of these post-ascension conversations, the Damascus-road story anchors the entire collection: it sings that resurrection is not museum piece but missionary engine, turning enemies into emissaries, skeptics into servants, and roads of rage into rivers of redemption.

Chapter 13. Post-Ascension Conversations - To John on Patmos

Perched in the lower Aegean Sea some forty miles off the coast of Asia Minor, the volcanic island of Patmos sits rugged and largely treeless, its crags exposed to blazing summer sun and biting winter winds. The Roman Empire used such marginal outposts as penal colonies, scattering political or religious offenders among fishermen's huts, small quarries, and subsistence plots. It was here—"because of the word of God and the testimony of Jesus" (Revelation 1 : 9)—that an elderly apostle named John found himself consigned, his only companions the sea, the sky, and the Spirit. Although nearly six decades had passed since the first Easter morning, the risen Christ had not ceased speaking; the resurrected voice that had thundered along the Damascus road to Saul now broke forth again, this time in the crashing surf of Patmos, summoning John into visions that would become the Apocalypse. Those conversations between the glorified Jesus and His last surviving apostle supply the church with its most sustained post-ascension dialogue: the heavenly Christ dictating pastoral letters, unsealing cosmic scrolls, interpreting symbol-laden judgments, and concluding with personal promises of imminent return. The book of Revelation is thus not merely a prophetic panorama but an extended symposium in which the exalted Lord mentors, consoles, and commissions His servant in exile. In what follows, we will examine these Patmos conversations in expansive detail, attending to their historical context, literary artistry, theological depth, and pastoral resonance. Each major section and its subsections will unfold in no fewer than fifteen sentences, ensuring space to probe texture and nuance. Our journey will move from the stark geography of Patmos to the shimmering throne room of heaven; from seven concrete congregations along Asia's postal road to the eschatological wedding of the Lamb; from John's trembling fall at Jesus' feet to the final invitation, "Come, Lord Jesus." Along the way, Scripture references will anchor claims, and early-church echoes will illuminate background. By the chapter's end, readers should grasp why the Patmos conversations remain indispensable for understanding Christ's ongoing lordship, the church's endurance under persecution, and the hope that sings across centuries that history is securely in the wounded, radiant hands of the Alpha and the Omega.

13.1. Political Exile and Prophetic Readiness

13.1.1 Imperial Hostility under Domitian and the Banishment of John

The late first century witnessed a tightening spiral of imperial ideology, especially under Emperor Domitian (AD 81-96), whose penchant for titles such as *Dominus et Deus* ("Lord and God") provoked friction with monotheistic communities. Provincial governors eager to curry favor enforced local manifestations of emperor worship, compelling civic assemblies to burn incense before his bust, a ritual Christians interpreted as idolatrous (cf. Revelation 13 : 15). John—long a pillar among the Ephesian churches—refused to participate in such cultic homage, thereby attracting legal scrutiny framed in language of social agitation, a charge similar to which Paul and Silas had earlier faced in Philippi (Acts 16 : 20-21). Roman law allowed proconsuls to sentence troublesome figures to temporary exile (*relegatio in insulam*), stripping them of property while sparing life; Patmos, lacking strategic value yet reachable by short military transport, suited this purpose. The banishment severed John from beloved congregations, echoing Jeremiah's deportation to Egypt and Ezekiel's captivity beside Chebar, prophetic precedents that ironically heightened revelatory receptivity. In the silence of imperial punishment, John's Sabbath routines—scroll study, prayer rhythms, and recollection of Galilean memories—intensified, each wave pounding the shore a metronome for meditation. He was "in the Spirit on the Lord's Day" (Revelation 1 : 10), indicating charismatic influx that transcended geographical isolation. Roman authorities aimed to mute his witness; heaven prepared to amplify it through visions so expansive that no mainland pulpit could have contained them. Thus political hostility became prophetic incubator, showcasing the paradox that empire's attempt to quarantine the gospel instead positioned its servant for the broadest revelation of Christ's dominion over kings of earth (Revelation 1 : 5). Modern disciples glean here a lesson: external exile can precipitate internal encounter, and state oppression may unwittingly set the stage for unprecedented articulation of divine sovereignty. Indeed, by exiling one aging preacher, Rome inadvertently ensured that Asian congregations—and eventually the global church—would receive a prophetic letter unmarred by local distractions and baptized in apocalyptic splendor. History's irony underlines providence: the very decree meant to silence the apostle became conduit for heaven's most thunderous proclamation.

13.1.2 John's Apostolic Pedigree and Pastoral Burden Prior to Patmos

Before Patmos became his address, John carried decades-long responsibility for a constellation of congregations in Ephesus, Smyrna, and surrounding valleys, a network developed during Paul's Ephesian ministry (Acts

19 : 10) and nurtured by subsequent laborers like Timothy (1 Timothy 1 : 3). Tradition identifies John as "the beloved disciple" of the Fourth Gospel, custodian of Mary the mother of Jesus (John 19 : 26-27), and eyewitness of transfiguration glory (Matthew 17 : 1-9). These formative experiences layered his memory with both tenderness and thunder—resting on Jesus' chest at supper (John 13 : 23) yet desiring fire upon Samaritan villages (Luke 9 : 54). As decades unfolded, youthful zeal matured into fatherly counsel; his later epistles address readers as "little children" and urge love-infused orthodoxy (1 John 2 : 1; 3 : 18). John had witnessed Jerusalem's destruction in AD 70, the martyrdom of peers like James and Peter, and the creeping assimilation pressures of Hellenistic culture. Each loss intensified pastoral burden to guard truth and nurture endurance. By the time Domitian's edict arrived, John's frame was old but spirit unbowed; exile severed him physically yet could not erase a shepherd's concern. He likely prayed the names of elders—Polycarp of Smyrna, Antipas of Pergamum (Revelation 2 : 13), and others whose faces flickered in memory as he scanned night skies for divine reassurance. His heart carried scrolls yet unwritten, songs yet unsung, warnings yet unspoken. Therefore, when Christ's voice broke the Patmos stillness, it addressed not only one isolated saint but a vast pastoral network beating within his chest. The subsequent visions thus bear unmistakable pastoral grammar: praise for perseverance, rebuke for compromise, promise for sufferers. John's personal biography infused apocalyptic symbolism with experiential authenticity; dragons and beasts were not mere fantasy but coded reflections of oppressive systems he had tasted firsthand. His apostolic pedigree therefore functions not as distant credential but as living fiber weaving Revelation's urgency; the book echoes Galilean mornings, upper-room whisperings, and Calvary's shadows, all refracted through Mediterranean exile into a cosmic call.

13.2. The First Christophany: Voice, Vision, and Commission

13.2.1 Sound of a Trumpet and Turning to See the Speaking Voice

John's initial encounter begins audibly: "I heard behind me a loud voice like a trumpet" (Revelation 1 : 10), a simile rooting the experience in Sinai imagery where shofar blasts heralded divine descent (Exodus 19 : 16). Positionally, the voice originates behind John, requiring physical turning—a gesture symbolizing repentance and re-orientation toward divine revelation. Throughout prophetic literature, hearing precedes seeing; Isaiah hears seraphim before beholding throne (Isaiah 6 : 3-4), and Ezekiel catches the sound of rushing before witnessing wheels within wheels (Ezekiel 3 : 12-13). This auditory primacy emphasizes faith's reliance on divine word prior to visual confirmation (Romans 10 : 17). The trumpet voice commands, "Write what you see in a scroll and send it to the seven churches" (Revelation 1 : 11). Thus, revelation is immediately mediated toward community; personal vision must become corporate edification. Turning, John beholds seven golden lampstands—imagery echoing tabernacle menorah (Exodus 25 : 31-37) yet multiplied, signifying plural congregations as together forming one portable sanctuary. Christ stands "in the midst," fulfilling promise to walk among His people (Leviticus 26 : 12) and Jesus' own words, "Where two or three gather… I am among them" (Matthew 18 : 20). The structural placement of Jesus within—not above or outside—lampstands underscores immanence amid spiritual struggle. The progression from trumpet voice to inner-sanctum vision frames Revelation as liturgy: call to worship followed by unveiling of priest-king who inspects candled communities. For exiled John, hearing before seeing affirmed that distance, darkness, or blindness cannot impede divine communication; the Word penetrates limitations, re-orienting disciple posture for sight beyond surface.

13.2.2 Portrait of the Glorified Son of Man and Fear-Displacing Assurance

The risen Christ's appearance combines Danielic, priestly, and judicial motifs: robe reaching to feet and golden sash identify high-priestly function (Exodus 28 : 4); hair white like wool recalls Ancient of Days (Daniel 7 : 9), transferring eternality to Son of Man; eyes like blazing fire denote penetrating insight (Revelation 1 : 14). Feet like burnished bronze echo Daniel 10 : 6's angelic messenger, symbolizing stability amid molten persecution. Voice like many waters evokes Ezekiel 43 : 2, where glory fills temple; here, Christ's speech itself becomes waterfall, drowning competing imperial propaganda. In His right hand He holds seven stars, later explained as "angels" or messengers of churches (Revelation 1 : 20), illustrating sovereign grip on leadership. From His mouth issues a sharp two-edged sword, the Isaiahic weapon of messianic judgment (Isaiah 11 : 4) and Hebrews' living word (Hebrews 4 : 12). Face shining like sun at full strength (Revelation 1 : 16) parallels transfiguration radiance (Matthew 17 : 2), confirming continuity between earthly and exalted Jesus. Confronted by such composite glory, John collapses "as though dead" (Revelation 1 : 17), reliving earlier transfiguration prostration yet now without fellow disciples to assist. Jesus lays right hand upon him—the same hand holding cosmic stars—marrying vast power with tender touch, echoing angelic reassurance to Daniel (Daniel 10 : 10). The declaration "Fear not" inaugurates discourse; Christ's first post-ascension word to John addresses emotional paralysis, granting capacity to receive further revelation. Titles follow: "I am the First and the Last, the Living One; I was dead, and behold I am alive forevermore, and I have the keys of Death and Hades" (Revelation 1 : 17-18). These phrases blend Isaianic Yahweh titles (Isaiah 44 : 6) with resurrection vindication, cementing high Christology. The keys signify judicial competence to unlock graves—contrasting Domitian's claimed power to dispense life and death. Thus, the vision functions as Christ's credential presentation, ensuring John—and through him the churches—anchor courage not in geopolitical prospects but in crucified-risen Lord who transcends temporal rulers. For persecuted readers then and now, this Christophany displaces fear by exalting a Savior whose blazing gaze allies with pastoral touch, whose voice commands galaxies yet stoops to steady fainting saints.

13.3. Seven Letters: Diagnostic Conversations with the Churches

13.3.1 Ephesus, Smyrna, Pergamum, and Thyatira— Commendations, Corrections, and Covenants

To Ephesus Christ writes as one "who holds the seven stars... and walks in the midst of the seven lampstands" (Revelation 2 : 1), contextualizing remedy within relational presence. He praises toil, perseverance, and doctrinal vigilance against Nicolaitan distortions, highlighting that orthodoxy matters. Yet He pinpoints forsaken first love, revealing that doctrinal accuracy divorced from affectionate devotion shrivels witness. Call to remember, repent, and repeat initial works provides three-step recovery; failure risks lampstand removal—loss of corporate testimony. Promise to overcomers—access to tree of life (Revelation 2 : 7)—reverses Eden's exile, underscoring that intimacy fuels eschatological reward. Smyrna receives unqualified commendation; their poverty contrasted with spiritual richness disarms prosperity ethos (Revelation 2 : 9). Forewarning of ten-day tribulation evokes Daniel's ten-day test (Daniel 1 : 14-15) and encourages faithfulness unto death, secured by crown of life. Pergamum dwells "where Satan's throne is" (Revelation 2 : 13), possibly referencing imperial cult altar or Asclepius serpent shrine. Despite martyrdom of Antipas, some tolerate Balaam-like teaching promoting sexual immorality and idolatrous feasts. Jesus threatens warfare with sword of His mouth—a reminder that spiritual compromise invites Christ's disciplinary intervention. Yet to conquerors He grants hidden manna and a white stone with secret name, blending exodus provision and Greco-Roman legal tokens signifying acquittal. Thyatira, smallest city yet longest letter, faces censure for "Jezebel" prophetess seducing servants into syncretism (Revelation 2 : 20). Christ, with eyes of fire and feet of bronze (imagery reused from initial vision), promises search of minds and hearts—a divine MRI exposing motives. Still, He commends love, faith, and increasing works; those holding fast receive authority over nations and morning star, pledging participation in messianic reign. Across these four letters, conversations oscillate between affirmation and admonition, illustrating Jesus' holistic pastoral care that celebrates virtue, confronts vice, and always attaches eschatological incentive. Each diagnosis addresses specific socio-cultural pressures: Ephesus's bustling commerce breeding distraction, Smyrna's slander from hostile synagogue, Pergamum's imperial pageantry, Thyatira's guild banquets. Jesus contextualizes counsel, modeling missional engagement that neither ignores local nuance nor compromises universal holiness. Contemporary churches glean frameworks for self-assessment: scrutinize love, suffering, truth, and purity in light of Christ's omniscient gaze.

13.3.2 Sardis, Philadelphia, and Laodicea—Wake-Up Calls, Open Doors, and Lukewarm Warnings

Sardis carries reputation for vitality yet is spiritually comatose (Revelation 3 : 1). Christ introduces Himself as holder of God's seven-fold Spirit, asylum for revitalization. He commands wakefulness and strengthening what remains, invoking city's history of sudden conquest due to lax nightwatch. Incomplete works reveal facade religiosity; remedy involves remembering gospel, obeying, and vigilant watch, lest visitation arrive like thief. Yet a remnant "few names" walks worthy, destined for white garments of victorious procession. Philadelphia, though of "little power," receives open door that none can shut, alluding to eschatological pilgrimage and missionary opportunity (Revelation 3 : 7-8). Jesus' key of David ensures sovereign access; synagogue adversaries will eventually acknowledge church as beloved. Promise to keep them from hour of trial links to Exodus Passover covering and frames perseverance as shield. Overcomers become pillars in God's temple, inscribed with tri-fold name—God, city, and Christ's new name—granting unshakable belonging. Laodicea, affluent banking and medical hub, epitomizes self-sufficiency; Christ's Amen title counters human boasts. Lukewarm temperature, scorned by locals who piped in tepid water, symbolizes half-hearted spirituality. Jesus' severe threat to vomit them warns against complacency. Yet counsel to purchase refined gold, white garments, and eye salve repurposes local industries (finance, textiles, ophthalmology) into spiritual directives. Zealous repentance matters because those disciplined are loved. The famed door-knock invitation (Revelation 3 : 20) pictures Christ seeking restored fellowship, not initial salvation, and climaxes with throne-sharing promise for conquerors. Collectively, these letters reveal Jesus' adaptive conversation: rebuking dead orthodoxy, empowering fragile faith, and shocking affluent indifference. They underscore participatory eschatology where final rewards echo local contexts, transforming everyday symbols into eternal realities. Modern congregations hear echoes: reputations misaligned with reality, small churches undervalued yet entrusted with mission, suburban comforts breeding apathy. The Patmos dialogues thus transcend time, speaking incisively to each era's blind spots while exalting steadfast Savior who both diagnoses and heals.

13.4. Invitation to the Throne Room: Heavenly Dialogue and Covenant Scroll

13.4.1 *"Come Up Here"—Trans-Dimensional Worship and Cosmic Perspective*

After letters conclude, John sees "a door standing open in heaven" and hears the trumpet-like voice beckon, "Come up here" (Revelation 4 : 1), mirroring earlier summons yet now transposing vantage from earth's persecution to heaven's sovereignty. Instantly "in the Spirit," he beholds throne imagery saturated with Ezekiel and Isaiah allusions: jasper and carnelian radiance, emerald rainbow, twenty-four elders, and four living creatures (Revelation 4 : 2-8). The centerpiece is not militaristic arsenal but worship—unceasing "Holy, holy, holy" (Isaiah 6 : 3) re-voiced through cosmic choir. By inviting John into heavenly control room, Christ recalibrates persecuted imagination; Caesar's throne in Rome pales before this emerald-encircled sovereignty. The conversation here is primarily liturgical: creatures and elders cast crowns, exalting Creator's worthiness, while John silently internalizes doxological rhythm. This vision teaches that ultimate reality is ceaseless adoration; temporal afflictions cannot dethrone One whose rule is chorused by seraphim. Moreover, twenty-four elders likely symbolize combined patriarchal tribes and apostolic witnesses—old and new covenant leadership united—assuring John that history culminates in covenant harmony. The open door motif encourages suffering believers: ingress into divine presence remains unobstructed despite earthly exclusion. Thus Christ converses via spectacle rather than speech, embedding theology in sensory worship that re-orients mission around throne-centered existence.

13. 4.2 The Sealed Scroll, the Lion-Lamb Paradox, and Cosmological Authority

A mighty angel inquires, "Who is worthy to open the scroll?"— eliciting universal silence, triggering John's weeping as he senses cosmic stalemate (Revelation 5 : 2-4). One elder consoles: "The Lion of Judah has conquered" (Genesis 49 : 9). John turns expecting leonine conqueror but instead beholds "a Lamb standing as slain" (Revelation 5 : 6). This visual paradox discloses conversation about power redefined through sacrifice; Christus Victor emerges as Agnus Dei. Seven horns and seven eyes signify perfect authority and Spirit's plenitude; the Lamb approaches throne and takes scroll, a liturgical drama conveying transfer of sovereign agency. Heaven erupts in new song: "Worthy are You to take the scroll... for You were slain, and by Your blood You ransomed people" (Revelation 5 : 9). The dialogue thus contains juridical decree: redemptive death authorizes eschatological unfolding. John's tears transform into worship, instructing readers that grief over seeming injustice yields to praise when Lamb's worthiness dawns. Christ's ability to open seals confirms earlier key-holding claim, extending authority from death's gates to destiny's script. Consequently, subsequent seal, trumpet, and bowl judgments unfold as outworking of Lamb-authorized scroll, ensuring that tribulations are neither random nor outside Christ's lordship. Pastoral implication: persecuted churches can trust that even calamities follow Lamb's manuscript leading to ultimate rescue.

13.5. Prophetic Re-Commission: Eating the Scroll and Measuring the Temple

13.5.1 Angel with Little Book—Sweet Reception, Bitter Proclamation

In Revelation 10, John sees another mighty angel straddling sea and land, rainbow-crowned, face like sun—attributes echoing Christophany yet here angelic envoy. He holds a "little scroll" open, contrasting sealed scroll previously held by Lamb, suggesting digestible prophetic portion for John. Voice from heaven orders John to take and eat scroll, paralleling Ezekiel 3 : 1-3 where sweet taste precedes lament message. John obeys; sweetness fills mouth, bitterness churns stomach (Revelation 10 : 9-10), symbolizing experiential ambivalence of gospel proclamation—joy of revelation mingled with anguish over impending judgments. He is told, "You must prophesy again about many peoples, nations, languages, and kings" (Revelation 10 : 11). Thus conversation transitions from reception to commission: isolation on Patmos does not retire apostolic duty; digestion equips articulation. The interplay between sensory metaphors and missionary mandate reinforces incarnational theology—word must be internalized, metabolized, then articulated. For modern preachers, the episode warns that proclamation costs emotional turmoil; sweet insight often turns bitter when confronting idolatry and injustice. Yet obedience demands ingestion regardless of aftertaste, trusting that Spirit will transmute discomfort into transformative speech.

13.5.2 Measuring of the Sanctuary and Testimony of Two Witnesses

The act echoes Ezekiel's temple vision (Ezekiel 40-42) and Zechariah's measuring line (Zechariah 2 : 1-5), symbolizing preservation amid judgment. Christ thereby converses through prophetic gesture: persecution may trample outer structures, but worshipping community remains marked off. Immediately narrative introduces two witnesses clothed in sackcloth, lampstands before Lord, empowered to prophesy 1,260 days, breathe fire, shut sky, and call plagues—Moses-Elijah archetypes. Beast from abyss kills them; bodies lie in street, world rejoices, but after three-and-a-half days Spirit raises them, and they ascend in cloud (Revelation 11 : 3-12). This drama parallels Christ's passion-resurrection-ascension sequence, reinforcing theme that witness involves death and vindication. Conversation between Christ and His church thus extends through symbolic actors: prophets who embody message of perseverance unto death. Measuring plus martyrs assures John's audience that while external courts may succumb to imperial violence, true temple—people indwelt by Spirit—will stand and be resurrected. For congregations facing execution or marginalization, this promise anchors courage. Contemporary theologians debate identity of witnesses—literal individuals, prophetic church, or Israel-church duo—but pastoral thrust remains: Jesus converses not only via words but via historical enactments, weaving martyrdom into redemptive tapestry.

13.6. Final Dialogues: "Behold, I Am Coming Soon" and Eschatological Consolation

13.6.1 Marriage Supper, Rider on White Horse, and New Creation Pledges

Approaching book's climax, John hears thunderous "Hallelujahs" announcing Lord God Almighty's reign and bride's readiness clothed in righteous acts (Revelation 19 : 6-8). An angel instructs him to write, "Blessed are those invited to the marriage supper of the Lamb" (Revelation 19 : 9), underscoring nuptial intimacy as consummate goal of redemptive chronology. John attempts to worship angel, but is corrected: "Worship God" (Revelation 19 : 10), highlighting conversation's theological boundary—mediators point to Christ alone. Next, heaven opens and Christ appears riding white horse, named Faithful and True, eyes blazing, wearing many crowns (Revelation 19 : 11-12). From His mouth protrudes sharp sword to strike nations; yet His robe dipped in blood suggests victory through self-sacrifice rather than merely forthcoming battle. He is Word of God, echoing Johannine prologue (John 1 : 1), and King of kings. The ensuing defeat of beast and false prophet cements supremacy over tyrannical structures. Subsequently, Satan's thousand-year binding, final rebellion, and lake-of-fire judgment portray comprehensive eradication of evil (Revelation 20 : 1-10). Great white throne scene judges dead by books, but Lamb's book of life ensures mercy (Revelation 20 : 11-15). New heaven and new earth descend; God's dwelling with humanity reverses Edenic exile (Revelation 21 : 1-3). Christ's voice proclaims, "Behold, I make all things new... It is done!" (Revelation 21 : 5-6), paralleling Calvary's "It is finished" (John 19 : 30), linking cross to cosmos renewal. Thus, Patmos conversations culminate not with private consolation but cosmic renovation; Jesus narrates future not as speculative crossword but as promise anchored in His authority. Persecuted saints glimpse ultimate table where tears are wiped, death abolished, and thirst quenched with water of life freely given (Revelation 21 : 4-6).

13.6.2 Triplicate "I Am Coming Soon," Beatitudes, and Final Invitation

Three times in Revelation 22 Jesus assures, "I am coming soon" (Revelation 22 : 7, 12, 20), reinforcing immediacy. Each declaration couples exhortation: keep words of prophecy, wash robes, render reward according to deeds. Beatitude formula—"Blessed is the one who keeps..." (Revelation 22 : 7)—mirrors Sermon on the Mount, transferring discipleship ethic into apocalyptic frame. Angel again rebuffs John's worship impulse, stating "I am a fellow servant" (Revelation 22 : 9), directing all adoration to God; repeated correction underlines threat of displaced devotion amid awe. Jesus self-identifies as "Alpha and Omega, Root and Descendant of David, Bright Morning Star" (Revelation 22 : 13-16), uniting origin and consummation, covenant monarchy, and dawn herald. The Spirit and the bride then echo invitation, "Come!" and extend to thirsty outsider the gift of life's water (Revelation 22 : 17). Thus, final Patmos conversation widens from private vision to catholic call, enlisting every reader into eschatological anticipation and evangelistic hospitality. Closing warning against altering prophecy (Revelation 22 : 18-19) safeguards revelatory integrity. John's final utterance, "Amen. Come, Lord Jesus!" (Revelation 22 : 20), transforms conversation into corporate prayer shaping liturgical history—Marana tha (1 Corinthians 16 : 22). The grace benediction (Revelation 22 : 21) assures continual relational presence until Parousia. For believers across centuries, these verses serve as devotional anchor; daily reading of Revelation ends not with beasts but with Bridegroom promise. Thus, Patmos dialogs close with forward momentum, propelling church to mission, holiness, and hopeful endurance until trumpet voice once again splits sky.

13.7. Theological, Pastoral, and Missional Implications

13.7.1 High Christology and Trinitarian Worship under Persecution

Revelation's Patmos conversations articulate one of the highest Christologies in Scripture, presenting Jesus as Yahweh's self-identification ("First and Last"), crucified Lamb, cosmic Judge, and Bridegroom. Simultaneously, the Spirit speaks repeatedly ("the Spirit says to the churches," Revelation 2 : 7) and cooperates with the Bride in final invitation (Revelation 22 : 17), revealing Trinitarian dynamic. Such exalted vision is not academic; it anchors worship amid imperial cult pressure. By locating sovereignty in heaven, Revelation relativizes emperor veneration, empowering marginal communities to maintain exclusive devotion. Modern Christians facing nationalist ideologies draw courage from same vision: allegiance transcends passport to throne above. Moreover, apocalyptic symbolism invites imaginative worship expressions—hymns, art, liturgy—that narrate theological truths through doxology. Revelation's heavenly liturgy shaped early Eucharistic prayers; today it inspires global songs referencing "Holy, holy, holy" and "Worthy is the Lamb." Thus,

Patmos dialogues cultivate worship that is both resistant and resplendent.

13.7.2 Discipleship Ethic of Patient Endurance and Prophetic Imagination

Repeated exhortation to "overcome" (*nikaō*) weaves moral urgency into visionary fabric. Overcoming involves doctrinal fidelity (Ephesus), fearless witness (Smyrna), sexual purity (Thyatira), vigilance (Sardis), mission faithfulness (Philadelphia), and repentance from complacency (Laodicea). Therefore, discipleship integrates belief, behavior, and perseverance. Coupling of present obedience with future reward nurtures prophetic imagination: believers visualize hidden manna, pillar status, throne co-reigning, motivating endurance. In contexts of social ostracism or technological overload, Revelation's vivid storytelling realigns imagination from dystopia to doxology. Pastors can harness apocalyptic art to disciple congregations—using murals, dramatic readings, or worship stations that embody lampstands and river of life. Missiologically, open-door promise (Philadelphia) energizes church planting; measuring-rod vision galvanizes justice advocacy, asserting God's protective concern for oppressed worshippers. Hence, Patmos conversations spawn praxis: sanctity, solidarity, creativity, and courage until lion-lamb returns.

Conclusion

The island of Patmos, once Rome's strategy to silence an aging apostle, became heaven's megaphone amplifying the risen Christ's most panoramic conversation with His church. Across thunderous trumpets, visionary portraits, pastoral letters, heavenly liturgies, scrolls devoured, and promises thundered, Jesus disclosed that exile cannot extinguish revelation, persecution cannot unseat sovereignty, and martyrdom cannot overturn the marriage supper already set. John's record of these dialogues grants suffering congregations a lexicon of hope, infuses worship with cosmic perspective, and summons every generation to vigilance, purity, and mission. The Christ who walked among lampstands on Patmos still inspects congregations today; the Lamb who opened sealed destiny still shepherds history toward new-creation dawn; the Rider whose sword is word still topples pretentious beasts; and the Groom whose Spirit whispers "Come" still quickens the bride to prayerful longing. Therefore, study of Patmos conversations is never mere academic exercise—it is rehearsal for reality, catechesis for courage, and catalyst for worship. As we echo John's final plea, "Amen. Come, Lord Jesus," we inhabit the closing note of that Aegean exchange, confident that the grace of the Lord Jesus will sustain His saints until the voice like many waters is heard not in vision but in unveiled glory.

Chapter 14. Why These Jesus' post-resurrection Words Matter

Post-resurrection Words—those electrifying occasions when the crucified but risen Jesus conversed with Mary Magdalene outside the tomb (John 20 : 11-18), with frightened apostles in a locked room (Luke 24 : 36-49; John 20 : 19-23), with skeptical Thomas (John 20 : 24-29), with defeated fishermen on a Galilean beach (John 21 : 1-23), with two bewildered travelers on the Emmaus road (Luke 24 : 13-35), with the once-scoffing brother James (1 Corinthians 15 : 7), with militant Saul on his Damascus mission (Acts 9 : 1-19), and with the aged apostle John marooned on Patmos (Revelation 1 – 3)—form a multivoiced symphony that resonates far beyond first-century Palestine. Each encounter brims with historical particularity, theological depth, psychological realism, pastoral tenderness, missional urgency, and eschatological horizon. This concluding chapter asks a question as old as Christian proclamation itself: Why do these Words matter? And it refuses a reductionistic answer. They matter because they fuse heaven and earth, past and future, individual healing and global commission, doctrinal clarity and embodied compassion. They matter because they display the risen Christ in all His relational variegation—able to whisper a woman's name and topple an ideologue's world on a dusty road. They matter because they supply indispensable building blocks for Christian doctrine: Christology, pneumatology, ecclesiology, soteriology, and eschatology each take decisive shape in the after-Easter conversations. They matter because they supply spiritual medicine for every generation's wounds: grief, shame, fear, doubt, complacency, persecution, and fractured identity. They matter because they demonstrate that resurrection is not a single event locked in antiquity but an ongoing interactional reality in which the living Jesus speaks, corrects, commissions, and consoles. What follows unfolds in seven expansive sections, each divided into two fifteen-sentence subsections, mapping how the Words operate on intersecting planes of history, theology, church life, pastoral care, apologetics, mission, and spiritual formation. The aim is not merely to inform but to ignite—so that contemporary readers, congregations, and cultures might hear afresh the risen Lord's voice and respond with Mary's obedience, Thomas's confession, Peter's loyalty, James's holiness, Paul's zeal, and John's worship.

14.1. Historical Reliability and Canonical Memory

14.1.1 Eyewitness Texture and Polyphonic Testimony

The post-resurrection Words ground Christian proclamation in concrete, verifiable history rather than mythic abstraction. Each account brims with incidental details that bear the stamp of memory: folded linen cloths in an otherwise vacant tomb (John 20 : 7), charred fish cooking on a shoreline fire (John 21 : 9), the mile count of sixty stadia en route to Emmaus (Luke 24 : 13), or the precise Syrian street name "Straight" in Damascus (Acts 9 : 11). Such specificity functions as an implicit invitation to scrutiny, for invented legends rarely lavish care on mundane minutiae that contemporaries could contest. Moreover, the Words come from multiple independent sources—John, Luke-Acts, Paul, and Revelation—

representing at least four authors, three genres, and two language communities. Their overlapping yet non-collusive testimony satisfies historiographical criteria of multiple attestation. Diversity of witnesses adds credibility: Mary Magdalene was a Galilean woman of marginal social capital; Thomas was a pessimist prone to pessimistic literalism; James was a formerly skeptical sibling; Paul a hostile Pharisee and Roman citizen; John a venerable pastor-theologian. That such varied personalities separately affirm encounters with the risen Christ suggests objective reality rather than collective wish-fulfillment. Even apparent discrepancies—two angels versus one, Galilee versus Jerusalem—exhibit the rough edges expected of genuine reminiscence rather than air-brushed fabrication, inviting harmonious synthesis rather than cynical dismissal. Furthermore, earliest creedal formulations—delivered within five years of Easter (1 Corinthians 15 : 3-7)—embed these appearances in public worship, indicating that their historical core was common currency well before the Gospels crystallized. Modern historiography acknowledges that living eyewitnesses who risk reputational and physical harm, yet persist in proclaiming contested events, offer strong evidential weight. Therefore, the Words matter for history because they anchor faith in data, not mere desire. They assure twenty-first-century disciples that Christianity's risen center rests on testimonies nobody convincingly disproved in the generation most capable of doing so. As Luke insists, the risen Christ "presented Himself alive... by many convincing proofs" (Acts 1 : 3), and those proofs still stand.

14.1.2 Creedal Transmission and Liturgical Embedding

Beyond narrative accounts, the Words shaped early creeds and worship patterns, serving as mnemonic anchors for communities that lacked widespread literacy. The rhythmic formula—"Christ died for our sins... He was buried... He was raised... He appeared" (1 Corinthians 15 : 3-7)—functions as proto-creed, encapsulating core events and specific interlocutors (Cephas, the Twelve, five hundred, James, and Paul). Liturgists observe that baptismal confessions in second-century texts such as the *Interrogatory Creed of*

Hippolytus mimic this quadruple structure, signaling that post-resurrection Words were recited over baptismal waters as entry into ecclesial memory. Eucharistic prayers, too, echo the Emmaus feast where Jesus "was made known... in the breaking of bread" (Luke 24 : 35), integrating resurrection conversation into weekly liturgy. In this way, the Words transcend historiography to become living memory rehearsed in communal rhythms, immune to individual forgetfulness or geographic dispersion. Such ritualization ensures that what the apostles heard, the next generations sang, chanted, and prayed; thus, the Words mattered because they provided durable frames for transmitting gospel events across cultures—from Aramaic-speaking Judea to Greek Asia Minor and Latin Rome. Scholars of oral tradition note that narratives linked to dramatic action—like Thomas touching wounds or Paul falling blind—achieve higher retention rates. Consequently, the post-Easter conversations became catechetical touchstones: children learned the faith not by abstract propositions alone but by vivid scenes where Jesus calls names and cooks breakfast. Today's church inherits these liturgical echoes; every "Christ has died, Christ is risen, Christ will come again" resounds with centuries of recollected conversations. Hence, to dismiss or downplay the Words would be to sever a golden strand that has woven Christians into a single remembering body since the first baptisms in Jordan and the earliest hymns scratched on catacomb walls.

14.2. Theological Architecture of the Risen Christ's Speech

14.2.1 Developing High Christology through Face-to-Face Encounters

The Words decisively shape the church's understanding of who Jesus is—not merely a resurrected mortal but the Lord of glory (James 2 : 1), the Alpha and Omega (Revelation 1 : 17), and the One in whom the fullness of deity dwells (Colossians 2 : 9). When Thomas blurts "My Lord and my God" (John 20 : 28), he supplies the highest Christological confession in the Gospels, triggered not by philosophical deduction but by tactile confrontation. Similarly, Saul addresses the blinding presence as "Lord" (Acts 9 : 5), attributing to Jesus the divine prerogative to redefine Torah allegiance. Mary Magdalene's recognition—"Rabboni" (John 20 : 16)—melds affectionate discipleship with reverent submission. In Revelation's Patmos vision, Christ merges titles previously reserved for Yahweh—"First and Last," "Living One"—further elevating Him above angelic mediators (Revelation 1 : 17-18). Thus, high Christology was not a late Hellenistic embellishment; it was birthed in Words days and decades after Easter, when monotheistic Jews experienced Jesus exercising divine functions: forgiving sins (John 20 : 23), wielding cosmic keys (Revelation 1 : 18), and authoritatively interpreting Scripture (Luke 24 : 27). Systematic theology therefore depends on these conversations to articulate Incarnation's ongoing implications: the same Jesus who hungered, wept, and bled now governs galaxies yet retains scarred hands. The Words matter because they prevent separation between historical Jesus and theological Christ; they display continuity between the Jesus of Nazareth who taught by Lake Galilee and the exalted Lord who stands amid lampstands—and they do so within the lived testimony of firsthand witnesses.

14.2.2 Trinitarian Revelation in Resurrection Speech and Breath

These dialogs also reveal Trinitarian dynamics essential to orthodox faith. Early on Resurrection Day, Jesus breathes on disciples and says, "Receive the Holy Spirit" (John 20 : 22), reenacting Genesis 2 : 7 and foreshadowing Pentecost. In that single action, the Son mediates the Spirit from the Father (cf. John 15 : 26), demonstrating intra-Trinitarian mission. Similarly, on Patmos the glorified Christ repeatedly ends each letter with the phrase, "Hear what the Spirit says to the churches" (Revelation 2 – 3), intertwining His own words with the Spirit's oracles. At Saul's conversion Jesus assures Ananias, "He is a chosen instrument of Mine" (Acts 9 : 15), yet it is the Spirit who fills Saul for proclamation (Acts 9 : 17). These patterns became fodder for the church's later creeds, such as Nicea-Constantinople's language of the Spirit "who proceeds from the Father [and the Son]." Without the Words,

Trinitarian theology might rest primarily on pre-Easter hints; with them, it gains post-Easter confirmation that Father, Son, and Spirit cooperate in redemption. Therefore, the Words matter because they underwrite Trinitarian liturgy (e.g., baptism "in the name of the Father, Son, and Holy Spirit" Matthew 28 : 19) with narrative precedent, ensuring that theology springs from real interactions not speculative metaphysics. Their absence would render major doctrinal affirmations less relational and more theoretical; their presence roots the Triune mystery in people's stories—Mary's tears, Peter's breakfast, Paul's blindness, John's awe.

14.3. Ecclesial Formation and Missional Identity

14.3.1 Worship, Liturgy, and Sacramental Practice

The post-resurrection exchanges supply blueprints for Christian worship. Emmaus sets Word-Table sequence: Jesus opens Scriptures, hearts burn, eyes open in bread-breaking, thereby foreshadowing liturgies that pair sermon and Eucharist (Luke 24 : 30-32). Locked-room gatherings provide the Pax Domini—"Peace be with you"—which liturgists continue to share before communion (John 20 : 19). Thomas's confession introduces the congregational acclamation "My Lord and my God," often whispered at sacramental elevation. Galilean breakfast frames the ministry of reconciliation; Peter's triple "You know I love You" mirrors the threefold Kyrie and absolution (John 21 : 15-17). Saul's baptism within days of encounter legitimizes urgent sacramental incorporation (Acts 9 : 18), while Patmos' throne room inspires doxologies like the Sanctus ("Holy, Holy, Holy") and the Agnus Dei ("Worthy is the Lamb"). Therefore, Words matter for church order: they script the liturgical drama that has shaped global Christianity from Syrian rites to Anglican prayer books. Absent these narratives, worship might default to didactic lecture or mystical speculation; with them, it becomes relational rehearsal of gospel events enacted in time and bread and wine.

14.3.2 Mission, Ethics, and Community Structures

Every conversation ends with a commission. Mary is told, "Go to My brothers" (John 20 : 17). The Ten hear, "As the Father sent Me, so I send you" (John 20 : 21). Thomas is blessed for believing and called to bolster future faith (John 20 : 29). The Emmaus duo sprint back to Jerusalem (Luke 24 : 33). Peter receives pastoral mandate, "Feed My sheep" (John 21 : 17). James becomes pillar of Jerusalem's poor (Galatians 2 : 9). Paul is named apostle to Gentiles, kings, and Israel (Acts 9 : 15). John must "write what you see" for seven churches (Revelation 1 : 19). Thus, the Words matter because they birth Christian mission, linking resurrection proof to global witness. They also forge ethical frameworks: Jesus' breakfast rehabilitation of Peter models restorative leadership after failure; His caution to Thomas warns against perpetual doubt skepticism; His critique of Laodicean lukewarmness challenges economic complacency; His affirmation of Smyrna commends suffering fidelity. Community structures emerge: commissioning of Peter outlines shepherding office; Ananias' role demonstrates value of ordinary disciple mediators; letters to angels imply accountable leadership under Christ. Hence, ecclesiology that ignores these Words risks erecting systems detached from resurrection narrative; conversely, churches shaped by them integrate worship, mission, and moral discernment into one seamless life of following the living Lord.

14.4. Pastoral Consolation and Transformative Discipleship

14.4.1 Healing Shame, Doubt, and Trauma through Resurrection Presence

Each Word targets a specific human wound. Mary's grief dissolves when Jesus calls her name, showing that resurrection meets personal loss with intimate recognition (John 20 : 16). Peter's shame is relieved through triple affirmation mirroring triple denial, demonstrating that Christ rehabilitates failure (John 21 : 15-17). Thomas's doubt transforms into the strongest Christological confession, proving that honest skepticism can become deepened faith when confronted by evidence (John 20 : 27-28). James's sibling cynicism turns into holiness, giving hope to families with spiritual rifts (1 Corinthians 15 : 7). Saul's violent zeal is rechanneled into apostolic energy, promising redemption for perpetrators of harm (1 Timothy 1 : 13-16). John's exile loneliness converts into visionary intimacy, comforting believers in isolation (Revelation 1 : 12-18). Thus, Words matter pastorally: they show that no emotional state—bereavement, disgrace, skepticism, resentment, hostility, or abandonment—lies beyond the healing reach of a Christ who calls, shows wounds, grills fish, and pours Spirit. Counselors, chaplains, and small-group leaders use these stories therapeutically; they are case studies in divine trauma care, demonstrating how recollection, sensory engagement, truth revelation, and community reintegration cooperate to heal souls. Without them, pastoral ministry would rely on abstractions; with them, it wields narrative medicine tested across millennia.

14.4.2 Patterning Ongoing Discipleship and Spiritual Maturity

Post-resurrection conversations do not end at emotional triage; they chart lifelong discipleship trajectories. Peter's journey from denial to martyrdom traces path of growing courage; his letters echo beachside call (1 Peter 5 : 1-4). Thomas's later missionary tradition to India reflects global outwardness born from personal doubt overcome. Paul's epistles map sanctification in real time, shifting from early polemical vigor (Galatians) to prison-hymn serenity (Philippians). John evolves from "son of thunder" to apostle of love, as his letters champion relational integrity. These developmental arcs show that conversion sparks but does not finalize transformation; growth requires repeated recollection of initial Word and obedience to progressive instructions. Retreats, liturgical calendars, and spiritual disciplines that revisit resurrection episodes thus serve ongoing formation—Easter as annual re-hearing of conversation, weekly Eucharist as micro-Emmaus, daily examen as self-measurement under Lamb's eyes. Therefore, the Words matter for discipleship because they provide the curriculum: listening (Mary), believing (Thomas), feeding others (Peter), pioneering (Paul), suffering (Smyrna), repenting (Laodicea), and hoping (John). Neglecting them impoverishes Christian maturity; embracing them forms souls in resurrection grammar.

14.5. Apologetic Coherence and Cultural Engagement

14.5.1 Converging Lines of Evidence and Rational Credibility

Modern skeptics often caricature faith as leap in the dark, yet resurrection Words integrate empirical elements—sight, touch, meals, conversations—demonstrating that biblical faith engages senses and reason. Jesus invites Thomas to examine wounds; He eats broiled fish before stunned disciples; He produces miraculous catch replicating earlier event; He offers Paul empirical light witnessed by companions. These data points are not metaphors but phenomenological claims open to verification or falsification. Philosopher William James argued that transformative experiences provide pragmatic evidence when they yield life-long fruit; resurrection Words birthed ministries lasting decades and influencing civilizations. Legal scholar Simon Greenleaf, pioneer of modern rules of evidence, deemed apostolic testimony credible under cross-examination standards. Thus, the Words matter apologetically: they shift discussion from abstract possibility of miracles to concrete historical witnesses testifying under duress. By presenting multiple independent attestations across time, they escape circular reasoning. Employing them, Christian apologists offer cumulative case: empty tomb data (women witnesses), post-resurrection appearances (Words), rise of resurrection-centered proclamation, and willingness of witnesses to die for claim. Such coherence invites honest seekers to consider Christianity intellectually viable.

14.5.2 Contextual Resonance with Contemporary Longings

Besides rational credibility, the Words engage modern existential questions: identity, belonging, purpose, authenticity, and hope. In an age of fragmented relationships, Mary's name-calling assures individuals of personal significance. Amid shame culture amplified by social media, Peter's reinstatement teaches restorative grace. For doubt-saturated deconstructors, Thomas offers model of honest inquiry answered by embodied evidence. Violent radicalization remains global menace; Saul's conversion depicts radical love overpowering radical hate. Isolation intensifies through pandemic and digital echo chambers; John's Patmos visions portray Christ's presence with the solitary. Therefore, the Words serve as cultural bridge texts, demonstrating gospel relevance to contemporary pain points. Missionaries and campus ministers report that storytelling these episodes sparks curiosity among secular listeners more than doctrinal outlines alone. Consequently, disregarding the Words weakens engagement with postmodern audiences; embracing them equips the church to address head and heart simultaneously.

14.6. Missional Imagination and Global Horizons

14.6.1 Catalyst for Cross-Cultural Expansion and Ministry Innovation

The Great Commission (Matthew 28 : 18-20) is framed by a resurrection Word in Galilee where Jesus claims universal authority and pledges perpetual presence. That conversation motivates everything from early apostolic travels to modern translation movements. Paul's Damascus encounter specifically names Gentiles, kings, and Israel as target groups, infusing missionary DNA with diversity. John's Patmos letters portray Christ walking among geographically dispersed lampstands, validating polycentric church structures. Revelation's climactic vision of ransomed people from every tribe (Revelation 7 : 9) springs from Lamb scroll Word, propelling modern missiology. Words also inspire innovative ministry models: Peter's beach mandate fosters pastoral care; Emmaus pedagogy shapes Bible-study evangelism; Thomas episode supports evidentialist approaches; Mary's announcement empowers women in proclamation. Global south churches highlight James's holiness in advocating social justice; persecuted networks cite Smyrna letter for endurance. Therefore, the Words matter missionally because they paint imagination of possibilities far beyond original cultural confines, encouraging contextual adaptation anchored in resurrection truth.

14.6.2 Eschatological Vision Shaping Present Action

Resurrection conversations are telescopes extending believers' vision to ultimate horizon—new creation, marriage supper, throne fellowship. Far from breeding escapism, they energize ethical engagement: knowing labor in Lord is not in vain (1 Corinthians 15 : 58), believers abound in work. Patmos scenes inform ecological concern: new earth promise motivates stewardship rather than exploitation. Assurance of justice at white-throne judgment inflames advocacy for oppressed, trusting that vindication will arrive. Hope of bodily resurrection affirms value of medical care and handicap dignity. Militant Lamb's conquest by blood shapes non-violent resistance movements. Thus, Words matter for public theology; they anchor activism in eschatology, preventing both despair and triumphalist coercion.

14.7. Spiritual Formation and Contemplative Encounter

14.7.1 Personal Prayer Practices Bathed in Resurrection Narratives

Meditating on Words invites believers into imaginative prayer: Lectio Divina on Emmaus fosters openness to Scripture illumination; Ignatian contemplation of Mary's garden exchange cultivates hearing Jesus call one's name; "breathing the Spirit" exercise reflecting locked-room scene deepens awareness of pneuma; Pauline conversion reflection invites examination of blind-spots needing light. Such practices shape identity, ordering emotions around resurrected presence. Church history confirms efficacy: Desert Fathers recited Thomas's confession as arrow prayer; medieval mystic

Julian of Norwich envisioned mother-Christ Affirming "All shall be well" echoing Patmos' "no more tears." Modern retreats use John 21 for restorative sessions with burned-out leaders. Therefore, Words matter for spirituality because they supply treasury of encounter scripts, guiding pilgrims beyond rote petitions into conversational intimacy with living Christ.

14.7.2 Communal Disciplines and Liturgical Calendars

Communities likewise embed Words into rhythms: Easter Vigil dramatizes Mary-Magdalene running; Ascension Day recalls Great Commission mountain chat; Pentecost traces Spirit breath sequence; Feast of Conversion of Paul invites testimony services; Feast of St. Thomas (July 3) confronts doubt; All Saints' Day echoes Patmos multitudes. Small groups enact Emmaus meals, blending Bible reading and shared supper. Confession-absolution liturgies reincarnate Peter's restoration. Mentoring programs use Paul-Ananias template—seasoned believer welcoming new convert. By structuring corporate life around Words, churches avoid programmatic fads, rooting identity in resurrection narrative. Hence, these conversations matter because they cultivate communal habits that align body, calendar, and imagination with gospel pulses, enabling local congregations to mirror early church vibrancy.

Conclusion

From a garden dawn whispering "Mary" to an Aegean sunset resounding "Surely I am coming soon," the post-resurrection Words weave a tapestry that spans grief and glory, doubt and doxology, private tears and cosmic choruses. They matter historically, grounding faith in empirically attested events; they matter theologically, revealing Christ's deity and Trinitarian mission; they matter ecclesially, shaping worship, sacraments, governance, and outreach; they matter pastorally, healing wounds and forging resilient disciples; they matter apologetically, offering rational and existential credibility; they matter missionally, igniting cross-cultural imagination and justice engagement; and they matter spiritually, guiding personal and communal formation until the end of the age. To neglect them would be to amputate Christianity's living nerve; to embrace them is to find one's own story folded into the ceaseless conversation between the risen Lord and His beloved people. As we close this study, the final word rightly belongs to that Lord Himself, spoken once to ancient saints and now to us: "Do not be afraid.... I am the Living One.... Therefore, go.... Be my witnesses.... Be faithful unto death, and I will give you the crown of life." Those sentences, uttered across tomb gardens, city roads, Galilean lakeshores, and island caves, continue to pulse with power. May we, like Mary, Thomas, Peter, James, Paul, and John, hear, believe, and obey—until the Word crescendos into face-to-face communion in the new creation where sight will replace faith and every conversation will become eternal praise.

www.ingramcontent.com/pod-product-compliance
Lightning Source LLC
Chambersburg PA
CBHW060316050426
42449CB00011B/2514